Clemence Dane and *Good Housekeeping*

Clemence Dane and *Good Housekeeping*

Modernity and Common Reading

Stella Deen

EDINBURGH
University Press

Edinburgh University Press is one of the leading university presses in the UK. We publish academic books and journals in our selected subject areas across the humanities and social sciences, combining cutting-edge scholarship with high editorial and production values to produce academic works of lasting importance. For more information visit our website: edinburghuniversitypress.com

Edinburgh University Press Ltd
13 Infirmary Street
Edinburgh EH1 1LT

First published in hardback by Edinburgh University Press 2025

Typeset in 11/13pt Sabon LT Pro
by Cheshire Typesetting Ltd, Cuddington, Cheshire, and
printed and bound in Great Britain by
CPI Group (UK) Ltd, Croydon CR0 4YY

A CIP record for this book is available from the British Library

ISBN 978 1 3995 1690 7 (hardback)
ISBN 978 1 3995 1691 4 (paperback)
ISBN 978 1 3995 1692 1 (webready PDF)
ISBN 978 1 3995 1693 8 (epub)

MIX
Paper | Supporting responsible forestry
FSC www.fsc.org FSC® C013604

This book is printed using paper from well-managed forests, recycling and other controlled sources

Contents

Figures

Acknowledgments

In writing *Clemence Dane and Good Housekeeping*, I have benefitted from support and assistance from institutions, colleagues, and family members. I am grateful to the State University of New York, New Paltz, for a sabbatical leave that enabled me to gain momentum. Several libraries and archives were indispensable, particularly in the early phases of my research. Abundant thanks go to the staffs of the Robert L. Carothers Library, University of Rhode Island, and of the British Library. Each made it easy for me to access bound volumes of *Good Housekeeping* and provided skillful assistance. I also thank the very able and efficient archivists at the Victoria and Albert Museum. Finally, Diane Courtney at Hearst generously answered many of my questions about editorial and business arrangements for the early days of *Good Housekeeping*.

The expertise and generosity of anonymous readers for Edinburgh University Press enriched the scholarship that informs this monograph. Claire Buck offered valuable insights, good advice, and humor at crucial stages of the writing process. Special thanks are due to Liz Evans and Megan Faragher for the generosity of spirit and keen intelligence that they applied to drafts of nearly every chapter, over a period of four years.

I am grateful to my mother, Rosemary Deen, for her unwavering and enthusiastic interest in my writing and for support of many kinds. Jason Taylor, Claire Deen Taylor, and Luke Deen Taylor have been loving, patient, and steady champions of this project. I owe particular thanks to Jason—who so often comes forward with an unforeseen and indispensable skill—for his technical help preparing the illustrations.

The cover image, Walter Granville-Smith's *Reading at the Beach*, is reproduced with permission of the Dowd Illustration

Research Archive, Julian Edison Department of Special Collections, Washington University Libraries.

Images from *Good Housekeeping* are reproduced courtesy of Hearst Magazines UK.

Illustrations from *The Hidden Orchis* and from *The Songs of Innocence* appear with the permission of The Medici Society Ltd.

Introduction: Clemence Dane, Modernity and Interwar Periodical Culture

In her monthly book page for *Good Housekeeping* between 1923 and 1933, Clemence Dane educated and entertained thousands of British readers. Positing a reader who seeks both intellectual stimulation and enjoyment, Dane's essays set forth literary critical principles and consistently demonstrate how new books gain interest and complexity as they are placed within literary traditions and enter into dialogue with predecessors. The serial essays provide an ideal forum for discussion of new books, topics of the day, and consistent literary-critical principles. And because the series appeared in a quality magazine read by comfortable, middle-class women, and in many cases other members of their households, Dane's corpus of *Good Housekeeping* essays provides significant data for the study of common reading during the interwar period. The length of Dane's tenure as a literary critic for *Good Housekeeping*, the long form of her essays, the consistency of her values and practices, and the fidelity of her audience all illuminate the importance of her essayistic criticism to histories of reading and of twentieth-century literary criticism. Dane's critical corpus clearly functioned to educate readers outside the university. In this para-curricular role, the essays express confidence in a shared literary heritage, model enjoyment of a wide variety of literature, and enjoin readers to play an active role in bringing forth good books.

Clemence Dane, the pseudonym of Winifred Ashton (1888–1965), came to the *Good Housekeeping* "Book Page" via her success as a novelist and dramatist. She had published the controversial *Regiment of Women* in 1917, a novel about the dangerous influence of a lesbian teacher over a vulnerable boarding-school student. *Regiment* was followed by the polemical *A Bill of Divorcement*, which enjoyed over 400 runs in the London Theatre when it opened in 1921. Yet writing was only one of many vocations for which this polymath was suited. Dane had trained at the Slade School of Fine Art from 1904–6; her accomplishments in painting and sculpture include a bust of Shakespeare at Stratford and three portraits in the National Portrait Gallery: an oil painting and bronze busts of Noël Coward and of Richard Addinsell. After a stint as a teacher in Ireland (1907–1913) and a brief career as an actress, Dane began a long, varied, and prolific career as a novelist, playwright, journalist, Hollywood screenwriter, radio dramatist, broadcaster, lecturer, and lay sermonist. She was both a prominent feminist intellectual and a middlebrow tastemaker.

Dane brought out a collection of feminist and social criticism, *The Women's Side*, in 1926. These essays, along with her regular book pages for *Good Housekeeping*, represent a relatively early phase of her career as a writer. Between 1918 and 1933, when Dane relinquished her book column at *Good Housekeeping* to take up screenwriting in Hollywood, she produced drama and fiction at a steady pace, including the experimental play *Will Shakespeare* (1923), a four-volume family chronicle, *The Babyons* (1927), the best-selling novel *Broome Stages* (1931), and popular detective fiction written in collaboration with Helen Simpson, *Enter Sir John* (1928) and *Re-Enter Sir John* (1932). But in her mid-forties, Dane was ready for a change that would broaden her outlook, and she turned to her agent, Curtis Brown, to organize an American tour. She had received numerous invitations to lecture, and these would finance the tour (Barrow 22). Dane was mesmerized by New York, but was soon packing for Hollywood, having signed with RKO Pictures for screenwriting (Barrow 24). Amidst absorbing collaborations for the cinema, Dane continued to contribute literary and social criticism to *Good Housekeeping* (resuming with the January 1934 issue), as well as for *The Forum*, *The North American Review*, and *The Living Age*.

Dane has been called "Britain's most influential, versatile and successful female writer" between the wars (Collis), but has only recently come out of relative obscurity.[1] One way to glimpse that influence is through the numerous networks she engaged and sustained. Dane's literary and professional circles included the Six Point Group, which from 1921 sought political, economic, and legal equality for women; and the Society of Women Journalists, where

[1] A resurgence of interest in Dane began with attention to her drama and fiction. See especially Maggie Gale. The first monograph on Dane's work, by Louise McDonald, appeared in 2021; and a scholarly conference on her life and work took place at The Institute of English Studies in October 2022. Significant attention to Dane's journalism in *Good Housekeeping* has come from Stella Deen and Alice Wood.

Dane served as Life President for twenty years. She was one of the four original members of the Book Society Selection Committee, Britain's first monthly book sales club, launched in 1929. Additional networks include RKO Pictures, the BBC, and the Detection Club—the last an informal association of mystery writers who collaborated on several round-robin crime stories (broadcast, serialized in *The Listener*, and appearing later in book form). In addition to broadcasting during the Second World War, Dane created radio programming, notably, *The Saviours: Seven Plays on One Theme*, with music by Richard Addinsell, a patriotic suite of plays about the legendary King Arthur (1940–1). And a network particularly close to Dane's heart was the friends and colleagues who gathered on many evenings in her Tavistock Street flat, which she leased from 1924 to 1959. 20 Tavistock was an "oasis of fertile conversation" whose source was Dane herself, a woman of "huge vitality" whose "wise, exciting talk and gift of words" often centered on history, religion, and theater (Thorndike). Each of these forums fostered Dane's professional and political growth and enhanced her collaboration with friends and colleagues. Additionally, Dane's writing was supported by formal and informal ties. Both her literary agent, Curtis Brown, and William Heinemann, who published *Regiment of Women*, were mentors and friends. Family friend Elsie Arnold served as Dane's secretary and became a long-term domestic companion. She was succeeded by Olwen Bowen-Davies. As observed by Stella Benson, they were the "wives" whose unseen labor supported Dane's notoriously long work hours (quoted in Collis). Dane's prolific writing career continued almost until her death.

Literary Culture in the Magazines

Periodical writing and reading were integral to the fabric of early twentieth-century British society and its economy. From political weeklies to little magazines to women's monthlies, periodicals disseminated news, information, and opinion, and many supplied readers with a continual stream of cultural reviews and literature, especially fiction. Periodicals fostered the sense of shared enterprise between readers and writers in periodical communities, and they participated in wider networks of dialogic exchange, collaboration, and rivalry. The commercial business of magazines had pervasive impacts on content, writers, and readers whose benefits and harms were fiercely debated. Even so, periodicals that gave significant attention to literature had a profound, generative effect on literary production and reception. Peter Marks argues that modernist magazines such as *The Criterion*, *The English Review*, and *The Adelphi* offered a forum for "avant-garde work as well as advanced criticism and theory," spurred experimental writing, and "provided avant-garde writers with sophisticated readers, and vice versa" (24). Carey Snyder concurs, considering how "magazines shaped the form and content of modernist women's writing" (166). We might make similar claims about other major literary magazines in this period, including *The London Mercury* and *The American Forum*, as well as intellectual weeklies such as *The Nation and Athenaeum*, whose literary pages were edited by Leonard Woolf.

Feminist and women's magazines were similar engines of literary production, and many enjoyed large circulations, making them central to the reception of interwar literary culture. *Clemence Dane and Good Housekeeping* joins an abundance of scholarship demonstrating this twofold literary significance. Recent, meticulously researched scholarship showcases the rich and diverse approaches to literary culture in interwar women's magazines: including work on *Woman, Woman's Weekly*, and *Modern Woman* by Fiona Hackney; on *Time and Tide* by Catherine Clay and by Barbara Green; on *Good Housekeeping* and *Vogue* by Alice Wood; on *Eve: The Lady's Pictorial* by Vike Martina Plock; and on *The Queen* by Sarah Lonsdale.[2]

The identity, ethos, and hierarchical status of a given magazine in the early twentieth century were fluid, as editors sought to broaden or reach new audiences, experimental features changed course, and publishers assessed their success competing for readers and for advertising revenue. But in what Barbara Green calls "the unruliness of print culture" ("Around 1910" 432), the ongoing transformations of a periodical were not merely a reflection of its internal network of publishers, editors, and writers, but additionally of its relationship to groups and organizations in a dominant culture that was "itself responsive to change" (Brooker and Thacker 17). Moreover, in another stimulus to external networks, journalists commonly wrote for multiple periodicals, often crossing magazine genres and market sectors. Writers' fluid movement across periodical titles suggests the instability and contested nature of cultural hierarchies, and points

[2] See Clay, *Time and Tide*; Green, *Feminist Periodicals*; Hackney, "*They Opened Up a Whole New World*"; Lonsdale, *Rebel Women*; Plock, "'A Journal of the Period'"; Wood, *Modernism and Modernity*.

to overlapping networks of writers and editors. This fluidity also reveals the woman journalist's saturation of and versatility within the cultural field. For example, in the 1920s Clemence Dane wrote for transatlantic literary reviews (*The Forum*, *The Bookman*, *The Yale Review*, *The North American Review*), intellectual and political journals (*The English Review*, *Time and Tide*), and middlebrow women's magazines like *Good Housekeeping*. Rebecca West contributed to *Time and Tide*, *The Bookman*, *The New Statesman*, and *Good Housekeeping*; and Virginia Woolf published reviews, essays, and fiction in the likes of *Vogue*, *Good Housekeeping*, and *The Times Literary Supplement*. This tiny sample hints at the feminist literary journalist's multiple interventions in culture: she participated in national cultural forums, advanced post-franchise feminist goals, entertained and enlightened fiction readers, articulated and disseminated tenets of twentieth-century literary criticism, and helped shape the subjectivities of common readers.

Clemence Dane's Journalism

Clemence Dane and Good Housekeeping will focus on Dane's book essays. Before turning our attention to this corpus, however, it is worth considering her broader role in interwar periodical culture. Dane's journalism for selected periodicals illuminates both her versatility and her high standing within journalistic networks, particularly before 1930. Authorship in multiple journals increased a writer's currency within periodical networks and facilitated the cross-fertilization of an authorial identity across titles.[3] Conversely, a journalist's identity in a given periodical conveyed and helped shape the magazine's distinct ethos. For example, the longevity of Dane's column for *Good Housekeeping*, unparalleled in her career, conveyed the alignment of institutional and authorial goals and allowed her to develop a unique authorial persona in *Good Housekeeping*. A composite picture of Dane's journalism across magazine titles confirms her prominence as a literary and social critic after the First World War and reveals the consistency of her interests and concerns.

The feminist, literary, and political journals in which Dane published opinion, essays, and cultural criticism variously shaped her

[3] In "Getting a Living," Fiona Hackney demonstrates that Leonora Eyles practised cross-fertilizing strategies so that her feminist and her socialist perspectives mutually enriched one another.

authorial identity as a journalist in the eyes of readers. As the author of monthly book essays in *Good Housekeeping*, Dane was at once a common reader and a literary expert, supplying her readers with reviews of new books and satisfying their deeper desire for literary history and intertextual connections. In the highly respected New York *Forum*, Dane belonged to a more rarified group of first-rank literary authors. *The Forum*'s front matter, whose ads constituted a snapshot of new titles in culture and politics, was followed by "Toasts": chatty, lively biographies for the contributors in a given issue. "Toasts" foregrounded writers' individuality, but also suggested their affiliation with one another in something like a club. Dane was an occasional writer for *The Forum*, contributing some ten articles between 1924 and 1935, with all but one published between 1924 and 1928. Within *The Forum*, Dane's stature was not only informed by the magazine's textual and commercial codes, but also by its cohort of frequent contributors, and even more immediately by the contributors to a given issue. For example, the May 1927 number included Clemence Dane's "Pegasus and Dobbin," an imaginative explanation for men's and women's different attitudes toward work; travel writing by D.H. Lawrence, "Fireworks"; Virginia Woolf's short story "The New Dress"; and the fifth installment of Willa Cather's *Death Comes for the Archbishop*. The common habitus of the *Forum* brought into alignment these writers from either side of the Atlantic and insinuated at that moment their shared status of major writers, a status that "Toasts" then further emphasized.

Dane's début as a journalist also sheds light on her standing within periodical circles. "A Problem in Education," an extensive criticism of single-sex education in Britain, appeared in *The English Review* in June and July 1918. Under its first editor, Ford Madox Hueffer (later, Ford), the *Review* was a venue for major writers, including Joseph Conrad, Thomas Hardy, and Henry James. Succeeding Hueffer in 1909, Austin Harrison maintained the high caliber of its creative work, while he enlarged the magazine's scope to include politics and social criticism (Vogeler 2). The publication of "A Problem in Education" indicates that early in her career, Dane was solicited for analysis of controversial social questions. A review of her second novel, *First the Blade*, appeared in the June 1918 *English Review*. In her first novel, *Regiment of Women*, Dane had addressed a topic she again attacked in "A Problem": the exploitation of the adolescent girl prone to "exaggerated hero worship" who is sent to boarding school and falls in love with a schoolmistress who "seeks to gratify her love of excitement" and power (Part ii, 39). But while the novel imagines a tragic outcome for the child, the social criticism proposes solutions as Dane draws on her experience as a teacher and as a boarding school student. The nonfiction locates the "problem" in a much broader segment of society—both the family and the societal standard of single-sex schooling. It recognizes the existence of "morbid and selfish" mistresses but hopes that they are rare and recommends an overhaul in education at home and in schools (39).

By situating Dane within a distinguished roster of *English Review* writers, Harrison identified her as an authoritative voice on a topic of social consequence. Harrison was committed to publishing controversial material (Vogeler 2), and "A Problem in Education" decidedly reached this bar. Dane calls attention to the infatuated girl's suffering in isolation and bewilderment and finds her to be the victim of the fear and shame that pervades societal attitudes toward sex. But what was controversial about Dane's approach was her contention that the system of single-sex education from primary schools through universities both reflects and perpetuates the estrangement of each sex from the other, as well as her call for co-education to remedy the dysfunction.

Dane's journalism in *The English Review* shares the concerns and the rhetorical approaches of her journalism for *Good Housekeeping* some five years later, where in essays like "The Educational Value of Acting in Schools" and "Some Questions on Divorce" she advanced educational initiatives and addressed social problems. Moreover, "A Problem in Education" aligned with the preoccupations of *The English Review* during this period in several ways. First, it contributed to the *Review*'s significant coverage, both before and during the war, of women's changing role. The *Review* had covered the suffrage campaigns, and in 1912 had sponsored a symposium that addressed the "sex war" and women's sexuality, psychology, morality, and capacity for strengthening the Empire (Vogeler 111–18, 196–7). Second, "A Problem in Education" contributed to debates in *The English Review* about the state of education in Britain (Vogeler 257–8). Third, the two-part "Problem in Education" appeared under the *Review*'s *War and Reconstruction* rubric, giving prominence to the essay's dimension of nationalism. Each of these themes suggests the dialogic engagement of "A Problem" with other textual material in the *Review* and invites new interpretations of *Regiment*.[4]

[4] Heather Julien reads *Regiment of Women* as a reflection of Dane's contradictory responses to feminist agitation for equal pay for teachers. Julien misdates the publication of "A Problem in Education" as 1926, when it was slightly revised for *The Women's Side*. The 1918 publication aligns it with *The English Review*'s broader

As Dane analyzes the harms of segregated schooling to both sexes, she calls attention to the crucial role of education to prepare strong citizens. "The most keen and ardent and impressionable of the children," she begins, those likely to "take the longest to shake off the effects" of misguided feelings for a teacher, are "just the very people who should be of most value to society" (Part ii, 43). The war's losses made it painfully clear how much the nation would need talented, clear-sighted, and devoted citizens to contribute to the efforts of reconstruction. In addition to students, Dane argues, teachers were an essential national resource, and they too had been disadvantaged by single-sex education: "How can they be fitted to prepare other people for adult life when, for practical purposes, they have never experienced it?" Dane underscores the importance of teachers, their insufficient pay, and their "immense responsibility" for "the whole future life of the nation" (Part ii, 45–6). Finding societal attitudes at the heart of the problem, and linking educational reform to the postwar reconstruction of Britain, "A Problem in Education" was characteristic of Dane's social criticism.

Being Modern, Reading as a Modern

Dane's journalism reached into history, the arts, and social reform, but literary culture—encompassing all of these—proved to be her forte. Dane's book essays functioned as a recurring, reliable component of the *Good Housekeeping* mission to inform busy wives and mothers, prepare professional women, and provide high-quality, stimulating material for hours of leisure.[5] In addition to fiction and poetry, the first issues of *Good Housekeeping* included articles in "departments" headed: *Furnishing and Decoration*; *Needlework*;

attention to educational reform and post-war reconstruction and thus invites recalibration of the critical view that the 1917 *Regiment* both supports an "anti-spinster" platform and reveals Dane's lack of support for teachers' pay increases (Julien 125–6). For example, "A Problem in Education" underscores the "common knowledge" that assistant teachers are "underpaid [and] overworked" (47).

[5] Following the success of the American *Good Housekeeping*, the National Magazine Company launched the U.K. edition in 1922. Its first editor, J.Y. McPeake, editor of *Nash's*, took assistant editor Alice Head with him to *Good Housekeeping*. Head became editor and managing director from 1924—when McPeake unexpectedly died—and remained in those roles until 1939. Head credits McPeake with *Good Housekeeping*'s ability to publish authoritative writers on the "burning subjects of the day" by following *Nash's* formula of paying them generously (Head 60–1). Priced at one shilling, *Good Housekeeping* was an immediate success, soon reaching a circulation of 150,000 (Braithwaite and Barrell 13).

HOME MANAGEMENT

WATCH THESE PAGES

THERE are always right and wrong methods of doing the hundred and one tasks involved in home management, and it is the object of this Department to help you to find the right methods and the best labour-saving appliances for each of these tasks. Consult these pages each month, and, if you need further information, write, enclosing a stamped addressed envelope, to Home Management, "GOOD HOUSEKEEPING," 1 Amen Corner, London, E.C.4

"Bell Out of Order"

Why Not Be Your Own Electrician?

By H. J. Birnstingl, A.R.I.B.A.

A FREQUENT cause of trouble in the house is an interruption or failure of the electric bell service. Yet for the most part the cause is some simple matter that can be repaired without calling in outside help. In the first place it will be as well to dispel a popular misconception, and that is that there is any danger of suffering a shock in handling the electric bell wiring. The voltage used in the bell circuit is usually three, four-and-a-half, or six volts according to the number of batteries used, and this is insufficient to give a shock to any part of the body except the tongue. The tongue, however, is so susceptible to small shocks that it may be employed as a useful "voltmeter" for very low voltages, and a quick test for a single cell is to place both poles on the tongue, and if this results in a sharp bitter taste it may be presumed that the cell is up to strength.

If a failure occurs, the first thing to ascertain is whether it is local or general. If the bell will not ring when any of the pushes are used it is probable that the fault is in the battery and this should be examined. First note if all the wires are properly attached to their terminals. The cells must be connected to each other in *series*, that is, the positive pole of one cell to the negative pole of the next, and the free pole from each of the end cells (one of which will be negative and one positive) must be connected to the electric circuit. If all the connections appear in order then it is probable that the cells have run down, and the easiest way to test this is to disconnect the cells from the circuit and from each other, and to taste one by applying the two poles to the tongue simultaneously as already described. If there is no taste or only a very faint taste, the cells are *dead*.

Electric bells are sometimes worked with dry and sometimes with wet cells. Dry cells cannot be recharged and must be thrown away and be replaced by the same number of new ones. If they are wet cells then some *exiter*, as the liquid in which the carbon and zinc poles stand is called, should be bought from the ironmonger. This is generally obtained in the form of crystals which dissolve in water.

If the cells of the battery, after testing, appear to be in good condition, and the connections are not loose, then the bell itself should be examined. If when the push is used it is found that the hammer of the bell moves forwards once, without hitting the gong, it is probable that it requires adjustment. The wooden cover must be removed and an adjusting screw will be seen held firm by a clamping screw. This must be loosened with a screwdriver and the adjusting screw, which has a platinum point pressing on a spring, slowly tightened until the magnets suddenly attract the armature to which the hammer is attached so that the hammer hits the gong once. The screw should then be turned back until the armature leaves the magnets. It is now as close to the magnets as it can be without being attracted, and the clamping screw should be tightened. This is the correct position for it.

If the bell still fails to work, the wires between the bell and the battery should

A battery of two Léchanche cells (liquid batteries) connected in series

26

Figure I.1 *Good Housekeeping* helped women develop both ordinary and extraordinary "home management" skills.

Fashions; *Home Management*; *Cookery*; and *Health and Beauty* (see Figure 4.1). Each issue also included numerous special articles whose titles were typeset on the tables of contents in the same font as that of the department headings. This approach to the tables of contents suggests the relative importance of special articles while emphasizing each issue as a miscellany. Beginning with Issue 1, a significant recurring series of articles was "X as a Profession for Women." From within the monthly women's magazine, Dane spoke in concert with other featured voices that together created a dynamic, forward-looking vision of modernity. Thus, in addition to the light they shed on the history of common reading, Dane's essays both illuminate the central role played by women's magazines in the construction of modernity and provide a strong case study of the major contributions of individual journalists in this project.[6]

Inseparable from their interest as constructions of the modern woman reader, Dane's essays contribute to a twentieth-century history of literary criticism. They shed light on the contemporary reception of new books as they unfold a rich record of engaging and principled reactions to new drama, poetry, fiction, and nonfiction. Moreover, they offer perceptive and often original commentary on literary genre and traditions. Dane engages with modernist and academic critics, though rarely naming them, as peers who pursue the same interesting questions that she does. She often identifies herself as a common reader and underscores her different judgment from more established critics. Bonding with her audience, she implicitly invites them to join her in "setting the record straight" as she champions an underappreciated writer or, adopting a more far-sighted perspective than her peers, counters their dismal predictions about the future of literary culture. As instances of this practice are discussed in the chapters, we will have occasion to observe that Dane created a forum in which middlebrow criticism by women could challenge rather than mimic highbrow criticism.[7]

[6] *Good Housekeeping* is one of several women's "service" magazines featured in Alice Wood's *Modernism and Modernity in British Women's Magazines* (Routledge, 2020). Wood expands on recent scholarship tracing modernism's "emergence in, engagement with, and, crucially, *mediation by* diverse forms of popular culture," including journalism (4). Supported by her observations regarding *Good Housekeeping*'s production, circulation, editorship, advertising, and features, Wood demonstrates persuasively—taking the May 1930 issue as her case study—that "within and beyond its domestic content," *Good Housekeeping* "urges the female reader to consider herself a modern subject and to negotiate her own responses to modernity" (51).

[7] Nicola Humble, Melissa Sullivan, and Sophie Blanch have argued that the middlebrow characteristically works "to affirm and renegotiate its own values" (Humble 21).

Dane's literary criticism considers both the text and the occasion for reading. The convention that the essay be occasional—prompted by an encounter, an ordinary thought, or a quotidian observation—illuminates the many connections in Dane's book essays between reading and postwar society. They treat reading within the contexts of modern woman's care of children and the home, consumerism, newly enfranchised citizenship, professional ambitions and concerns, and the two-sided ethos of self-improvement and leisure. They also express a humanistic interest in the role of good books to prompt ethical reflection and to nourish human spiritual sensibility, the subject of Chapter 4. These topics resonate with *Good Housekeeping*'s periodical codes, the set of material, textual, and human elements that determine to a large extent the identity of the magazine.[8] In this case, the topics and attitudes reflected in Dane's book essays often reinforce and are reinforced by those of other articles, illustrations, ads, and fiction in *Good Housekeeping*, which in any single issue assembled a composite picture, a polyphonic statement of female modernity. As the book chapters will document, while *Good Housekeeping* evokes and constructs this complex modernity, Dane's addresses to readers additionally posit a single, multi-faceted reader whose roles, experiences, and moods are in flux.

Insofar as Dane's book pages use new books as a springboard for broader discussion, her construction of good books provides a distinctive response to the quintessential question of how to be modern. Dane's ongoing and evolving solution to this question prompts innovation in the form of the essay; her essays are of aesthetic and literary value both in themselves and for the light they shed on the continual innovation called for by a periodical writer who adopted each month a fresh subject and a new set of books. In attending to the craft of Dane's periodical essays, I follow Kate Campbell's recognition that journalism's "interest and identity extend beyond" its knowledge content and her call for attention to its form and style ("Introduction" 8). Dane works with such recognized essay forms as the rambler, in which the essayist follows the rhythm of her own "thoughts, memories, and observations" (Good 75); the constellation, in which an image or theme unites disparate objects;

Moreover, "middlebrow writers, artists and designers understood, capitalised upon and often celebrated key differences between the modernist and middlebrow spheres" (Sullivan and Blanch 6).

8 Jerome McCann, George Bornstein, and Matthew Philpotts have each made foundational contributions to theorizing bibliographic and periodical codes.

Figure I.2 In line with *Good Housekeeping*'s vision, Norah McGuinness's illustration for "As You Like It" captured women's multi-faceted experience of modernity. Courtesy of Hearst Magazines UK.

the fragment, which adopts the trope of the beautiful object that is about to decay; the portrait, which creates a likeness of its object; the epitome, offering miniature replicas of its object; and others, examples of which will be explored in each chapter.[9]

[9] My characterization of essay forms in this paragraph is indebted to Good.

Clemence Dane's Tenure at *Good Housekeeping*

Even on the basis of her early literary successes, Dane was a "celebrity" writer, and *Good Housekeeping* included her name on the cover of the inaugural issue of *Good Housekeeping*. Dane's first articles were on social questions, informed not only by her success as a writer but by her varied professional experience. For example, "The Educational Value of Acting in Schools" (1922) and "Art and the Academy" (1923) were informed by her training in the visual arts and acting. Dane's first article for *Good Housekeeping*, "Some Questions on Divorce" (1922), a companion of sorts to *A Bill of Divorcement*, made good on the magazine's promise to present "burning issues of the day." The editors encouraged the presentation of controversial topics in the form of dialogue, often using a sidebar on the table of contents to indicate the "pro" and "con" positions of two writers. Balancing the controversial opinions Dane voiced, Mrs. Belloc Lowndes was invited to present a rebuttal in the next issue underscoring "why easy divorce would be disastrous in England" (Table of Contents for April 1922). Dane agreed to contribute more such articles on social and cultural questions; the third (May) issue touts the "well-known writers," Dane among them, whose columns will appear over the next few months. In the fall of 1923, Dane evidently entered into contract with *Good Housekeeping* for a regular book essay; in Volume 4 she "inaugurates the monthly book page," as announced on the first-page spread of "The Twelve Best Books for Women" in October. Dane went on to publish substantial book essays for some ten years, most between 4,000 and 7,000 words, for a total of about 120 essays for *Good Housekeeping*.

Within *Good Housekeeping*, Dane's touted credentials were her published novel and play, but as her monthly book pages unfolded it is clear that her real authority lay in the breadth of her literary knowledge, her ability to offer historical perspectives on literary questions, her abiding enjoyment of books and reading, and the ease with which she explored literary history and traditions to shed light on new books. These were repeatedly demonstrated in Dane's monthly book essays for *Good Housekeeping*. Yet in addressing her readers, Dane does not invoke disciplinary expertise, emphasizing instead her "long established habit of reading," her participation in a wide readership of good books. She appreciates innovations in literary form and language, yet she characteristically emphasizes the contribution of such originality to literary traditions. A lover of Victorian books, she more often sees twentieth-century continuity with, not rupture from, the past. And against critical fashion, Dane often situated books within the context of their authors' biographies.[10] Word play, metaphor, and, above all, a thick carpet of eclectic literary allusion and quotation fill her essays. She evokes a shared literary culture and extends it through discussion of new books.

The Modernity of Journalism

As Bingham and McAleer have pointed out, historians of reading have often neglected the role of newspapers and magazines in shaping and reflecting Britons' experience of modernity (Bingham 1; McAleer 10). It was in the interwar period that "national daily newspapers became part of everyday life, read by a majority of the population" (Bingham 1). Yet the influence of periodicals in the reading life of twentieth-century Britons has often been denigrated, the source of everything from light, "human-interest" stories, sensationalism, fragments, and "trash"; and decay of the English language.[11] By the end of the century, many observers believed, journalism had relinquished its responsibility to educate the public, offering entertainment and sensory stimulation in its place. And the role of women in this decline did not go unnoticed.

The reputed "feminization" of the press can be dated from 1896 and the first issues of *The Daily Mail*, Bingham finds. Before then, the national morning press was dominated by in-depth political and financial coverage, written for an audience of educated men who were "expected to have the leisure to work carefully through the paper column by column" (Bingham 23). But Alfred Harmsworth (later, Lord Northcliffe) explicitly courted women readers, devoting two columns to fashion and domestic matters and incorporating human interest stories and serialized fiction with particular appeal to women. Establishing "women's pages," other papers followed his lead. And as the chief spenders of the domestic budget, women readers became indispensable to advertising revenue. Display ads

[10] As Chris Baldick puts it, modernist criticism evolved "a new language and new procedures for the examination of literary works as autonomous objects of inquiry, no longer to be confused with the lives or philosophies of their authors" (*Criticism and Literary Theory* 66).

[11] For a discussion of journalism characterized by trash, see Campbell, "Journalistic Discourses."

targeting the female consumer especially reshaped the style, tone, and content of the Victorian newspaper (Bingham 27–31).

To some critics, however, the feminization of the press was synonymous with the decline of its traditional educative function (Campbell, "Journalistic Discourses" 41; Collier, *Modernism on Fleet Street*). Yet as Campbell argues, the role of journalism to observe and report on ephemera, fragments, and impressions predates the outsized influence of the female magazine reader in the first decades of the century. The modernity of mid-nineteenth-century journalism, Campbell finds, arose from its sustained contrast to the forms of perception and knowledge gleaned by the learned reader of books. Against the deep coverage of a book, the journalistic treatment of surfaces seized the essence of a moment or rendered "a vast map of embodied events and living detail" (Bagehot 976, qtd. in Campbell, "Journalistic Discourses" 44). The very contrast between depth and surface—which Northcliffe was to recast in gendered terms—delineated in the earlier period the perceptual modes and cognitive processes that pertained respectively to the book author and to the journalist.

Numerous women's magazines of the 1920s retain most elements of Northcliffe's successful formula for courting women readers. *Good Housekeeping*, for example, constructs women's concerns as both diverse and modern, pertaining both to public and private spheres. What has been underappreciated, however, is the degree to which this quality magazine restored "depth" to the modernity of journalism. From its inaugural issue, *Good Housekeeping* sought out experts and allotted them a generous word limit. Regular columnists such as historian and barrister Helena Normanton and critic Clemence Dane consistently presented modernity in dialogue with history, counterbalancing the magazine features highlighting more transient phenomena such as "Spring Fashions," "Your Summer Garden" or "The Ideal Home Exhibition."

Dane's body of criticism repeatedly formulates modernity as an opportunity to bring the new into dialogue with the traditional, the ephemeral into relation with the enduring. An overview of her role in *Good Housekeeping* illustrates how the seriality of her journalism facilitated Dane's fulfillment of this formula. As *Good Housekeeping*'s long-standing critic, Dane made a major contribution to its mission, announced in the inaugural issue in 1922: to meet the needs of leisured, financially comfortable women readers who sought to improve themselves. Yet far from merely instructing readers or providing them with lists of everyman canons, Dane spoke about books within the broader experience of modernity, which she characterized as a tension between continuity and change. In essays like "Autumn Lists" (1929) and "Fragments That Remain" (1926) Dane might characterize and celebrate ephemeral beauty, while in essays such as "American Primitives" (1924) or "Things That Go Bump in the Night" (1924) she showed readers that good new books can be illuminated when they are set within well-established Western literary traditions.

To consider this tension between the enduring and the ephemeral, the traditional and the modern, we might observe that in the wake of the First World War utter change may well have been the perceived reality of most Britons. And most narratives of modernism emphasize its rupture from the past. Yet modernity may be better understood as the search for a way to put the new in relation to the old. In different ways, canonical critical essays from this period, including Eliot's "Ulysses, Order, and Myth" and Woolf's *A Room of One's Own*, insist that pathbreaking writers will make use of literary tradition in fresh ways. Although scholars do not typically turn to periodicals like *Good Housekeeping* for further examples of this trend, magazines were in fact perfectly poised to deliver each month a combination of consistency and novelty. Moreover, as Ann Ardis observes, monthly magazines that did not proclaim their literary focus are among the untapped vehicles for the circulation of literary discourse in this period (21).

In what follows I will characterize the modernity of Clemence Dane's work for *Good Housekeeping* in two ways. First, Dane positioned her essays with respect to modernist and academic criticism and vis-à-vis mass journalism. Her *oeuvre* is a record of her contributions to modern debates about what, when, and how to read, contributions in which she carved out a generous territory for discussion of reading as a modern woman. Second, Dane's essays show how literary journalists could take advantage of the seriality of the periodical and its miscellany to develop a sustained and infinitely varied conversation about books and reading.

Dane's monthly book pages collectively provide a record of non-academic literary criticism in the interwar period. This record reveals an ongoing, sometimes combative dialogue with academic literary criticism as well as continued resistance to reading habits dominated by the consumption of formulaic and degraded exemplars of literature. In some essays, the daily press epitomizes the derivative thought and mechanical language that spills over into formulaic novels. The "standardised times" make it more difficult to find "writers with minds and styles that are their own!," Dane proclaims in "Remarks About the Universe" (1929). "You do not ask of every writer that he should be a genius ... But you do ask of every individual that he should think for himself and not merely obey his newspaper or his party" (42). Dane associates newspaper content with "snippets," but approves her own implied audience's "capacity to swallow large doses of words and information" and their "desire to know more about the subjects which cannot be dealt with in snippets" ("Spring Fashions" 35).

In essays such as "The Kingdom of Me" and "Remarks About the Universe," both the daily paper and formulaic novels provide a foil for the books under review that "really rouse and quicken my interest, startle or annoy or lure me into thinking seriously about them" ("The Kingdom of Me" 61). The daily paper likewise casts Dane's literary journalism in a favorable light.[12] Thinking seriously as one reads is one example of the effortful reading practices that Dane hopes to foster in her readers. The reflection, meditation, and reasoning implied in "thinking seriously" contrast to the "casual reading" of newspapers, which encourage the reader to pass unreflectively from a report of atrocities in Morocco to a debate about public art in London ("Capes of Good Hope" 111). And while Dane did not invalidate what she called "light" reading, she curtailed the occasions for indulgence in it. Such delimitation of legitimate, casual reading left plenty of room for Dane's frequent construction of alternative reading practices for modern readers of *Good Housekeeping*, readers who in the very first issue of the magazine are understood to take "a wholesome and intelligent interest in the affairs of life" ("The Reason for *Good Housekeeping*").

Serious thinking, the desire for in-depth information, and independence of mind all characterize the space and time for reading good books and set them apart from casual newspaper reading and light literature. Against the newspaper's snippets of information, Dane's criticism establishes the conditions for appreciation of new books by setting them in literary-historical contexts and promoting their intertextual dialogue with an eclectic assortment of books. It may come as a surprise then, to learn that Dane distinguishes her periodical criticism from academic criticism just as determinedly as she contrasts it to mass journalism. Against the newly established

[12] As Kate Campbell, Patrick Collier, and Catherine Clay have demonstrated, journalism was the frequently denigrated other that served to foil "pure" and enduring forms of literature. This denigration continues in later twentieth-century distinctions.

rigors of academic methods, Dane advocates for a holistic appreciation of literature, engaging intellectual, somatic, sensuous, and emotional registers.

To call Clemence Dane a literary critic is to recognize that she evaluated literary texts, located them within literary traditions, and enlivened them through intertextual discussions that might range across centuries. Additionally, I call her literary criticism for *Good Housekeeping* "book essays" because their scope extends well beyond that of book reviews. Frequently, Dane offers guidance and commentary about reading: reading for pleasure, the experience of rereading good books (and cautions about limiting "light" reading), and reading for active citizenship. Like the nineteenth-century "man of letters" who wrote for "a relatively unified group, intelligent, educated, middleclass and serious-minded" (Shattock 13), Dane did not consider serious reading or intellectual musing to require specialization or regulation by academic protocols; nor did she confine these to literary matters. Her articles for *Good Housekeeping* and other journals include social criticism, both within book essays and separately from them. In some book essays, discussion of a recently published book is merely a springboard to the social and humanist questions raised by that book. For Dane, the two forms of critical practice, literary and social, were continuous. Her wide ken hearkens back to the Victorian man of letters, who kept his readers informed about a range of topics beyond literature, including "history, politics, religion and economics" (Shattock 13).

The practice of literary criticism had undergone significant changes when Dane began to work as a journalist. Increasingly "withdrawn from public life" the literary critic now served a smaller, more elite constituency within a university setting (Atherton 180). He no longer wrote with the circumstances and the taste of the common reader in mind. The division between academic and common readers, and between professional and "amateur" forms of authority, are just two of the fracture lines that altered the production and reception of literary criticism in the late nineteenth and early twentieth centuries. As the study of English literature began to take hold as a university discipline in the late nineteenth century, it fueled a series of debates about the kinds of learning that would constitute academic curricula. The English universities pursued diverse approaches, but also shared important elements: curricula increasingly emphasized forms of knowledge that could be supported by "the factual bodies of knowledge associated with the text's language, sources and historical background" (Atherton 81). In turn, a new emphasis on literary history laid out the historical influences between writers and "made explicit" the literary canon (Guy and Small 381; Atherton 29).

As these changes took place, the Victorian journalist critic who wrote for a general, educated audience was superseded by the professional literary critic in an academic institution. (By the turn of the century, Guy and Small find, literary criticism had been included in university studies of English literature.) For one thing, the authority of the critic now rested in his credentials and professional position in an academic institution and not merely in his literary sensibility and wide reading. Other changes, too, dramatically altered the landscape in which literary criticism was produced and read. The expansion of literacy in the late nineteenth century had fractured the relative unity of the mid-Victorian readership, while improved technologies for printing and distribution had facilitated the emergence of a stratified and robust early twentieth-century print culture. Yet although the determination and nature of the literary critic's authority were shifting, readers still sought literary guidance and opinion from daily, weekly, and monthly journals, critics continued to write it, and journals continued to provide it, albeit by targeting more specific audiences.

This sketch of the professionalization of literary criticism bears on Clemence Dane's journalism in several ways. First, while the professional critic is often contrasted to the "amateur" critic, Dane's case suggests that *literary journalist* is a more apt contrast to the academic critic; this designation also calls attention to the renaissance of the essay genre in this period. Dane is a literary journalist in the sense that she discusses and evaluates literature, but also insofar as she composes her essays with attention to literary design and with an understanding of English and European essay traditions. If the purpose of academic criticism is to provide information or develop judgments, Dane's journalism additionally seeks to provide literary pleasure.

Second, the professionalization of literary criticism influenced Dane's essay craft. Her journalism for *Good Housekeeping*, *Time and Tide*, and *The Forum*—magazines that targeted an educated audience—reflect contemporary debates about the purpose of literary criticism and the nature of the critic's authority. Dane rarely refers to specific schools of criticism, but the literary critic who has boxed himself into a rigid literary theory is the occasional butt of light criticism, as is the case in "Fools in the Forest" (*Good Housekeeping* 1925) and "Near Home and Far Off" (*Good Housekeeping* 1925). While not specifically hostile to an emerging modernist or academic criticism, then, Dane's criticism is openly resistant to academic or artificial delimitations of the literary. Dane's is the freedom to appreciate literature holistically, and she transmits these same freedoms to her readers. Positioned outside the university, Dane is not bound to emphasize objective standards or scientific methods for textual analysis. Moreover, both the occasional nature of the essay genre and Dane's status as a literary journalist liberate her to adopt an eclectic approach to books, to espouse a catholic taste, and to adopt unconventional forms of authority that implicitly challenge academic approaches to literature.

Dane wrote for *Time and Tide* from its earliest issues, publishing "Blake at the Tate Gallery," "Japanese Prints," and "Two Eyes" in 1920. This journalism precedes her regular essays in *Good Housekeeping* and thus illuminates some of the ways in which she positioned herself with respect to academic debates. Her first article for *Time and Tide* demonstrates her substantial preparation as a literary critic. "Two Eyes," whose title alludes to the Brothers Grimm fairy tale "One Eye, Two Eyes and Three Eyes," proposes a typology by which "to criticise, to appreciate the writers of our age" (32). Dane identifies three classes of writers, each setting out on a racetrack behind a different leader and each group aiming for a different goal, a different point on the track. To flesh out this schema, Dane draws on Goethe's notions of the True, the Good, and the Beautiful, aligning these with one-eyed, two-eyed, and three-eyed vision, respectively. She discusses writers as far-flung as the twelfth-century Benedictine monk Jocelin of Brakelond and James Joyce. John Galsworthy is the featured "two-eyed" writer, the "truest representative" of his group, a novelist who entirely merges his art and his message (34).

So far, Dane is working alongside, not in opposition to, her academic counterparts. She is engaged like them in questions of canon formation, she identifies purposes ("to criticise, to appreciate"), proposes a schema for the formation of judgments, discloses the values that inform such judgments (the True, the Good, the Beautiful), and provides wide-ranging textual examples to support her analysis. Yet "Two Eyes" does not read like a scholarly article, beginning with its endorsement of the "appreciation" of literature that cannot be supported with evidence. Dane further diverges from an academic community through the metaphor of children collaborating on a jigsaw puzzle that pervades the essay. "To your story-lover," Dane writes, "literature is a jig-saw puzzle, and the picture to be made a ladder of fame. On each rung there is room for just one author and the fun, of course, lies in fitting favourite authors into their proper places" (32). Dane suggests that literary critics are ordinary readers, beginning in childhood and continuing through their lives as readers.

It is to this ordinary reader that Dane turns her attention near the end of her essay to describe the purposes of their criticism and of hers:

> But all this jig-saw puzzling out of literary personalities does not, of course, pretend to be criticism. It remains a game that one plays because it amuses us and doesn't hurt them. What reader wants his criticism to take effect? Who really wants Carlyle to chasten his superlatives, or Dickens to suppress Little Nell, or The Triumphs of Temper cut out of the history of Literature? Such blurs are part of the charm. Criticism surely is a first aid to the audience rather than to the artist, and such as is here attempted is pertinent only if it simplifies the attitude of the reader to the genius of the writers concerned. (33)

Writing in this passage for the benefit of the modern common reader, who remains an "intelligent, educated, middleclass and serious-minded" reader, Dane no longer works alongside her academic counterparts. The common readers' canon is not restricted to masterpieces, but embraces the flaws and idiosyncrasies of favorite writers; "such blurs are part of the charm." Dane also announces her divergence from the academics' development of methodologies and bodies of knowledge to be used by the scholarly community. She emphasizes instead the common readers' different goals as critics—playing "a game ... because it amuses us"—and as readers of criticism: acquaintance with theories that can increase enjoyment by "simplifying the attitude of the reader to the genius of the writers concerned."

The Serial Advantage

Dane shared the academic critic's interest in classifying books to facilitate readers' understanding of literary genres and traditions. Yet the modality of the monthly magazine, so different from the professor's lecture, freed her to speak to her audience with ever-new purpose, each month varying her tone and her essay form to suit the occasion. Her book essays show how literary journalists could take advantage of the seriality of the periodical and its miscellany. As Laurel Brake has observed, the periodical created reader expectation, whetted their appetites, and encouraged them to return, subscribe (125). Dane used each month's column to describe a consistent persona's new encounter with books, people, natural objects, or social phenomena. Dane's serial book essays thus created a successful formula of continuity plus novelty.

In its inaugural issue, the editors of *Good Housekeeping* announced a "great feminine awakening": women were rousing themselves from "apathy and levity" and were taking "a wholesome and intelligent interest in the affairs of life" ("The Reason for *Good Housekeeping*"). In line with this vision, Dane invoked and constructed a multi-faceted modern woman who sought knowledge and aptitude, but who also read for enjoyment, and thus was free to satisfy her curiosity, indulge in nostalgia, or range far afield in her imagination. The seriality of the periodical essay was perfectly suited to address modern woman's multiple facets as well as the contingent material and psychological circumstances in which she read. Dane's essays frequently evoke an individual setting and mood for reading; collectively, they acknowledge manifold, individualized occasions for woman's reading. "Jefferies of the Fields" (1927) provides a good example. When the essay begins, the critic-persona has been woken up early by birdsong and is casting about for something to read that will suit her humor, one that will resonate with the birds. The first several paragraphs are structured by the chain of associations that run through the persona's mind, including an impressive list of neighborhood birds, their individual songs, and an observation about how "as the centuries go by" Britons become more and more out of sync with the natural diurnal cycle. Unable to fall back asleep, she tries "Jane Austen, that refuge from every form of boredom," who was nonetheless "useless at five o'clock in the morning" (73). Yet the mere mention of Austen prompts her to share her own opinion on the topic of Austen and the country: "I think she loved the country, but her love scarcely gets into her books" (73). Quoting from *Mansfield Park*, she finds that what Austen includes, if not the country, is her protagonist's yearning for it. The persona's search continues, ostensibly because her mood demands a very particular kind of book. This endearingly dramatized search makes the point that one's choice of reading varies with one's local conditions; it also provides the pretext for Dane to unfold a personal canon of books about the English country.

In the opening paragraphs of "Jefferies of the Fields," Dane thus demonstrates the leisured reader's freedom to range among many moods and dispositions. Dane's treatment of each iteration in the serial as a novel occasion for reading, matched with books to suit these occasions, squares with the reputed ephemeral truths of the personal essay. Implicit in the tradition of the personal essay is the idea of encounter with an object and the record of the knowledge arising from that encounter only (Good 4). Emphasis on the provisional conclusions of the personal essay has led commentators to distinguish it from the academic paper. As Graham Good demonstrates in his impressive history of the European essay, the two kinds of essayistic practice have diverged in part by virtue of the development of disciplinary values that have shaped the academic paper. While modernists should be recognized for their practice of the personal essay, Good argues, as modernism gained acceptance in academia "the essay was being replaced by the professional article as the form of literary criticism" (179). Just as academic critics honed the professional article, as a periodical essayist in the modernist period, Dane adapted her essays to the conventions of periodical writing and the editorial policies of *Good Housekeeping*.[13] But it was not just her adherence to the magazine mission that led to Dane's innovation in the periodical essay, as I will demonstrate. It was also the periodical essayist's freedom to treat each iteration in the serial as novel, exploratory. Each encounter with a new set of books prompts fresh mutual illumination of critic-reader and book.

In the chapters that follow, I will argue that Dane's critical essays depart from the emphasis on novelty and on contingent knowledge in the personal essay by welding its "spirit of encounter" to enduring structures and principles. One such structure is the sensibility that such reading implicitly fosters. In contrast to the contingency of the *Good Housekeeping* reader's encounters with books and her multiple roles in modern society, her sensibility—as Dane envisions it—is a facet of her self that accretes, becoming enriched with the passage of time. Through her very reading of books of the hour, the multi-faceted and mobile woman furnishes herself with the language and the interior structures of feeling. Jane Austen, it turns out, is not quite "useless at five o'clock in the morning," for Dane opens and then quotes from *Northanger Abbey* and *Mansfield Park*. Dane is Fanny Price's double when Fanny finds it sad to "lose all the pleasures of spring" and when she realizes how much she "derive[s] animation both of body and mind" from "the opening of leaves in her uncle's plantations and the glory of his woods" (qtd. in Dane 73).

[13] One such adaptation is the essayist's incidental or deliberate dialogue with other voices. For example, Dane's first articles on social questions constitute a debate with other voices on a topic, as I discuss in the case of "Some Questions on Divorce."

As much as the imagined reader of Dane's essays shifts roles freely and adopts a variety of dispositions, she simultaneously stabilizes her cognitive and emotional faculties; her self-knowledge and capacity for feeling are figured as forms of identity that are nourished with each new reading encounter.

Dane vicariously feels what Fanny Price feels because she is an experienced reader, schooled in the conventions of reading novels. Thus, the most stable of Dane's enduring critical structures is literary tradition. The critical, if not the personal, essayist must depart from the emphasis on novelty found in the personal essay, as well as its practice of extending merely provisional conclusions, so as to impart principles and knowledge to her readers. In addition to describing her experience reading a new set of books, in each essay Dane introduces a dialogue between these books and literary tradition, a second mutually illuminating encounter. Thus, while the book essays for *Good Housekeeping* present a series of fresh but transient reading experiences, they also present the stability and the solidity of literary tradition. The critic's knowledge of tradition is a second source of stability, as it gives rise to her confident expression of critical principles. As Adorno says of Proust, the essayist critic offers us "the knowledge of an experienced [person]" ("Essay as Form," qtd. in Good 177).

Chapter 1, "Books That Endure," situates Dane's *Good Housekeeping* journalism within two contemporaneous cultural phenomena: the rise of university English Studies and critical debate about the perceived dichotomy between ephemeral journalism and enduring literature. While Dane's authorship of a monthly book page might have aligned her in this period with the transience of journalism, I argue that, on the contrary, she quickly gained the authority of a literary critic and the trustworthiness of a confirmed book lover. The chapter illustrates Dane's relation to European traditions of the essay and argues that she made innovative contributions to classic essay forms. Dane's strength as a critic, however, arose not only from her essay craft, but also from her brilliant deployment of a formula native to the periodical series: repetition plus variation. Nearly each month, she situated new books within long-standing literary traditions. Across more than a decade of book essays for *Good Housekeeping*, Dane taught her readers that, far from clashing, tradition and innovation were the very foundation of books that endure.

Chapter 1 illustrates Dane's critical principles through analysis of four major essays that appeared in the 1920s *Good Housekeeping*: "Melpomene and the Fat Boy," "Things That Go Bump in the

Night," "The Poet v. the Talkies" and "Near Home and Far Off." Collectively the essays demonstrate Dane's support for cultural innovation that at once addressed the unease of the decade and grew out of traditions of poetry, fiction, drama, music, and even film. "Books That Endure" concludes that concurrent with the university's development of cognitive approaches to literature, the para-curricular forum of Dane's monthly book page endorsed the pleasure of aesthetic forms, both large and small, as well as the rich insight to be gleaned by rereading a beloved book after a passage of time.

Chapter 2, "Common Readers and the Varied Pleasures of Reading," situates Dane's theorization of the common reader with respect to Samuel Johnson, Hugh Walpole, and Virginia Woolf; and it demonstrates her engagement with contemporary social and cultural concerns about reading. These include the formation of taste, the somatic, emotional, and cognitive responses to books, the commercial domination of book production, and the common reader's responsibility to participate in critical dialogue about national literary culture. Dane models and stages such cultural dialogue. The chapter shows that she welcomes opportunities to link books and reading to cultural trends already garnering popular interest, such as the artifacts unearthed in archaeological digs; and it reveals Dane's assertive dialogue with academic and modernist literary critics, particularly for the purpose of acknowledging and often departing from their judgments in matters of literary genre, literary reception, the status of the author, and more.

The periodical community of *Good Housekeeping* writers and readers was thus always informed by and articulated with external stakeholders, members of a wider community. Yet, Chapter 2 shows, Dane's book pages particularly cultivated the periodical community by encouraging readers to imagine others different from themselves yet to whom they are bound by virtue of the shared experiences reflected in books. Yet affection and nostalgia only begin to describe the links between members of the community. Capitalizing on the consistency and variety that are unique to the serial, Dane provided literary instruction for readers, stimulated their imaginative and critical engagement with challenging texts, and endorsed their freedom to enjoy a variety of books. By modeling and fostering many forms of reading pleasure, she protected this "purpose" for reading against a culture of advancement that fostered reading to gain others' approval or to become credentialed.

Chapter 3, "The History of Ourselves: Cultural, Rural, and Matriarchal Legacies," demonstrates that in a period of instability following the war, Dane used her book essays to develop readers' understanding of their many-faceted heritage. The essays variously explore the cultural traces of a buried matriarchal past, the continued force of archetypal patterns in literature, and the threatened legacy of Britons' rural heritage. Dane often constructs British cultural, rural, and political traditions as endangered legacies, even as she insists that they be tapped into as resources that can correct the moderns' foreshortened view of literary and political history and provide guidance for action in the present. Vitally innovative, literature both illuminates and keeps alive this heritage, which Dane represents unfolding through the collective unconscious or in English national life. Modernity as construed by *Good Housekeeping*, these essays show, was capacious enough to affirm the legacies of cultural history expressed in both popular and elite media.

Chapter 4, "The Boundary Stones of Belief," argues that Dane played a significant role in affirming and stimulating the moderns' spiritual, ethical, and imaginative faculties. Drawing on texts from both Western and world traditions, Dane traces the biblical forms and mythic patterns that structure the religious literature of the past and that continue to inform modern societal dilemmas. A believer herself, Dane is nonetheless interested in the secular expressions of archetypes. "Cities of God" offers a good example. In that essay, Dane explores both religious representations of holy cities and secular manifestations of the age-old division between builders and razers. In Dane's essays about belief, ancient religious myth continues to inflect modern literature, and both of these in turn illuminate modern secular society.

In addition to her support for religious belief, Dane actively participates in the period's exploration of a range of alternative beliefs. Impressive in historical and literary scope, Dane's essays of belief collectively establish a clear link between the human imagination and the human capacity for belief, and between belief and ethical responsibility. They prompt readers to recognize new forms of belief, enlarging its territory, and to set the boundary stones between belief and skepticism far from the center of their lived experience.

In each of the essays featured in "The Boundary Stones of Belief," Dane recognizes how individual media may influence readers' cultivation of hope or of apathy. I argue that Dane's essays of belief are conceived and developed to counter a mode of reading that she believes contributes to apathy: the passage from one, perhaps disturbing, newspaper item to a pleasantly distracting one. Dane reflects critically on the newspaper's ability to bring global events into the homes of readers and yet allow them to remain emotionally distant from the human atrocities so often reported. She calls on literature to assume—or resume—its responsibility to restore magnitude to the representation of crisis and suffering.

Chapter 5, "The Voice of Women," expands the focus of earlier chapters to examine five major feminist writers for *Good Housekeeping*: Violet Bonham Carter, Clemence Dane, Helena Normanton, Rebecca West, and Rose Macaulay. Together they formed a virtual community for the advancement of women's political subjectivity in the 1920s and beyond. They address such topics as women's psychological and political readiness for active citizenship, the reading and education that best fosters women's political subjectivity, their ethical capacity, and the influence women might wield as they expand their participation in the public sphere.

Dane published a monthly essay (and sometimes two a month), with Helena Normanton's contributions not lagging far behind. When we add articles by Bonham Carter, West, Macaulay, and numerous one-time authors, it becomes clear that the regularity and concentration of feminist voices in *Good Housekeeping* in themselves amount to a kind of strength, to which we must add the coincidence of the concerns the journalists individually address. To prepare women for active engagement in the civic sphere, they collectively developed rich rhetorical strategies, including advice about reading, warnings about the cost of political apathy, encouragement in the form of reader-journalist mirroring, and the craft of satirical and comic relief in the face of women's baffling new civic responsibilities. These essayists formed a feminist critical mass within *Good Housekeeping*, alongside domestic and fashion features, that has only recently garnered critical attention.[14] Within this collective effort, Clemence Dane's book page reveals the versatile role of literary discourse to inform and enhance debates about citizenship in *Good Housekeeping*.

[14] See Wood, *Modernism and Modernity in British Women's Magazines* and Deen, "Remarkable Obscurity: Portraits of Professional Women."

Chapter 1

Books That Endure

There is some irony in Clemence Dane's repeated recourse to the platform of a monthly magazine from which to urge readers to choose books that endure. In addition to deploying an ephemeral vehicle, the periodical essay, in which to advocate for enduring literature, Dane inflects her essays with awareness of the much-discussed dichotomy between literature and journalism. For much of the nineteenth and twentieth centuries, writes Kate Campbell, journalism stood for a "factual, conventional, heavy-handed commercial practice, the antithesis of literature's integrity and creativity" ("Introduction" 1). Journalism propagated the idiom of street life against the reasoning of books; it stood for the scraps and fragments against proper knowledge.[1] Dane participates in this detraction of journalism in essays like "A Bunch of Daisies" (1924), in which she valorizes literary writing and denigrates newspaper writing. Using the example of a lecture summarized in a newspaper, she argues that however much it may have gripped its audience, it is useless as literature until remodeled.

> [A] verbatim report [in a newspaper] leaves out for you the pause, the smile, the turn of the body, the movement of the hand, all the eloquent trifles which in literature are supplied by that delicate manipulation of word and phrase which we call style. (29)

For the most part, however, Dane's essays exempt the woman's monthly magazine from the forms that constitute literature's other: popular novels, pulp fiction, the daily newspaper.[2] And perhaps this

[1] See especially Campbell, "Journalistic Discourses."

[2] One exception is "A Bunch of Daisies," in which Dane characterizes her readers as "you who skim these monthly summaries." She buttonholes the reader: "But, as it is, does a vague dissatisfaction ever depress you as you hurry to your library, as you tick off the latest novels on your list?" (92).

exemption is justified. Not only has the periodical essay constituted a convergence of literature and journalism (Brake 122), yoking two modes of discourse that have been polemically separated, but additionally Dane enjoyed the status of a regular columnist, giving her a cultural presence that overrode the transience of the journalist's utterances. And she used that cultural authority to widen the divide between the ephemeral and the enduring. In her essays the "sex" novels and thrillers *du jour* contrast to new books that Dane illuminates within long-standing literary traditions and that promise to become classics. And against the overproduction and rapid consumption of "light" literature she urged effortful reading and the discovery of "new beauties" with each rereading of beloved books.

The tension between the ephemeral and the enduring that characterizes the work of the periodical essayist, as well as the apparent polarity between modernity and tradition, figure prominently in Dane's book essays. Her repeated and varied development of these themes suggests her value to study of the period's discursive construction of high and low forms of journalism. In her book essays, Dane figures popular novels as ephemera that foil enduring literature even while she models broadbrow reading. And her own craft of classic essay forms—the epitome, the rambler, the constellation, and others—affiliates her with *belles lettres* and sets her periodical essays apart from newspaper writing. Dane's literary-critical essays for *Good Housekeeping* thus contribute to the history of common reading, and, as I argue below, particularly inform us about the pedagogical campaign carried on in quality women's magazines to protect the territory of literature against the incursion of commercially motivated reading matter and of new mass communication technologies such as the dictaphone and the talkies.

This chapter considers exemplars of Dane's literary criticism in which she draws on the tension between books of the hour and books that last, to establish principles for the evaluation of poetry, fiction, and drama. Dane's substantial body of literary criticism, some 120 book essays, provides a compelling case study in the influence of the "Book Page" in the women's monthly magazine. Key to that influence, I will argue, is the authority of the so-called amateur critic. Nominally marginalized with respect to the rising status and influence of academic critics during this period, Dane's literary criticism in fact enjoyed a wide and enduring audience, albeit one largely restricted to the prosperous middle classes. The denigration of journalistic criticism notwithstanding, Dane's literary-critical corpus reveals a powerful forum, the women's monthly magazine, in which the journalist critic, far from occupying a marginal or embattled position, enjoys proliferating forms of authority. She makes her début for *Good Housekeeping* as a novelist- and dramatist-critic, identified and characterized on the magazine covers as well as through editorial insets. But it is the succession of monthly essays that establishes her strong rapport with readers, democratizes the essayist's authority, and soon makes editorial publicity for Dane superfluous; through iterations of her book essays, Dane takes on the authority of an essayist-critic. By the end of 1928, when *Good Housekeeping* solicited responses to an extensive "reading questionnaire," Dane was among the most revered of *Good Housekeeping*'s regular columnists. Reporting on the results of the survey in March 1929, the editors find that "Clemence Dane's articles came in for a considerable amount of appreciation, and so did those of Lady Violet Bonham Carter, Jessica Cosgrave, and St. John Ervine" ("The Results of Our Reading Questionnaire" 144). Dane contributes to the distinguished history of the European essay and joins the ranks of critics from Samuel Johnson to William Hazlitt to Virginia Woolf. The high/low divide that Dane addresses in her criticism is mirrored in her own status: a critic who rises above the newspaper woman's report of transient controversies and trivial events, a woman of letters steeped in the history and art of the essay.

Skillful exemplars, Dane's serialized essays find individual forms for her affective and intellectual responses to modernity, books, and literary genre. They epitomize both the versatility of the essay form and its occasional nature, qualities underscored in recent critical work on the essay. Traditionally, the essayist shapes experience according to her individual sensibility and need not rehearse received authority. This freedom from established wisdom has often been linked to the unsystematic nature of the essay's concepts and designs; as Graham Good characterizes its stance: "What happens happens *to me* and has no design other than what I can give it ... The world is chaotic and disenchanted, but also free for me to order it 'for now'" (22).[3] Yet other theories of the essay depart from this conception of its provisional design to depict a reciprocal anchoring of concept and concrete object or phenomenon. In *The Origin of German Tragic Drama*, Benjamin describes the essay as the salvation of phenomena by means of eternal ideas: "Ideas are timeless constellations, and by virtue of the elements [of phenomena] being

[3] Both Good and Gualtieri offer insightful discussions of the essayist's freedom from received authority and of the provisional character of her expression.

seen as points in such constellations, phenomena are subdivided and at the same time redeemed" (34). Dane's critical essays, I will argue, carry on this tradition of the salvation of ephemeral phenomena by means of "timeless constellations" of literary traditions, whose designs she sketches for her readers as they take up the books of the hour, one by one. Through her work for *Good Housekeeping*, the essayist-critic freely considers topics of the day, which she combines with analysis of literary traditions and new books that can illuminate those topics. Illustrating the virtually limitless, generative power of books to speak to the experience of female modernity, Dane's essays repeatedly teach readers to see how an individual book is embedded in an established tradition.

The authority and freedom of periodical essayists like Dane were strengthened by the rise of English Studies in the 1920s and 1930s. Outside the disciplinary strictures of the academy, the periodical essayist, sometimes called an "amateur" critic, enjoyed the freedom to adopt heterodox methods, idiosyncratic points of view, and eclectic canons. She had no stake in performing the gestures of the new disciplinary practitioners by upholding objective standards, testable methods, and verifiable results. Thus, she surveyed, upheld, and celebrated a wider literary territory.

Dane's essays reflect a sometimes-contentious divergence between the academic critic's and the journalist critic's assumptions and goals. Good has observed that "the essay remains a focus of individual resistance to 'systems' of various kinds, political, intellectual and cultural" (185). Indeed, resistance to academic practice helps the essayist define her distinct identity. Especially as represented in Dane's essays about literature that endures, the academic critic condescends to notice only a narrow range of what the public reads, while the journalist critic freely tastes of both popular and highbrow literatures, for she has learned the importance of "giving the public, not the intellectual but the ordinary everyday public, what it wants" ("American Primitives" 185). A more impassioned opposition to academic critical practice comes in "Goliath Slings the Pebble Back," an extended allegory about the battle of the brows, in which Dane proclaims: "I don't believe that poetry can be assessed in the schools and the critical columns: I don't believe that poetry is a question of brains and head. I believe that poetry is a question of ear and heart" (409). As this last example suggests, Dane's position outside of academic criticism strengthens her affiliation with the resistant tradition of the essay.

But if Dane's literary criticism gains power through its dialogic tension with the "objective" methods of academic criticism, that is in part because like the university professor, Dane's aims are pedagogic. *Clemence Dane and Good Housekeeping: Modernity and Common Reading* makes the case that Dane's serially published book essays provide what I have called their para-curricular instruction of readers; that is, their work to cultivate well-informed and self-directed women, only a small proportion of whom were likely seeking degrees at university ("Cultivating Citizen Readers"). Along with such regular *Good Housekeeping* columnists as Helena Normanton and Violet Bonham Carter, and in addition to occasional or singly featured columnists, Dane's literary criticism suggests that our study of women's quality magazines in this period has underestimated this para-curricular function.

The nature of Clemence Dane's authority as a book essayist for *Good Housekeeping* illustrates the centrality of mainstream literary journalism both to female modernity and to histories of reading. This authority helps account for her strong cultural presence both within and beyond *Good Housekeeping*. This chapter will demonstrate the development of Dane's authority from a "virile" intellectual, based on her success as a novelist and a dramatist with name recognition in major London theaters, to an integral authority based on her demonstrated wide reading. As literary critic for *Good Housekeeping*, Dane spoke to readers across a ten-year period, a span of time that enabled her to build readers' confidence in her dual roles of expert and common reader. In the essays discussed in "Books That Endure," she stands alongside her readers on the plain, linked to them by the shared conviction that reading is "the most fascinating occupation that life can offer" ("Monuments" 59). But her knowledge of literary traditions simultaneously places her above her *Good Housekeeping* readers, on a peak from which she gains a long historical perspective. Like the *Good Housekeeping* readers, Dane experiences the pleasures and the frustrations of a modern book industry. The surfeit of new books published makes some readers treat books as so many sweets to be consumed; while agents within the nexus of book publicity and distribution encourage readers to select light, easily digested fare. Characteristically, Dane does not condemn these experiences, but acknowledges her own appetite for them. At the same time, in her educative role, she speaks with the authority of an expert, albeit one outside the university, whose "long-established habit of reading" ("Interesting People" 88) affords wide vision and has acquainted her with deeper reading experiences, especially those that tap into universal and archetypal human emotions. As we will see, the literary journalist's claim to an authority based on book loving and on

LET CLEMENCE DANE HELP YOU TO FIND THE MONTH'S BEST BOOK

WOULD you not value the help of so discerning a critic as Miss Clemence Dane in the selection of the books you read?

And if that help was augmented by the advice of Hugh Walpole, J. B. Priestley, George Gordon and Sylvia Lynd, would you not feel confident of being recommended only the most "worth while" books of the day, and of thus saving much valuable reading leisure?

Yet this care-free selection of the best modern books is only part of the service which is rendered free by the **Book Society**.

Each month the distinguished committee named below meet to determine their choice from among the manuscripts submitted to them in advance by the leading publishers—the pick of the publishers' own lists.

This selected book, together with a supplementary list of other recommended good books, and the committee's criticism of each, reaches members of the **Book Society** on the morning of its publication.

The list is a guarantee against disappointment; for anybody to whom the first book doesn't happen to appeal, is free to exchange it within five days for any of the other specified books.

NO ENTRANCE FEE

There is no entrance fee to the **Book Society**. You pay only the bare published price of the monthly book and remember, chosen books are always likely to be first editions.

These books you will receive before the rest of the world. They are inexpensive and ones you'll want to keep.

The high literary standing of the Selection Committee makes it impossible for you to miss any really good modern books.

In the monthly Book Society News you get a real, live criticism, and you are guaranteed against disappointment by the supplementary lists.

NO SUBSCRIPTION

The invaluable service you receive costs nothing. Think of the time and trouble that membership of the Book Society will save you.

Never to miss an outstanding book; *never* to waste a moment of your precious leisure on a worthless book; *never* to have to wait your time for the book that everyone is discussing; *never* to run the risk of buying a book which will disappoint you. All these "nevers" are ensured by membership of the Book Society—a membership that costs you nothing.

Below you will find a printed form entitling you to a Free Booklet which tells in more detail the story of the Book Society. Take time by the forelock—send it off to us to-day.

YOUR COMMITTEE

HUGH WALPOLE
(Chairman)
J. B. PRIESTLEY
GEORGE GORDON
(President of Magdalen College)
CLEMENCE DANE
SYLVIA LYND

IT COSTS YOU NOTHING TO JOIN

MRS. SYLVIA LYND

GEORGE GORDON

J. B. PRIESTLEY

HUGH WALPOLE

You may send me, without cost to myself, your **FREE BOOKLET** explaining how the Book Society operates. I understand that this involves me in no obligation to subscribe to your service.

Name..............................
(Mr., Mrs., or Miss)
Address..............................
....

THE BOOK SOCIETY, LTD., 38 Grosvenor Place, London, S.W.1

Advertised Goods are Good Goods. 159

Figure 1.1 Dane enjoyed the dual authority of expert and common reader. In 1929, the new Book Society capitalized on readers' confidence in Dane to promote its book-of-the-month club. Courtesy of Hearst Magazines UK.

decades of reading sets her apart from the trained literary scholar and marks out her distinctly different guidance to readers.

Wide vision and deep reading experiences are the anchors enabling Dane and her readers to resist total immersion in the immediacy and contingency of ephemeral reading matter, both the periodical in which Dane's essays appear and popular novels such as the romance and the shocker. Far from merely helping readers to fill hours of leisure, Dane's literary criticism modeled how wide reading would afford the literary-historical perspective needed to evaluate new books and to contribute to the longevity of good books.

If Dane's double role solidified her ready sympathy with readers' immersion in the immediacy of new books, as well as her long-sighted wisdom, her authority was also important to the editorial vision of *Good Housekeeping*. Dane was among the first regular columnists for *Good Housekeeping* and was promoted, in alternately masculine and feminine guises, both as a successful dramatist and novelist and as an intellectual. Such a construction suggests the relatively new, controversial position of the woman journalist in the early 1920s. Dane's first four articles for *Good Housekeeping* were social, political, and cultural criticism. A controversial piece on divorce law reform, "Some Questions on Divorce," appeared in the inaugural issue of *Good Housekeeping* (March 1922); and was strategically counterbalanced by a more family-friendly topic for her second article, "The Educational Value of Acting in Schools" (November 1922). There followed an article on the perceived decline in religious faith; and the series concluded with a review of exhibits in the art academy. In this initial sequence of four articles, then, the apparent extent of Dane's expertise, while it did not always bear a direct relation to her authorship of plays and novels, included politics, social mores, education, religion, and culture. *Good Housekeeping* curiously underscored such remarkable breadth of intellect with indicators of masculine strength: "Miss Dane's article shows a virile and logical mind at work on the problem. She states facts arrestingly and points to a way out."[4] At the same time, a large photograph of Dane on the first spread reveals feminine beauty and a readiness to speak directly to readers about all things literary. Holding an open magazine, she gazes at *Good Housekeeping* readers and authenticates both her own expertise and theirs, that of common readers.[5]

[4] This comment appears as an inset on the first page of "Some Questions on Divorce."

[5] For a discussion of Dane's skill in her historical essays in reaching both students of literature and ordinary readers, see Deen, "Cultivating Citizen Readers."

A third affirmation of her credentials lists the titles of her publications beneath her byline.

In selecting a journalist who initially offers breadth rather than specialization, *Good Housekeeping* positioned itself as a magazine that included but transcended the staples of the women's domestic magazines, a trend noticed by recent scholars working in women's print media.[6] Thus, even while the inaugural editorial emphasized the home—"We believe that the time is ripe for a great new magazine which shall worthily meet the needs of the housekeeping woman of to-day"—it simultaneously affirmed modern women's wish to be in touch with the political and social world beyond the home. Thus, readers were promised that "The burning questions of the day will be reflected each month in articles by women in the public eye, known for their sound grasp of their subject—by women who can lead women, and who are fearless, frank, and outspoken" ("The Reason for *Good Housekeeping*").

Dane's first four articles certainly addressed such "burning questions." Yet in masculinizing Dane's first contribution, the editors reflect contemporary anxiety about the authority of the woman journalist. As Patrick Collier demonstrates, women were understood to be the major consumers of the new, degraded journalism. Their appetites drove the perceived transformation of "the daily newspaper from an outlet for sound political news and opinion" to—especially at the hands of press barons like Lord Northcliffe—"a purveyor of gossip, news 'tit-bits,' oddities, and garish crime coverage" ("Journalism Meets Modernism" 188). As writers of news about women, women journalists were also implicated in the reputed decline of journalism. A regular contributor to *Good Housekeeping*, even St. John Ervine joined in the critique of a "womanised" popular press and marveled at the readiness of newspapers to "print 'powerful articles' by young ladies not long enlarged from school on the reform of Marriage or the reorganization of Sex or the overhaul of Religion," topics that Dane herself covered in the first issues of her column (qtd. in Collier, "Journalism Meets Modernism" 188). In pointing out Dane's "virile and logical mind at work on the problem," the editors distinguish Dane's longform essays from light journalism, tidbits, and gossip, and associate

[6] See Hackney, "'Women are News'" 117–18; Giles 123; and Wood, *Modernism and Modernity*.

her voice with intellectual force. It is pertinent that this tack of masculinizing the woman journalist did not last, as I discuss below.[7]

Dane's first "book page" for *Good Housekeeping* did not appear until October 1923, but *Good Housekeeping* promoted her well before then as a "brilliant dramatist and novelist" (Volume 2); as a rising star "who won distinction both as a novelist and dramatist with a rapidity that was startling"; and as a "shrewd critic" (Volume 3). Within a short time, Dane passed from celebrity to the credibility of an expert but common reader. *Good Housekeeping* stops finding it necessary to authenticate Dane's expertise, so that in the "Headliner" for *Good Housekeeping* 5.2 (April 1924), she is simply "Clemence Dane."

The breadth of Dane's grasp of modern society and culture remained a cornerstone of her authority even while it was doubled by her practice of common reading. As we have seen, Dane's amateur authority arose first from the breadth of her knowledge in society, religion, and the arts, not from her specialization. Second, it is affirmed each month as an intrinsic function of the serial: the satisfactory product of the previous month is repeated, with variation on stable elements, in the next month's issue. Dane was thus well-positioned to meet *Good Housekeeping*'s promise that it would address multiple facets of the modern woman's life, including her wish to employ leisure time intelligently, to be well-informed, and to hear both sides of the issues of the day.

This chapter features four essays that illustrate Dane's characteristic approaches to the evaluation of literature in the 1920s. In "Melpomene and the Fat Boy," "Things That Go Bump in the Night," "The Poet v. the Talkies," and "Near Home and Far Off" Dane shows readers how to identify books that endure, and even how to make them endure. In these essays we can hear an ongoing, sometimes combative dialogue with academic literary criticism as well as continued resistance to reading habits dominated by the consumption of mass, formulaic, and degraded exemplars of literature. The literary-critical tenets themselves illuminate Dane's appreciation for the new, the topical, and the modern, along with an assurance

[7] If it is easy to find detractions of the woman journalist in this period, it is also the era that registered a "seismic shift from conceptualizing femininity in terms of self-effacement to the view of women as agents of literary production" represented by such initiatives as the Hogarth Press, the *Wheels* anthology, the Seizin Press, and The Hours Press (Dowson 536). See also Hackney, "'Women are News'" and Collier, "Journalism Meets Modernism."

that archetypal patterns, or long-standing literary traditions, or tried and true recipes for good books, undergird the new.

"Melpomene and the Fat Boy"

The women's magazine was an ideal vehicle for this project to present the continually new faces of familiar, stable structures. Periodicals were central to women's experience of modernity because their seriality allowed magazines to approach the idea of the modern in endlessly new ways. Regular "departments" organizing tables of contents—modern childrearing, contemporary housing design, new household products, cultural reviews, and installments of serialized fiction—all these built the formula of repetition plus variation into magazines like *Good Housekeeping*. Yet if a single issue of *Good Housekeeping* facilitated readers' engagement with the *now*, it simultaneously demonstrated how often the new could be set in the context of venerable traditions. The temporal rhythms of the present were established through articles, photographs, illustrations, and ads highlighting the new spring fashions from Paris or the upcoming Ideal Home Exhibition. These were balanced by long features that celebrated (and sometimes deplored) the modern by surveying its emergence from a coherent history. Helena Normanton writing on law and politics, and Clemence Dane on books, regularly provided this reassuring historical view: good trends had the support of precedent, while regrettable modern phenomena could be turned around with guidance from the past.[8] In this way, the *Good Housekeeping* reader was encouraged to keep pace with modernity, to contribute to its efficiencies, and relish its pleasures, but also to cultivate a thoughtful and informed understanding of the past's sustaining function. Normanton's two articles in Volume 7 illustrate the second of these rhythms. In "Women Justices of the Peace" (1925), Normanton celebrates the Sex Disqualification (Removal) Act of 1919, which has restored to women "the ancient office of Justiceship of the Peace. The word 'restoration' is used advisedly" (64), she adds. Normanton then reels off a list of six women who served under monarchs from Stephen to Queen Mary, including the Countess of Chester under Stephen; an unnamed woman under

[8] Helena Normanton (1882–1957) took advanced degrees in History and in French, lectured and wrote on feminist issues, and became the first female barrister to practice in England (Workman).

Edward I; Nicolla de la Haye under King John; Margaret Countess of Richmond under Henry VII; and Lady of Berkely under Queen Mary. Normanton even unearths evidence of a woman commoner in Sussex, "named Rouse, girt with the sword of knighthood," who "habitually sat upon the Bench as Justice at Assizes and Sessions" (64). But later, women forgot the "*roles* played by their greater ancestresses." Characteristically, Normanton draws on history to emphasize what has been restored in modernity rather than to proclaim its revolution from the past.

Normanton's conception of modernity as a renewal of women's proven strength recurs in many of her *Good Housekeeping* essays. Clemence Dane's book essays adopt a similar approach as they set new books within well-established literary traditions. And some of Dane's essays, including "Melpomene and the Fat Boy" and "The Poet v. the Talkies," guide readers to books that endure in order to reverse instances of contemporary cultural deterioration.

In "Melpomene and the Fat Boy" (1925), Dane deplores an accelerating audience demand for "shockers" and advises readers more often to choose tragedy, as defined by Aristotle's *Poetics*. A spokesman for the shocker, Dickens's "fat boy" of the *Pickwick Papers* strives to make our flesh creep, while tragedy, sponsored by the muse Melpomene, elicits the pity and fear that bind us to others. Dane's critical authority in "Melpomene" is based on her wide-ranging knowledge of tragedy and its relatives, including the shocker, which she legitimizes by identifying its proper role to flavor "one's rest hour." Finally, with the same expertise that marks her historical view, Dane identifies modern generic innovations such as the tragi-comedy. In this final section of the essay, Dane's critical judgment again plays a role, this time to distinguish inadvertent combinations of tragedy and comedy from deliberate, successful ones.

Yet Dane's authority is not confined to her erudition. In "Melpomene," as in each of the four essays discussed in "Books That Endure," the confidence inspired by author and critic Clemence Dane is doubled by her *bona fides* as a common reader. She is one with her readers, anticipating their thoughts and feelings, which likewise arise in her own mind and heart. In "Melpomene," Dane's ordinariness produces her affective response to tragedy and compels her readers likewise to embrace awe, terror, pity, or rapture, which ancient Greek audiences validated in ritual spectatorship. Dane illustrates how such emotions could overwhelm ancient audiences through the story of Phrynichus, whose tragedy induced such suffering in the spectators that he was heavily fined.[9] Thus while Dane begins "Melpomene" exercising her critical acumen, what claims her sustained interest is literature's ability to stir pity and fear within us. These emotions are dangerous, but the turbulence they bring moves us beyond ourselves to a state of sympathy for others. "The blackest villain in hell must at least be grey to himself," says Dane. "It must be possible for the watcher to say of him—'I shudder, but I understand: and understanding I feel pity as well as terror'" (131).

Contemporary audiences, however, prefer sensation to emotion. In "Melpomene and the Fat Boy," Dane identifies a deterioration in the culture of reading, epitomized by excessive consumption. With the expansion of the periodical press after 1870 "a spate of new publications encouraged not discrimination and refinement but demand for more of the same, 'light' entertainment" (McAleer 3). Dane cites bookseller data that for every reader of classical tragedy there are 100 readers of crime thrillers. Detective fiction in this period attracted all classes of readers and was the exception to the general rule that popular fiction was consumed by lower middle-class and working-class audiences (McAleer 8). Frequently lumped together with cinemagoers, readers, especially women readers, were accused of bypassing their cognitive and moral faculties to satisfy an insatiable appetite for stimulating media that could be quickly ingested (Littau 21, 156). Dane likewise adopts a discourse of consumption to develop her own criticism of shocker readers. She even hints that such reading is akin to addiction, capturing a related nineteenth-century worry memorably expressed by Alfred Austin in 1874. No sooner did fiction readers finish one book than they "hunger for another," he observed, calling this tendency a "vulgar, detrimental habit, like dram-drinking" (qtd. in Littau 42). Dane concurs. "If the shocker habit 'puts me off' *Wuthering Heights*, for instance; if it makes me pronounce *Tess of the D'Urbervilles* long-winded, or *Lord Jim* obscure," then it does more harm than "any of the other habits by which we debase our long-suffering bodies" (22). In suggesting that immoderate shocker reading is a vice, Dane demarcates low texts to be consumed from high texts to be contemplated.

In the first part of "Melpomene," Dane is unusually didactic, as she takes readers to task for their excessive consumption of thrillers. In dialogue with a voice who opines that "surely the public can be left to indulge its love of the thrill in moderation," Dane replies,

[9] The tragedy in question was *The Capture of Miletus*. The Athenian tragic poet Phrynichus flourished around 500 BC ("Phrynichus").

"But can it? But does it? Isn't this ever-increasing modern craving for mental and physical 'creeps' a sign that we are living far too sensationally already?" (131). Yet even as she criticizes this modern trend, Dane acknowledges that shockers and tragedy capitalize alike on a primordial human response to others' pain. She also admits her own occasional enjoyment of thrillers; and her use of the first-person pronoun lowers the finger of blame she had pointed at readers:

> I seem to be abusing shockers. I don't mean to do that. I get far too much amusement and enjoyment out of them to be so ungrateful. I want my daily shocker at lunch after a morning's work as much as a haymaker wants his glass or so of cider in the hot middle of the day. It may not be exactly nourishing; but it gives one's rest-hour a flavour. (22)

This characteristic humility marks the essayist's double role as expert and as common reader. Dane's erudition cements her expertise, while her admission that she, too, enjoys shockers positions her within the body of flawed common readers to whom she speaks. Equality with her readers allows her to speak knowledgeably about their taste and habits. In "Melpomene and the Fat Boy" we can see Dane making this transition from critic to common reader, first evaluating Melville's reputation and then arguing that his humanity is more important than his technique:

> Not least among these tragi-comedians is that writer who was so little appreciated in his lifetime, and is now, perhaps, overpraised—Herman Melville. Yet why should one grudge praise—even if his "how" does not appeal so strongly to the reader as his "why." What a man makes of his soul matters, after all, so much more than what he makes of his craft [.] (132)

No critical expertise is needed to evaluate "soul," and as she urges her readers that Melville's "soul" is more important than his "craft," Dane communicates to her audience as one common reader to others. Dane's didacticism is additionally deflected through her rhetorical turn away from modern readers toward the shared cultural territory of the audience in "The Nightingale." For Dane this fairy tale illustrates the wisdom of choosing genuine, full human responses to art, even if painful ones, while resisting simulated ones. The Japanese emperor who forsakes the real, brown bird for the shiny simulacrum of the nightingale and its song is a brilliant analogy for the reader of shockers. More examples are drawn both from ordinary and from sophisticated registers, with Dane exclaiming in one case, "What a queer public we are! We actually like our pine apples tinned" (22). She theorizes that we shun the torment of watching the real nightingale press a thorn against its heart as it sings and so we choose the clockwork nightingale's song. "The Nightingale" then becomes an objective correlative for the wisdom that it is better to experience pain than find an ersatz experience. Thus initial blame for this instance of cultural decline is recast as readers short-changing themselves by selecting an inferior product when a superior one is available.

But superior descendants of tragedy are available, if readers know where to look for them. In her ensuing discussion of tragi-comedy, Dane demonstrates that enjoyment of these modern developments depends on readers' appreciation of their ancestors and classical and Shakespearean tragedy. "Melpomene and the Fat Boy" thus delivers one of Dane's core critical tenets: the modern gains meaning and vitality by its dialogue with the classical. Dane distinguishes between high and low genres but declines to fix them to specific authors or to correlate them with readers' brows. Her survey of tragedy crosses literary periods and genres, boosting confidence in her versatile mind and encouraging that disposition in her readers.

By understanding a genealogy and a hierarchy of genres, Dane's readers can evaluate literature based on a spectrum of rhetorical effects ranging from spine chills to emotions. To some extent, then, the essayist-critic is not unlike the university lecturer on drama who supplies generic definitions and examples and confirms a canon of great writers that will include Socrates, Shakespeare, Emily Brontë, and Hardy. Like a scholar, for example, Dane cites leading theorists on tragedy: "To be tragic the right must contend against the right in two human creatures, says Hegel" (131). But Dane's essay soon departs from the neat categories of high and low genres that might comprise the heart of a university lecture. Such divisions are academic, that is, theoretical, but the experienced reader knows that the evolution of literature depends on hybridization of high and low, as Melville's tragi-comedies will illustrate.

Dane identifies the different effects of tragedy, horror, and comedy and begins a survey of writers. Here too the neat classifications break down. Shakespeare is revered as a tragedian, but has also written shockers. In the case of *Othello*, for example, Shakespeare is more like Frankenstein, whose cold intellectual force leads him to create the monster Iago. The many rhetorical turns in "Melpomene and the Fat Boy," each of which introduces and illustrates critical concepts, require critically thinking *Good Housekeeping* readers.

But rather than restricting herself to a purely intellectual approach to her topic, Dane keeps in play personal, intellectual, somatic, moral, and emotional registers and shapes an essay that responds to these manifold dimensions of reading. Her invocation of the body, first in the analogy that likens thrillers to the haymaker's draught of cider, then in her warning readers to cut down on shockers just as they would curb a vice, is particularly striking. Far from watering down the complexity of canonical literary criticism, Dane's essays exemplify the periodical critic's work to enrich the purely cognitive dimension that increasingly delimited academic and modernist reading in the interwar period.

Turning from shockers to tragedy, Dane probes beneath the sensations of the body to consider the tragic figure's soul and the spectator's heart. Tragedy should play a role in our lives, Dane has taught us, because it arouses "fellow-feeling in the watcher's breast." Dane practices this ethos in the last paragraphs of her essay, leaving behind altogether her concerns about reading choices that stimulate mere sensation, in order to explore our contemplation of "soul" when we read tragedy. She does so by eliciting our pity for suffering artists. Her first plea is somewhat mocking—"pity those [such as Marie Corelli] who break their hearts to give us tragedy, and see—all we can say is—'A good shocker!'" (132). There follows an intriguing succession of geniuses who are "strangely mocked by their own temperament" (Byron, Webster) and who fall short of crafting tragedy through "some flaw in character or judgment" (132). Dane's survey, organized from unsuccessful tragedians to nearly successful, builds pathos until she reaches the tragi-comedian Melville, on whom she lavishes her richest imagery, so as to inspire our awe and pity. Melville's case is so compelling that Dane seems positively unwilling to turn from him to his fictional characters:

> [I]f ever a man had a vasty deep of a soul, it was Melville. He reminds one of those flimsy, gigantic shadows thrown by travellers, they say, from mountain tops on clouds, or a creature of the third day of creation wandering in a world half made, the waters barely parted, the naked land sweating in the first sunrise. He writes with power of elemental creatures like himself, clothed awkwardly in seaman's slops. (132)

Comprised of elemental stuff, both base and elevated, Melville is a "creature" in the process of becoming fully human, and he thus inspires our pathos. An artist, he creates "elemental creatures like himself" in two further senses of "elemental." He breathes life into the raw material around him and elicits in his audience the most elemental, primordial of human responses to spectacles of suffering. Dane recommends *Billy Budd* and *Moby Dick*, inviting her readers to marvel with her at "how Melpomene and the Fat Boy can reign together in a human heart" (132). The debased genre of the shocker has not been relegated to a lower class of readers, but remains at the core of human response, along with pity and fear. Characteristically, Dane ends the essay declining to maintain academic categories and welding the modern to the classical. "Melpomene" concludes with Dane's inclusion of both high and low literary genres in the heritage of her readers.

"Things That Go Bump in the Night"

In "Things That Go Bump in the Night" (1924), Dane links the determination of great literature to a writer's innovation in a tradition. In addition to her emphasis on innovation, Dane locates the achievement of individual writers within a recurring cycle of collectively produced folk literature. Adopting an anthropological perspective, Dane argues that although they may rise and fall in literary quality, ghost stories continue to be written and read because they help us to explore the enduring human question of what happens to us when we die. This anthropological approach aligns Dane superficially with the "scientific" methods of criticism then infusing university study of literature, but she ultimately establishes the distinguished heritage of the ghost story on the basis of common reading, not through scientific research. As a book lover rather than as an academic critic, Dane "amused [herself] the other day by making a list of the best ghost stories of the last hundred years, and was astonished at the pack of famous names it involved" (134). The anthropologist's graph of the rise and fall of supernatural literature explains why we will continue to read it, but Dane's authority in the eyes of her readers is based on the breadth of her common reading. And yet Dane's knowledge draws no lines between expert and novice *Good Housekeeping* readers, for "Things That Go Bump in the Night" characterizes and dramatizes a community of readers who relish the chills and thrills of the supernatural. Characteristically, Dane endorses a holistic reading praxis that includes cognitive, emotive, and somatic responses. And by valorizing equally the cognitive and affective sides of reading, Dane makes the point that both elite and popular ghost stories can be great.

Dane argues that the ghost story is a communal form that progresses through historical cycles of vitality and decline. This long view of literary history provides assurance that an apparent, present-day degradation in the form represents but a temporary phase in its evolution. A short-range perspective might lead us to pessimistic conclusions: "the modern" ghost story, belonging to the last hundred years—"is a kettle of very different fish from the leviathans of the great days" (32). It has "dwindled, petrified, and grown self-conscious" (32). But a long-range view suggests that the ghost story might be on the verge of a renaissance. Dane sketches the history of the ghost story. Beginning in "a half true tale told over the fire by the people of Tutankhamen's day" (32) and orally transmitted, it later becomes great literature "in the hands of the Homers and the Shakespeares," "only to be dragged down to its 'horrid happening' level once more by the Mrs. Radcliffes and the Monk Lewis's [sic] and all the other sensationalists" at the nadir of the cycle (32).

Dane refutes the idea that ghost stories do not belong to "the very cream of literature" (32). She calls out the "modern trick of sniffing at the ghost story as something 'a little better than a Holmes, a little dearer than a Dell'—as something to be enjoyed shamefacedly" (32). Her views trouble what by 1924 was an accepted view of an absolute divide between elite and popular or mass literary forms.[10] As Dane characterizes them, however, neither the form nor the audience is monolithic and unchanging. Rather, both elite and mass forms are characterized by instability, continual transformation, and versatility, molded in each era and by each storyteller. Dane nonetheless implies that great practitioners of these forms are needed to wrest the tradition from—or at least counterbalance the effect of—those "who are eager to achieve the thrill without bothering about the form" (32). Genius may be necessary to create great literature out of what has previously been immature or disorganized or unconscious developmental steps. But "to say that a ghost story is worth reading

[10] Even by the end of the nineteenth century, the outcomes on reading habits of broad societal changes—compulsory education, a new quotient of leisure for the working classes, and the expansion of the press—seemed clear to most observers: publishing houses, subscription libraries, newspapers, and popular magazines would happily encourage the reading public's reputed insatiable appetite for formulaic, "light," and sensational entertainment. In the pre- and postwar periods, the most salient source of this divide between popular and elite reading material was arguably the rise of modernist movements that rebuffed the idiom and the short forms of the newspaper and sought both to restore the prestige of literary language, to designate its special readership, and to craft vehicles for a newly understood and more complex reality.

generally means that a man of genius has held the pen" (134)[11]—that is, until the advent of May Sinclair's *Uncanny Stories*, which inaugurates a rise in the historical cycle. Beyond her hint that the genius may come from, and is dependent for material on, the folk, Dane does not probe the origin of "genius," for example, as Virginia Woolf does by exposing its cultural construction as male and by revealing its dependence on education, money, and a room of one's own. Instead, Dane constructs her essay so that May Sinclair emerges like a gem on a beach of pebbles, by virtue of a significant innovation.

Nonetheless, the intersection of genius and gender is important to Dane, who hypothesizes that Sinclair's innovations have a gendered source. The ghost story, Dane tells us, has been epic, dramatic, and narrative; and is now entering a new phase, characterized by Sinclair's focalizing the stories through the ghost rather than through the terrified human being. What attracts Sinclair is "not so much the ghost story as the ghost. That is perhaps because she is a woman. Most women write from the inside outwards, and Miss Sinclair most of all" (136). Here Dane celebrates less the genius of Sinclair than the fact that the genius is a woman and the ensuing effects on the tradition: "because it is a woman of genius instead of a man of genius who is interesting herself in this particular form of art, it is once more, after many years, altering its whole character, just as the whole character of the novel altered when women began to use it as a means of expression" (136).[12]

Yet innovation in the ghost story cannot be merely cerebral or aesthetic. The great writer must be sensitive enough—must tap into the primordial dread, superstition, and pity that make ghost stories popular—to evoke these in her readers. In keeping with her advocacy for emotive and somatic, not merely cognitive appreciation of ghost stories, Dane's art of the essay provides the enjoyment of sensory motifs. "Dusk," for example, is the territory into which ghost story writers must journey and the ground on which they meet readers. A realm "peopled by untouchable terrors," dusk is a liminal place beyond our solid knowledge. It is, nonetheless, "a land that is perhaps peculiarly fascinating to writers because they can bring back from it the best stories in the world if only they have the courage" (32). This country is a literary tradition whose subscribers

[11] It is noteworthy that Dane believes both the "unconscious" beginnings—materials on which the likes of Shakespeare will draw—and the "man of genius" are needed. Debates about how far great thinkers were independent of thinking in the mass were active in the Victorian and modernist periods. See Beer 34–6.

[12] "Things That Go Bump in the Night" anticipates *A Room of One's Own* (1929).

are limited, not by demonstration of erudition, but by willingness to abandon the signposts of mimetic truth. Dane returns strategically in the essay to "dusk," a metonymic shorthand for the writer-reader partnership built on feelings of dread and superstition. This evocative trope illustrates an essay craft that imitates the features of the literature under discussion. Following Lukács, Dane practices a critical essay that is "mimetic as well as creative; it aims at a kind of truth, as well as imaginative response" (Good 17).

Dane's para-curricular guidance to *Good Housekeeping* readers hinges on her endorsement of this fusion of truth and imagination. Her non-scientific "dusk" captures both the sensuous phenomena and the equivocal, liminal experience of reading the literature of the supernatural. In an oblique put-down of modernist experiments that she deems merely technical, Dane insists that great stories expand our feelings. "I do not believe in art for art's sake" (138), she says, comparing Sinclair's "Their Fire Is Not Quenched" favorably to her novel *Harriet Frean*:

> A tale that, with every grace of technique, can also make you say to yourself—"There, but for the grace of God"—is a more valuable thing than the tale told merely to prove that the writer can tell it. *Harriet Frean* was great craft, but this story of what comes of sinning the unforgivable sin is great art. (138)

"The Victim" proves Dane's contention that "in Miss Sinclair's hands, though the suspense, the thrill, the—dusk, as it were, is triumphant, fear has gone from the ghost story" (138). Now Dane returns to her theory of the woman writer's innovation in the tradition. It is not just that Sinclair is good at "dusk." Her profound attention to her ghosts' feelings paves the way for "understanding" that is inseparable from empathy, from the writer's and readers' journey together into the dusk. Sinclair's treatment of the ghost story gives us "the heart of the disembodied creature ... in all its fears and desires, its piteous limitations and superb liberties" (138). As a result, "Awe, pity, even horror, Miss Sinclair puts into our hearts, but she cannot put fear, because in its place she has already put understanding" (138).

For all her appreciation of May Sinclair's *Uncanny Stories*, the abiding purpose of "Things That Go Bump in the Night" is to characterize the tradition. As in other "books that endure" essays, Dane assures her readers that through ordinary reading, they engage with a stable and distinguished heritage. "The strange mixture of terror and delight with which we regard the supernatural is one of the oldest and most deeply rooted characteristics of humanity" (32), she says, and then quickly surveys the most horror-provoking biblical, classical, and European examples:

> Who, having read, can forget the meeting of Ulysses with his dead mother over the pit of blood, which, tasting, "then she knew I was her son," only to vanish like a sleep when Ulysses stretched out his arms to her. Who can forget the shamed dreadful figure of Deiphobus whom Aeneas met in hell, or the blood of Abel crying from the ground, or the story of Samuel rising like "a god coming up out of the earth" to terrify Saul, or that magnificent ghost story in The Ere Dwellers of Thorgunna and the Bedhangings and the Trial of the Ghosts? (32)

In this wide-ranging survey, Dane establishes her own critical authority. But rather than creating an intimidating distance from her *Good Housekeeping* audience, Dane reels off these titles much as a restaurant proprietor posts the menu of dishes to be enjoyed upon entrance to the restaurant. And it is on the basis of pleasure that Dane posits a community of readers who are susceptible to the chills and thrills of the ghost story. Their rapport is strengthened by Dane's ironic construction of a "superior" sort of reader who is too rational to be enticed by tales of the supernatural. "Why do you laugh?" Dane asks her. "Are you one of those superior people who don't believe in ghosts?" (32). In dramatizing various readers' self-inclusion or self-exclusion from the cohort, Dane acknowledges the interwar trend to designate readers' brows. But characteristically, she expects and encourages them to travel freely across such borders. If the professionalization of English Studies led academic critics to develop and advocate a "scientific" method of study whose results would be measurable, then we must look to such para-curricular fora as *Good Housekeeping* to find the endorsement of catholic taste. It is in this spirit that "Things That Go Bump in the Night" conducts a series of humorous, dramatic turns by which the superior reader turns out to be inferior. Dane invokes and pretends to envy this reader at the outset of the essay:

> It must be so convenient to be able to take a short cut at night through the churchyard, such a churchyard as ours, with a black thunder-cloud of a yew-tree that dates from William Rufus, and Scroogian railed-in graves with their stone lids sliding off the oozy brickwork to right and left of the path. (32)

Through the delicious, sensory ghost story tropes—churchyard, graves, yew tree—Dane invokes its historical (William Rufus) and literary (Scroogian) roots, the tightly woven common culture that both reader and reviewer enjoy. And so the skeptical reader, excluding herself from this community of readers, is ultimately the object of Dane's pity: such a person is impervious to the incomparable thrill of the ghost story. If she feels no fear, she is also short on imagination. Indeed, pity for this unsusceptible reader soon replaces the persona's "envy": "In a word you do not know what *dusk* is" (32). With the triumph of "dusk," Dane places at the top of her list of books that endure those that engage readers' body, mind, and emotions.

"The Poet v. the Talkies"

In "The Poet v. the Talkies" (1929), Dane reviews the recent publication of a collection of playlets by Gordon Bottomley; praises his revival of verse drama; and admires his ability both to express the spirit of the age and transcend it.[13] Bottomley's verse drama reveals the beauty of spoken English, restoring it for an audience satiated with the "hideous" speech of the talkies. The beauty of Bottomley's dramatic speakers' voices and language arises in part from his paring away story and spectacle; Dane's essay makes the case that poetry, including verse drama, should dispense with realism. She welcomes experimentation, specifically citing Bottomley's adaptation of the Japanese Noh dramatic form. But her essay also insists that a great poet must combine innovation and tradition, which in "The Poet v. the Talkies" leads to the wisdom that the most important of human emotions remain constant in any era. Beneath the moderns' postwar fatigue of spirit, behind the "crude" entertainment of the cinema, and beyond the sensational best-seller—as great poetry intuits—is the unchanging human desire for rich experience and profound emotion.

"The Poet v. the Talkies" offers a good example of Dane's alignment with major commentators on the role poetry might play in shoring up the cultural standards eroded by modern mass entertainment. Most clearly, I.A. Richards's *Practical Criticism* (1929) found that "good poetry" might become "a powerful weapon for breaking up unreal ideas and responses," that is, received ideas susceptible to crude distortion, especially in the hands of less educated readers (Richards, *Practical Criticism* 248–51). Dane likewise recognizes

[13] Bottomley was one of the "Georgian poets" whose work appeared in a series of five anthologies between 1912 and 1922, published by Harold Monro and edited by Edward Marsh (Baldick, *The Oxford English Literary History* 90).

the challenges that poetry presents in the context of a highly stratified reading public. But she departs from the views of Richards, F.R. Leavis, and Q.D. Leavis in her confidence that the audience for great poetry extends beyond the educated minority to include "the half-educated," albeit in cringingly condescending terms. Bottomley's verse drama, she says, "satisfies not only the pleasure of the educated in subtleties of thought and speech, but the need of the half-educated for simplicities of feeling" (150). Mainstream literary journalists like Dane, we can see, both criticized cultural trends of the day and supported the moderns' desire for something better.

Dane sees the poetry and verse drama of Thomas Hardy, only recently deceased, as evidence for her case that a great poet must fuse modernity and tradition. She sprinkles her discussion with a series of variations on this motif. Hardy speaks powerfully to the experiences and emotions of the modern age, but his words are steeped in the wisdom of long experience that make him an "Elijah" among prophets. "Hardy is our To-Day as well as our Yesterday," Dane proclaims (57). As she casts around for a replacement, she seeks someone who is "truly rooted in tradition and is yet an innovator" (57). Dane's notion that modernity can be supported by and is not incompatible with tradition is a staple of her criticism, and in "The Poet v. the Talkies" it sounds a note of reassurance. She asks "Who alone to-day expresses the spirit of the age, yet is apparently independent of the poetic habit of the age?" (57).[14] The "poetic habit" suggests that modern society has become enthralled to commercial mechanisms and formulaic self-expression. Dane's particular concerns are the "vulgarity" of the English language in the talkies and the commercial imperatives of the theater. In "The Poet v. the Talkies," Dane presses Bottomley's poetry into service as a beacon pointing the way to cultural health. The modern rhythms of Bottomley's poetry transcend the merely literary, capturing the war-torn spirit of jazz and modern dance and expressing their craving for intense emotion and their longing for release from the present.

In its emphasis on the role poetry must play not merely to resist the abasement of cultural standards but also to assuage Britons' unrest, "The Poet v. the Talkies" is representative of Dane's cultural criticism. In these essays the audibly "composite discourse"

[14] The idea that literature should express the dominant ideas of its time is not new, but Dane's coupling it with the criterion that the poet simultaneously transcends his time recalls Hegel's specific formulation of it: "For Hegel *Zeitgeist* means that one is aware of one's time but reflects critically on it in order not to be asphyxiated by the spirit of that particular time and historical period" (Klikauer 25).

of criticism means that while Dane retains her role to ensconce new books within literary traditions, the humanizing agency of criticism takes the upper hand (Baldick, *The Social Mission* 9). In "The Poet v. the Talkies," Dane raises a number of concerns about modernity: the dominance of a commercial mass culture, its endangerment of serious poetry and drama, and the loss of a unified audience for culture. In the context of crisis, Dane's Arnoldian approach to the new books under discussion considers their salvific power. In particular, the poetry of Gordon Bottomley presents a solution to each face of cultural disintegration. The voices of those poets who both express and look beyond the unease of the closing decade are those that will endure; this is Dane's reassurance to *Good Housekeeping* readers in "The Poet v. the Talkies."

One major concern is the new commercial mass culture, epitomized by the talkies. For many onlookers, cinema embodied all that was pernicious about modern mass culture. I.A. Richards worried about a direct cause and effect relationship between "'aesthetic' and ordinary experience," making "the average superfilm" responsible for "a disorganization which has its effects in everyday life." Audiences, he believed, were substituting the clichés proffered by producers for their own experiences: "The extent to which second-hand experience of a crass and inchoate type is replacing ordinary life offers a threat which has not yet been realized," he warned (*Principles* 217). Dane surely counts on her audience's familiarity with such warnings, while expressing a specific concern about the crude rendering of human speech in the first all-talkies: "The talkies have already begun to teach us our horrid lesson: they are teaching even the crudest ear how hideous modern speech can be."[15] Dane's focus on the quality of speech in the cinema sets up her contrast with the beauty of speech in contemporary verse drama. "But now a poet has come upon the platform to teach us how beautiful modern speech can be.[16] We are watching the duel between the talkies and the speaker, between the robots and the poet" (150).

[15] In 1928, the first continuous "all-talkie" in Europe, *The Terror*, elicited critical dismay about the possibilities of language in film. Reviewing *The Terror* in *The Observer*, C.A. Lejeune lamented "the invasion of more sound in an already rowdy world" (qtd. in Hutchinson).

[16] Such appreciation bolstered feelings of nationalism. Baldick notes that English Studies gained a hearing during this period in part because it appealed to national pride in the language as well as the literature; he discusses the Newbolt Report (1921) in this light (*The Social Mission* 82, 80–9).

Yet Dane is not among those who augur the end of high culture as audiences revolve hypnotically from film to film. "The Poet v. the Talkies" is an essay in which Dane welcomes artistic innovation, and on this topic Bottomley will claim her sustained attention. She begins "The Poet v. the Talkies" with brief praise for H.G. Wells's newly published *The King Who Was a King* and its vision of "the new art, film making" (57). Dane is sympathetic to Wells's account of the symbiosis between novelists lured by lucrative film rights and an industry clamoring for stories to repetitively fill a few molds. She shares his conviction that writers must break free of novelistic methods to realize the distinct possibilities of camera and sound inherent in film. And just as Wells is eager to "get off the ground of the realistic story-film" (qtd. in "The Poet v. the Talkies" 57), Dane singles out Bottomley as an innovator in drama who "escape[s] from realism and representation." As theatrical elements such as stage, scene, and lighting are minimized, the poetry in drama becomes clear, while its spiritual and psychological dimensions emerge (148, quoting Bottomley's "Preface" to *Scenes and Plays*).

Dane's concern about the commercialization of culture includes the theater. She alludes to a division between the commercial mainstream theater and the uncommercial fringe theater that Baldick dates from the Independent Theatre Company's attempts from 1891 to produce the works of Henrik Ibsen for English audiences. Subsequently, the Stage Society promoted the work of George Bernard Shaw and others. Such experimental or controversial literary drama was relegated to small, suburban theaters. The dominance of the commercial theater continued after the war: comedy and melodrama were the staples that diverted urban middle-class audiences and guaranteed significant profits for theaters and producers (Baldick, *The Oxford English Literary History* 114–15). But Dane singles out Gordon Bottomley and John Masefield as holdouts against the lure of commercial success: "To the modern manager there is no money in verse plays and our poets are accustomed to accept this point of view. Not so Mr. Bottomley, who, it is clear enough, believes fiercely that if there is no money in verse plays, at least there are hungry audiences waiting for them" (148). As we will see, Bottomley's indifference to popular acclaim frees him to dispense with narrative and to adopt the visual and poetic rhythms of the stage drama.

Closely related to the commercialization of literature is the disintegration of a unified audience. The acceleration of mass literacy in the late nineteenth century, accompanied by the expansion of the press, exacerbated the splintering of the reading public. It was F.R. and Q.D. Leavis who were to develop the most extensive critique of the twentieth-century reading public and its contrast to the Elizabethans. In Shakespeare's day, Q.D. Leavis claimed, "the masses were receiving their amusement from above," instead of being separately catered to by popular novelists and the cinema (85). Dane likewise identifies more and less educated audiences, and at the end of her essay evokes the different needs that Bottomley fills for each. But she makes her first argument for Bottomley's greatness by appointing him the successor to Thomas Hardy and by appealing to an implied unified audience: "When we said, a year ago, 'our greatest living poet,' we meant Thomas Hardy" (57), who had died in 1928. The sweeping "we" leaves no room for contemplation of a "sensitive minority" of poetry readers vs. a best-seller-reading herd. The nation mourns the recent death of Hardy, whose undisputed towering stature leaves little doubt, Dane implies, that the fragmented reading public can again cohere if a great poet comes along. From there it is a short step to confirming Bottomley's readiness to take Hardy's place. Dane signals the achievement of this consensus through proleptic retrospection knitting together the future and the past: "in years to come we should probably look back to the year when Bottomley's book of playlets, *Scenes and Plays* was published as we now look back to the year of the *Lyrical Ballads*" (147). While for Leavis, a unified reading public belonged to a distant era of English history, for Dane it has only recently been suspended, with Hardy's death in 1928, and is within sight of restoration, with the advent of Bottomley. Viewed from the lurching present and its splintered reading public, the future looks unsteady. But through the agency of Bottomley's verse drama, the nation may once again be unified. Bottomley's verse drama may be "the beginning of a new drama, a drama that will satisfy a Georgian audience precisely as Shakespearian verse forms satisfied the Elizabethan audience" (150).

While Dane acknowledges an enervation in many postwar cultural expressions born of despair, in each examination of a modern trend she yokes that despondency to desire for something better. Thus, jazz dance expresses "the sense of being crowded out of life, of having right to no more than a foothold upon earth. But it expresses other things—the desire for continuous experience, for rich and vivid emotions: it is the dance of 'letting go'" (150).[17] The great

[17] Modern dance for many connoted both hedonism and decadence. John Lucas illustrates this point in a brief analysis of Noël Coward's *The Vortex* (1924). The

literature of the era must recognize and build on the desire for continuity and for profound human experience while assuaging postwar despair.

Bottomley's poetry does just this. It expresses "rich and vivid emotions"; and its rhythms illuminate the common elements in a range of modern experiences. In dramatizing "things done long ago and ill done": "the burning of a castle and its inmates, the blotting out of a clan, the torment of a woman in child-birth," Bottomley illuminates "human nature irrespective of time" (150). Yet he also expresses modernity by setting these "ancient thoughts" to "rhythms as modern as the song of machinery" (150). Returning to her familiar formulation in *Good Housekeeping* of modernity in dialogue with tradition, Dane asks "Now why are these lovely sounds" of Bottomley's poetry "so new and yet so familiar?" (148). They are "the rhythm of a pounding train" (148) or a "wheeling aeroplane" (150) and of "dancers in a modern ballroom" (150).[18] Bottomley's *Scenes and Plays*, Dane believes, can lead modern audiences away from the most degraded forms of culture.

Dane's endorsement of Bottomley's "escape" from realism and her deployment of symbols of transcendence like the airplane mark the shared territory of "The Poet v. the Talkies" and modernist theories of poetry. When the scope of literary criticism of the early twentieth century is expanded to include periodical essays in quality magazines, such as Dane's, we find a rich dialogue between modernist and mainstream criticism. Yet the continuity of concerns across canonical criticism and periodical literary criticism does not fully account for the interest to contemporary scholars of "middlebrow" journalistic literary criticism. Such similarity in fact illuminates different bases of critical authority and divergent assumptions about the goals of reading books that endure.

For example, while Dane repeatedly contrasts poetry and popular culture, her approach to poetry in "The Poet v. the Talkies" makes none of the pleas for effortful reading that she makes in essays like "Near Home and Far Off," discussed below. Instead, Dane sets herself at a distance from the growing movement advocating close

characters' habitual "cocktails, cigarettes, casual affairs ... [are all] identified through, the mania for dance music" (114).

[18] In *Mrs. Dalloway* (1925), Virginia Woolf similarly suggests the visual and auditory power of modern engines of speed briefly to unify a wide swathe of Londoners: "Then suddenly, as a train comes out of a tunnel, the aeroplane rushed out of the clouds again, the sound boring into the ears of all people in the Mall, in the Green Park, in Piccadilly, in Regent Street, in Regents' Park" (21).

analysis of poetry. Her goal is patently not to *train* readers to attend carefully to the complex verbal texture of a poem; she takes a less cognitive approach than Eliot, Riding and Graves, Richards, and Empson.[19] A personal experience crystallizes her concept of poetry. As a nervous passenger in an ascending airplane, Dane is suddenly seized by the feeling, not the belief, of the clouds' proximity to eternity, and the poetry of Gordon Bottomley springs to mind. Rather than emphasize the complexity, irony, and ambiguity in poetry, Dane singles out the power of rhythm—whether verbal or adumbrated by a machine—to capture the plain reader's feelings about the present day and to anchor that experience to an enduring, and therefore reassuring human truth.

"Near Home and Far Off"

> "The two most engaging powers of an author" are "New things are made familiar, and familiar things are made new." (Samuel Johnson, *The Lives of the English Poets*: "Pope")
>
> "The test of a writer's skill" is to counter the popular belief that there is a tremendous difference between "This End of Somewhere" and "The Other End of Nowhere." (Clemence Dane, "Near Home and Far Off")

In "Near Home and Far Off" (1925) Dane teaches her readers to exercise both near and far-sighted literary judgment: to take pleasure in beautiful replicas of the world we know, and to suspend disbelief so as to realize gains not within sight on first acquaintance with a book. Dane attends both to the writer's role to inspire belief and to readers' role to respond to that invitation. On their side, fiction writers must develop imaginative worlds that erode readers' conviction that "this end of somewhere" holds no surprises and that "the other end of nowhere" has nothing in common with what they know. Linking her valorization of belief and her promise of beauty is Dane's enticement of her readers to reread, a testament of faith that will lead them to discover new beauties in books that endure.

[19] Laura Riding and Robert Graves, I.A. Richards, and, later, William Empson, all deplored the plain reader's reputed tendency to look for a prose paraphrase of a poem. Instead, they demonstrated poetry's complex associations, fusion of thought and feeling, as well as its enriching irony (Richards) and ambiguity (Empson). See Baldick, *Criticism and Literary Theory* 78 ff.

Engaging Dane's creative and critical skills, offering both enjoyment and guidance to readers, "Near Home and Far Off" intervenes in contemporary debates about taste in art. Against the grain of the period's many expert reading advisors who caution that the formation of taste is a kind of training, Dane endorses common readers' critical competence to designate writers as "masterful" and empowers them to find that very different sorts of writers each may reach the highest levels of achievement. And as she defends her own catholic reading tastes, Dane tacitly rejects judicial critics' call for fixed criteria of literary excellence. Likewise, she holds her ground against the new academic discipline of English Studies claiming criticism as its exclusive purview. Readers need not seek expert advice, Dane judges, but must take an active role in the discovery and enjoyment of beauty. For the richness of literary works to be revealed, they must immerse themselves, reread, and accept the writer's invitation to believe in his created world. In her pragmatic approach to literature, Dane shifts authority to determine literary excellence from the credentialed critic to the engaged reader.

Advice about how to select one's reading material and how to shape one's taste was not new in the 1920s. Publishers, editors, library directors, educators, and critics all launched initiatives to steer aspiring readers toward classic literature. But what was new was the identification of readers by their disposition rather than their social class. As Melba Cuddy-Keane argues, "the nineteenth-century goal of conveying a putatively superior culture to the lower classes is replaced by the twentieth-century work of developing the skills and abilities of anyone able and willing to participate in collective cultural activity" (118). Efforts to define and reach this new kind of common reader included published lists of "Hundred Best" books; commercially successful volumes of literary criticism, including Virginia Woolf's *Common Reader* series (1925, 1935); and advice manuals such as Arnold Bennett's *Literary Taste: How to Form It* (1909). Periodicals also joined in this work, notably *John O'London's Weekly* (1919–54), which founder and editor Wilfred Whitten conceived of as a literary paper "for readers not 'high-brow,' but eager to know their way amongst the masterpieces" (Waller 93). When it folded in 1954, *Time* magazine remembered *John O'London's*:

> Its readers were mostly young people just acquiring their literary education and oldsters belatedly seeking theirs, with a scattering of professional writers. The weekly ran a literate section on English grammar and word usage, carefully recommended good books, [and] had a steady circulation of 80,000. ("The Press")

Dane's literary criticism participates in these efforts to empower the common reader.

At the outset of "Near Home and Far Off," Dane dramatizes her recent dispute with a critic who declares the "indisputable fact that it was impossible to enjoy both Bach and Beethoven." But, Dane laments, "when it comes to books, how such a ruling would limit one's pleasure and profit!" "Beauty is beauty," she protests, "whatever dress she wears" (50). In opposition to "rules," Dane posits our instinctive or spontaneous apprehension of beauty. She sets herself the task of convincing this dogmatist that two vastly different works of art can each be assessed as "masterful." But she will not do so with "indisputable facts."[20] Instead, the essay repeatedly epitomizes the beauty it finds in beloved literature. Literary gems in the form of tropes and metaphors, as well as descriptions of small works of art duplicate for readers, rather than explain or theorize, aesthetic pleasure.

In jettisoning academic and objective evaluative criteria, Dane joins an early twentieth-century critical current that favors personal and intuitive aesthetic responses. Chris Baldick posits Pater's *The Renaissance* as the advance guard in a movement that would incorporate Spingarn's "direct intuitive encounter with the imaginative source of the artist's expression," but would also include figures such as Arthur Quiller-Couch, A.C. Bradley, George Santayana, and Irving Babbitt, all of whom sought to rein in, without eradicating, the "free play of taste" with "stabilizing control and correction" (*Criticism and Literary Theory* 29). Following these critics, Dane models a subjective response to literature while voicing the enduring critical tenets that allow us to share our responses with others. The form in which she undertakes this dual activity, however, is not a lecture or treatise but an essay that pays tribute to the principles and styles of Joseph Addison and Samuel Johnson. Dane focuses on two contemporary novels, John Masefield's adventure *Sard Harker*, and Hugh Walpole's *The Old Ladies*, in the realist tradition. Thus, in keeping with the hallmark of her essays for *Good Housekeeping*, Dane foregrounds two works of modern literature within a conversation about classic literary principles, while her own essay makes the familiar neoclassical principles and tropes new. "Near Home and Far Off," in fact, epitomizes Samuel Johnson's precept that writers

[20] Dane distances herself from one approach to literary history: "scientific scholars" inductively discovering the "laws of literary development" (Baldick, *Criticism and Literary Theory* 33).

most engage our interest when "new things are made familiar, and familiar things are made new" (*The Lives of the English Poets*: "Pope").

The Essay as Epitome

> Art, indeed, is often requisite to collect and epitomize the beauties of nature. (W. Shenstone, qtd. in "Epitomize")

As an essayist critic, Dane attends in "Near Home and Far Off" as much to essay craft as to illustration of critical principles. Across her body of work, she demonstrates versatility in such forms as the "rambler," the "constellation," and others. "Near Home and Far Off" showcases the essay as epitome, as two eighteenth-century definitions of "epitomize" suggest. A concentrated vision or small compass,[21] the essay "collect[s] and epitomize[s] the beauties of nature."[22] Practitioners of the English essay have long been drawn to the epitome; indeed, the seventeenth-century *Essayes or Moral Discourses on Several Subjects* celebrates the essay as a form that displays to the reader "an Epitomy of himself, and the world together." In this formulation, the author seems to have in mind both the useful knowledge of "men and manners" to be found in the essay and the "wit, and eloquence, (the ornaments of the Pen and thought)" that one is likely to find in essays (*Essayes or Moral Discourses* 32).[23] "Near Home and Far Off" is infused with such ornaments, figures of beauty such as landscapes and sculptures,[24] which both afford pleasure and illustrate aesthetic principles such as "[A work of art] triumphs not on account of its material but through the artist's management of the material" (172). Dane's multiple miniature figures replicate the works of art enjoyed by visitors to museums—and readers. For example, her account of Walpole's craft

[21] One apposite, eighteenth-century definition of *epitomize* is "to put into a small compass; to concentrate" ("Epitomize").

[22] The source of this *Oxford English Dictionary* citation is W. Shenstone, *Works*. (1768) II. 106.

[23] N.S. Thompson Elbert explains that the authorship is disputed, though sometimes attributed to Thomas Culpeper (8).

[24] Even in metaphors comparing literary passages to beautiful landscapes, Dane evokes Samuel Johnson, for example, in his memorable conclusion to a comparison of Pope and Dryden: "Dryden's page is a natural field, rising into inequalities, and diversified by the varied exuberance of abundant vegetation; Pope's is a velvet lawn, shaven by the sithe, and levelled by the roller" (*The Lives of the English Poets: Pope*).

in *The Old Ladies* doubles as a description of a Chinese carving, while the instance of the carving as epitome exemplifies an art that seems without artifice, no other than the raw material from which it is created:

> *The Old Ladies* is like one of those Chinese small intricate carvings in jade or carnelian, in which the amazing beauty of the group itself, its conception, composition, line, shape, story, is drowned and in a sense obliterated by the changing, flooding colour of the material itself, that shines through the shape it has been given. (172)

While at first the beauty of the object seems artless, a closer look uncovers the artist's craft: "And yet it is the shaping and polishing, naught else, that has released the colour, and turned a lump of stone into a jewel of price" (172). Both novelist and essayist create the beauty that audiences enjoy, but then the baton is passed to readers, who must become effortful, immersive readers.

In addition to literary replicas of tiny works of art, Dane supplies epitomes in the form of favorite eighteenth-century tropes, self-contained figures of delight. Antithesis is a staple of comparisons: "But if Mr. Masefield's problem is our ignorance, Mr. Walpole's difficulty is our knowledge" (172); while chiasmus links the two figures who approach one another from different starting points: Masefield has to "make the marvelous customary and credible," while Walpole has "to make us realise that the commonplace can be marvelous" (172). These tropes, within an essay of comparison reminiscent of Johnson's comparison of Pope and Dryden in *The Lives of the Poets*, bring Dane to the critical principle that two writers may come from widely separated terrain yet both embody beauty.

Each writer's objective is to make the reader believe in his tale. As Dane foregrounds belief, we realize another way in which "Near Home and Far Off" invites us to contemplate epitomes. For novels are small worlds in which we believe, so convincing are the replicas of our worlds that we find in them. As audiences comprehend these replicated worlds, they are called upon alternately to admire familiar things made new or to delight in new things made familiar.

In "Near Home and Far Off" Dane teaches her readers to toggle between these "near" and "far" critical perspectives so as to take the full measure of writers' achievements. But ultimately what one likes depends on taste. Dane shows *Good Housekeeping* readers that while critical principles can resolve an academic argument, true confidence in their own taste will develop only with rereading. Through

Figure 1.2 "For to want to re-read a book and not be able to get hold of it is as bad as having toothache on Saturday evening," Dane proclaims in "Mrs. Robinson's Bag." Illustration by Norah McGuinness, courtesy of Hearst Magazines UK.

the pleasure of rereading good books, Dane implies, a reader comes to resemble a lover who has wooed his beloved patiently, attentively, and appreciatively:

> To buy a book is not to possess it! Indeed, almost any book that one dearly loves may only be said to have been acquired after half a dozen readings at least. It is impossible to reach such a book's heart at a sitting. At the twentieth reading and the hundredth "dipping" you will still find yourself uncovering beauty after new beauty, discovering a hidden scheme, and realizing that the familiar sentences are serving the author in twenty subways, instead of the plain surface one of first acquaintance. (175)

The touchstone of great literature, then, can be found in the "ever-receding waters of the story," a gift that draws the reader into an intimate relationship and transforms her into a rereader:

> This receding quality, as of waters perpetually withdrawing from the enriched ground, so that, as you follow after them, you tread on ever greener pasturage and rarer flowers, is one of the tests by which you may distinguish genius from talent. Shakespeare had this quality beyond all writers, this gift of making you feel, each time you re-open a play of his, that now and only now have you grasped his full meaning, that all your previous readings have been mere preliminary. (175)

In a compelling instance of many in the essay, Dane suggests that reading is never a static experience, because it unfolds in time. The temporal experience of reading a novel, itself a pleasure, can be extended over months or years by rereading. This temporality thus holds up the promise of ever-new beauty to be discovered in a beloved book to which one returns repeatedly. The same principle applies to the relationship between the periodical essayist and her reader. *Good Housekeeping* readers enjoy immediate, but ephemeral beauty, for Dane's periodical essays, which each live but a month, are laden with miniature beauties in the form of images, tropes, and metaphors, while they display for readers' anticipation the beauty of enduring books featured in each essay.

With its emphasis on aesthetic pleasure, "Near Home and Far Off" exemplifies an area of literary criticism in which essayistic criticism excelled. The professionalization of English Studies required the establishment of normative standards, including the conventions of citation, the historical sourcing of evidence, and the institutionalization of archival and source material (Guy and Small 379–80; Baldick, *Criticism and Literary Theory* 32–3). But Dane and other theorists of common reading reject the notion that the deepest appreciation of literature arises from objective methodologies. And even at Cambridge, the first Chair of English Studies, Professor Arthur Quiller-Couch, resisted the idea that such objective practices sufficed to characterize the trained student of literature. In his inaugural Cambridge lecture in 1913, Quiller-Couch proposes that the goal of university study of literature is "an improvement of sensibility," not knowledge of literary history or command of terminology. Yet that sensibility nonetheless distinguishes the scholar from the ordinary reader, and it does so by his "trained judgment":

> the man we are proud to send forth from our Schools will be remarkable less for something he can take out of his wallet and exhibit for knowledge, than for being something, and that "something," a man

> of unmistakable intellectual breeding, whose trained judgment we can trust to choose the better and reject the worse. (*On the Art of Writing* 27)

In contrast with Quiller-Couch, we have seen, Dane crafted essays demonstrating that great art—replete with the delights of music and imagery—could appeal primarily to the senses and thus to the untrained reader.

Another mark of the trained scholar's sensibility, Quiller-Couch unfolds, is his intuition of literary style. But since style "evade[s] all tests," he cautions the Cambridge students to evade the charge of "mere dilettantism" by studying "such definite beauties as we can see presented in print under our eyes" (*On the Art of Writing* 31). While Dane shares Quiller-Couch's appreciation of "definite beauties," such appreciation is not for her the exclusive mark of "the initiated man" (*On the Art of Writing* 32). Through the effortful reading practices modeled in "Near Home and Far Off," Dane expects that enjoyment of the "concrete beauties" will be open to her audience of "earnest amateurs" in equal measure to Professor Quiller-Couch's "initiated men."

The essays discussed in "Books That Endure" are representative of Dane's corpus of literary criticism for *Good Housekeeping* and suggest the remarkable breadth of her critical approaches. Often she shows readers the link between genre—tragedy, the ghost story, poetry—and a desired rhetorical effect. Dane's attention to literature's readers extends to the carefully chosen vehicles for her critical principles. These concepts unfold in enticing, image-rich passages, such as her evocation of the "ever-receding waters of the story" in "Near Home and Far Off." Or they are delivered succinctly, in maxims, as when Dane pronounces in "The Poet v. the Talkies" that "in every age," the ability both to express and to be independent of one's era "differentiates the reflector of his decade from the interpreter of his century" (57). Both vehicles encouraged readers to make their own selection of books that fit such memorable formulations.

For *Good Housekeeping*, we have seen, Dane exemplified the authority of a celebrity author and helped establish the high standards intrinsic to the brand. Simultaneously, through her persona of book lover, she established her own and her readers' authority as common readers. Dane's empowerment of book readers fell squarely within the mission of *Good Housekeeping* to cultivate modern woman's manifold roles within the domestic and public spheres. But if Dane's journalism informs us about the importance of talented journalists to *Good Housekeeping*'s agenda, it also reflects a wider, and underappreciated, trend in interwar women's print media. In this chapter, I have argued that Dane's long-form and original essays are typical—not exceptional—of women's journalism in quality magazines. Throughout the decade, they filled a para-curricular role for thousands of women readers, most of whom were not enrolled in university courses, who wanted to inform themselves and to connect with "interesting people" through their love of good books. Writing her book pages in the 1920s and beyond, Dane entered into dialogue with literary modernism, approving innovation that was not merely brilliant and that would have a lasting impact on literary genre. She also critiqued the effects of mass communication technologies on the sensibilities of book readers. Far from occupying a sequestered space in a battle of the brows, Dane's journalism was a platform for her vigorous contributions to contemporary cultural debates.

Chapter 2

Common Readers and the Varied Pleasures of Reading

Clemence Dane's book essays speak to and celebrate the common reader. In this chapter I investigate Dane's conceptualization of common readers' taste, their somatic and cognitive pleasure, and their critical acumen. Treating a number of book essays written in the 1920s, I demonstrate Dane's validation of reading pleasure in an era that increasingly associated pleasure with sensual debasement or contamination by the growing dominance of the cinema, the daily paper, and the formulaic best-seller. Closely associated with pleasure, taste figures prominently in Dane's essays. Over more than a decade, Dane took advantage of magazine seriality to address this personal topic in multiple and nuanced ways. She intervenes decisively in contemporary debates about taste, staking out her positions in dialogue with middlebrow tastemakers and with modernists, particularly in essays on poetry. Finally, Dane stresses the common reader's responsibility to exercise critical judgment in a way that will impact the success or the failure of current and future books.

Far from static, enjoyment, taste, and judgment are developed and shared in the *Good Housekeeping* periodical community. Dane models the common reader's enjoyment of good books; and her reviews of new books implicitly circulate that enjoyment within the community. Moreover, many essays evoke the intimacy of community members, as they valorize books that affirm readers' sympathetic connection to one another. Additionally, Dane repeatedly discusses the need to defend good new books critically so as to keep them in circulation, especially in a climate of increasing highbrow influence. In Dane's periodical community, then, different tastes are respected at the same time that critical principles are adjudicated so as to be more effectively practiced by members. Indeed, as Dane demonstrates in "Fragments that Remain," common readers' shared taste and critical principles may prove decisive in their collective defense of misunderstood great writers.

In essay after essay, the weight of common readers' consensus is the source of middlebrow confidence: the conviction that literary value is not the unique purview of university professors and the editors of little magazines, but is a matter for wide cultural debate, much of it unfolding in periodical venues that include well-respected weeklies, quality magazines, and modernist little magazines.

The Common Reader Theorized and in History

The book-loving public have been variously termed the common reader (Johnson, Woolf), the unknown public (Wilkie Collins), the man on the street plus a little culture (Hugh Walpole), the earnest amateur (Dane), and the writer's partner (Dane). The term *common reader* engages foundational concepts invoked by Samuel Johnson, especially the reading modes practiced by this reader and the power of this public to decide which books shall receive "all poetical honors" (*Lives* 360). Dane's consciousness of this power is addressed at length in her 1929 address "The Writer's Partner," where she distinguishes between the colleagues who form professional associations for, among other purposes, shop talk, and each writer's partner, the ordinary reader. This "partner" demands that the writer tell stories about himself and his neighbors, in short, about humanity in general, and turns against the writer if he continually strays into territory of interest only to cliques. These readers, and the opportunity to turn them into "confirmed book lovers," are the driving force behind Dane's essay series for *Good Housekeeping*. She shares Richard Altick's conviction that "the capacity to find knowledge, inspiration, escape, and sheer delight in reading is latent in far more people than have ever become confirmed booklovers" (*English Common Reader* 374).

Early twentieth-century literary critics and reading advisors alike conceptualized an amateur reader. Emerging implicitly from her book essays, Dane's theorization of a book lover, who determines her own purposes for reading, can be compared to several other contemporary theories, including those of Virginia Woolf and Hugh Walpole. Walpole's *Reading*, with its three chapters titled "Reading for Fun," "Reading for Education," and "Reading for Love," would seem to align well with topics that Dane's essays address, and Dane and Walpole were colleagues who served on the first panel of judges for the Book Society, modeled on the American Book-of-the-Month Club.[1] Moreover, Dane quotes with approval Walpole's epithet for the amateur reader, "The Plain Man," who is in turn "The Man in the Street plus a little culture" (qtd. in Dane, *Tradition* 13). But Walpole's view of the amateur reader only superficially resembles Dane's. *Reading* gives little attention to the range of a given reader's cognitive and emotional responses, which are of great interest both to Woolf and to Dane. Walpole is interested in the socio-cultural phenomena surrounding reading, such as the curation of a private library. For example, he describes the "beautiful old deep red Morocco" binding of his Chapman's *Homer*, a book that "has played a great part in [his] life" (70). He is also preoccupied with societal types of amateur readers, even entertaining his audience with caricatures of eccentric book lovers, such as the one who makes himself at home in one's private library, pulls books off the shelf, and uses a pencil to mark fine phrases in selected books (76). These characteristic passages ultimately betray Walpole's limited knowledge of actual readers. His caricatures of readers undermine his ability to imagine a community of readers and to include his book audience in the community.

Walpole does nod to the creative power of the book lover, whose disposition and temporal-spatial location influence his response and thus help "write" the next book: "no book is written by its author ... an author merely collects notes for a certain suggested work and ... every reader then writes the book for himself" (78–9). Yet Walpole's "plain men plus a little culture" designate a set of readers affiliated as book lovers only in a loose sense and exert little force in a wider, perhaps national, literary culture. In contrast, both Woolf and Dane theorize a common reader who "differs from the critic and the scholar" and who thus plays a crucial role in shaping literary culture (Woolf, "The Common Reader" 1). Both concur with Johnson's identification of the common reader's power and role, as Johnson expresses it in his life of Thomas Gray: "I rejoice to concur with the common reader; for by the common sense of readers, uncorrupted with literary prejudices, after all the refinements of subtilty and the dogmatism of learning, must be finally decided all claim to poetical honours" (*Lives* 360).

Following Johnson, in "The Common Reader" Woolf measures this amateur reader against the critic and the scholar, emphasizing

[1] The other judges were J.B. Priestley, Sylvia Lynd, and George Stuart Gordon. See Figure 1.1.

his independence with respect to these: "He reads for his own pleasure rather than to impart knowledge [the scholar] or correct the opinions of others [the critic]" (1). With respect to his influence on a shared literary culture, Woolf agrees that the common reader will have "some say in the final distribution of poetical honours" and points out the paradoxical relationship between the power of this judgment—"so mighty a result"—and the apparently hapless activity ("hasty, inaccurate, and superficial") to which it gives rise. The important thing, however, is not that the structure be beautiful or that it be sound, but that it serve his creative purpose to imagine a whole. Woolf's common reader thus creates a temporary structure to which she and other common readers can refer, for the purpose of pleasurable learning comprised of "affection, laughter, and argument" (1). The last of these three terms in particular suggests the purpose of reading to converse with others.

Pleasurable learning also figures in Dane's theory of common reading. She addresses an audience of "earnest amateurs" who want to learn through their experience and enjoyment of art. As she says in "Bridges," the "plain man" expects "his theatre, his gallery, his library, to educate as well as amuse him" (51). In practice, Dane adopts a variety of pedagogic approaches; yet in her common reader essays, instruction is always subordinated to the evocation of leisure and of freedom to read across literary brows. Above all, Dane cultivates readers' confidence in their own taste and judgment. As my discussion of Dane's "Fragments that Remain" will show, common readers' confidence, which we might well designate "middlebrow confidence," allows them to fend off with gentle satire the interference of expert critics and positions them to rescue and retain in circulation good books that might otherwise founder in the competitive market.

Both Dane and Woolf reject the assumption on the part of contemporary reading advisors that the common reader needs expert instruction. She learns instead through discovery, conversation and first-hand experience of art. In "Biographical" (1927), Dane recommends reading Blake's poetry before embarking on Max Plowman's new *Introduction to the Study of Blake*, so that "you yourself know something of Blake's own work and have conceived your own idea of his place in the world" (182). And in "Why?" (1934), Woolf urges readers to bypass the university lecture and learn via conversation and reading at home. Some lectures, Woolf concedes, may be valuable, but can best admit the learner's questions and responses outside the hegemonic space of the university. Read the printed lecture at home, Woolf urges, where you can do so at your own pace and reflect critically upon it. Thus, Woolf emphasizes the learner's right to the space and time in which to form her own judgments. She again hints at the common reader's authority, and even extends it to her imaginative freedom, when she describes the reader's erection of a ramshackle structure, her intuition of the structure built by the writer, which may go no further than her own mind and provide satisfaction only to herself ("The Common Reader").

For Johnson, common readers' authority is derived not from "the dogmatism of learning" but from "common sense" made possible by their freedom from "literary prejudices." This authority, moreover, arises from their numbers, their consensus, their sense-in-common.[2] Dane's reader is constructed within a periodical community of readers, and for this reason another sense of *common*—what is shared or communal—resonates more decisively in Dane's work than in Woolf's "The Common Reader." Dane's book essays clearly spurred the formation of an imagined community, whose members do "not personally know their fellow-members ... yet in the minds of each lives the image of their communion" (Anderson 6). The communion is made possible by the medium of print, which enables members "to find common ground, to recognize each other across differences of space and time" (Anderson; Beetham, "Periodicals" 232). The seriality of the magazine strengthens this recognition across time and space. Dane's persona is developed over months and years of addresses to book lovers, who follow Dane's monthly column and develop common attitudes toward books and reading. As Margaret Beetham puts it, the periodical press constituted "a series of overlapping networks" of communication "in which cultural values and social norms ... were worked through" ("Periodicals" 235). Dane acknowledges that readers may share principles and attitudes without sharing taste. Indeed, Dane's affirmation and reaffirmation of literary-critical or social principles each month, while respecting the individuality and contingency of taste, represents one of the feats of her corpus of essays. Exploring Dane's ethos for common reading in turn yields a strong example of how a single periodical writer entertained and instructed readers, while also mobilizing them to exert their collective power in the cultural marketplace.

[2] Additionally, as Laurie Kaplan has written, Johnson "credits the Publick with his own fine sense of social responsibility and rationality."

Taste

Samuel Johnson, as we saw, posits common readers' banding together to form a virtual community. Both Woolf and Dane build on this idea. If the outcome of the virtual community is critical consensus, its inception is the affection that binds book lovers to one another. Woolf posits a reader bound to others by "affection, laughter, and argument." Dane concurs. Moreover, in multiple book essays, Dane explores fluctuations in taste, even within a single reader, and uses that circumstance to encourage readers' sympathy with others who are differently positioned.

Dane's essays facilitate discussions of taste within the periodical community and bring about recognition of shared experiences. She believes that one of the affective bonds between common readers is nostalgia for the past, which books and illustrations may indulge. The books discussed in "Keys of Heaven" (1924), "The Painted

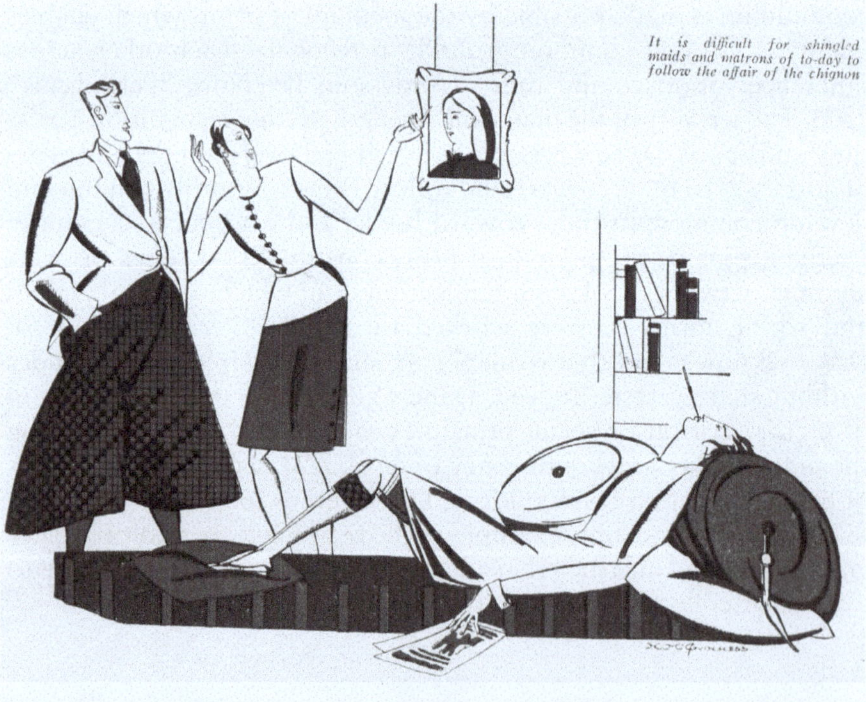

Figure 2.1 Only illustrators can "convey convincingly the look of vanished fashions to a reader unacquainted with them." "The Painted Past." Illustration by Norah McGuinness, courtesy of Hearst Magazines UK.

Past" (1927) and "Eighteenth-Century Amazons" (1928) affirm readers' feelings about common childhood experiences, feelings so unanalyzed that readers may register them primarily as sensations. In "The Painted Past," for instance, Dane asks why it is so pleasant to link present and past. "Are we indeed but our fathers and mothers 're-enlarged upon the earth'? Do we half recognize, I wonder, with a homesick thrill, cold hearth-stones, dead faces, forgotten years?" (120). She assumes that everyone feels this "homesick thrill," and that books that connect readers to the past thus also bind them to one another. Dane likewise explores primordial responses to books in "Eighteenth-Century Amazons" and "Keys of Heaven." These essays invoke bonds of sympathy and affection along Romantic lines, including the bond between parent and child, the sympathy between author and reader, and the mutual recognition of readers who have shared a childhood recaptured in books. In these essays Dane valorizes essential human bonds and shows how they are affirmed by reading.

Dane's book essays emphasize that taste is dependent on time, place, and individual disposition. In "As You Like It" (1926), Dane quarrels with friends and colleagues who accuse her of inconsistency if they detect a change in her pronouncements of what she likes. She openly admits that taste is vagrant, erratic, and unpredictable. It is "one of the world's marvels how even people in sympathy with each other, agreeing over all questions of principle, can stare at each other bewildered when it comes to questions of taste" (191). But "As You Like It" does not find this condition to lead to chaos. In contrast to modern tastemakers' efforts to help audiences form "good taste," Dane slyly points out that the most enduring and revered of writers, Shakespeare, may have been successful precisely because he understood how mixed was the taste of even a single audience member. Yet taste can still be principled. The "prime enemy of good judgment is the convention that, having once said, 'Them's my sentiments!' it is the act of a renegade to change them" (192). Dane maintains that "to change your opinion of the best method of enforcing a principle, does not mean abandoning the principle itself" (191).

Both "As You Like It" and "First Flights" emphasize that taste changes over time. These essays show Dane's careful attention to the nature of taste and its imbrication with cultural factors. In "As You Like It," Dane objects, "How childish for one man to twit another with an extract from a speech spoken a dozen years before. The man is twelve years older, and his mind has actually grown and changed with his body's changes!" (192). In "First Flights" (1926) Dane addresses the topics of taste and critical evaluation in relation to authors' first novels. She rationalizes readers' taste—it is best understood in the contexts of custom and association—before acknowledging the instability of taste, particularly with respect to readers' age. We like what we can place within the bounds of what we already know: "we depend, in order to appreciate, on an accustomed eye" (45). Dane's theory is similar to Pierre Bourdieu's *habitus*: the attitudes and tastes are shaped within our social milieu, but in contrast to Bourdieu's conception of ingrained taste, Dane emphasizes change over time. How might a single reader's taste change, then, over her lifetime? Dane considers factors like the growth of a reader's historical knowledge and the larger perspective that often brings tolerance.

"First Flights" acknowledges the differences in book lovers' taste based on their age; and it counts these as opportunities for connection rather than as sources of friction between readers. The middle-aged lover of books "is perpetually plagued by the conviction that the days of good literature are over," because he forgets "to allow for the glamour of association and custom," that is, how powerful and lasting are the impressions we form in the first twenty years of reading. In fact, what a "young untrained mind likes, it likes with an ungrudging intensity" (45). While the young welcome new ideas, Dane seems particularly concerned about middle-aged intolerance for them. "[I]t is tragic enough, this incapacity of the age that is, to appreciate the age that is to be.[3] For new ideas he hates: anyone would! It is absurd to pretend that we like new ideas once we are over thirty. If we discipline ourselves sufficiently to accept them, that is surely enough to expect in the way of broadmindedness from the sobering middle years" (45). The middle-aged reader's mere tolerance of new ideas makes her an ironic partner for the young writer, who comically offers what such a reader might be ill-equipped to read. For first-venture writers express new ideas, Dane continues, but "held by the glamour of their classics," stick to tried and true forms. So, when the literary beginner breaks from this trend and instead "gives in a fantastic, delightfully blown new bottle a sound wine," the middle-aged reader "hugs himself" (45).

The gap between young and middle-aged readers' taste might be a problem for writers who want to reach a broad audience. Or it might be a problem for a reviewer speaking to multiple generations of women readers. By explaining and expressing tolerance for these gaps, Dane encourages readers to bridge them by broadening

[3] Dane will later invite us to imagine "the age that was," for example, to imagine the sensation that *Sense and Sensibility* and *Wuthering Heights* created in their own time.

Figure 2.2 Illustration by Edmund Dulac for *The Green Lacquer Pavilion*, reproduced in Dane's "First Flights." Courtesy of Hearst Magazines UK.

their taste. Time, destabilizing all fixed things, is on the side of these readers. Dane makes this point by juxtaposing a variety of time spans in "First Flights." Against periodical time, the monthly succession of magazine issues, Dane posits several slow, subjectively experienced times, including

- Time as experienced by the young, whose taste is shaped by custom and association.
- Time as experienced by the middle-aged.
- The time that turns a novice writer into an accomplished one.
- The era and the society that shapes any writer's production.

The passage of time brings greater experience and understanding, which in turn are likely to inform one's taste and rationalize it. Thus in "Eighteenth-Century Amazons," Dane addresses her older audience members and invites their agreement with her: "As you get older, don't you find that your taste slowly and steadily heads away from the novel and towards history, essay and poetry?" The youthful imagination may need to be nourished by novels, but "Middle age prefers to learn the facts that inspired the novel" and allow experience to feed its imagination (34). In contrast to the student and the professional critic, the common reader's taste and judgment are shaped by her life experience.

If patience and tolerance prevent hasty judgment in readers, they also benefit writers. For slower time also applies to the achievement and the stature of an individual writer. His first book may provide only a clue to his gifts and qualities, while by the third novel of a newcomer, "you begin to know where you are with him, can make guess whether he is to become your grandchildren's classic or merely one of those rows of books on a dusty shelf that the same grandchildren will pull out to chuckle over" ("First Flights" 45). The fluidity of the partnership between changing writers and changing readers suggests the rewards of open-mindedness on all sides.

Just as taste should be understood in the context of one's generation and age, so should readers consider "age" in the sense of the spirit of an era and its effect on writers. Dane's attention to the reception of an individual writer—yet another time scale—brings her from review of newly published "first flights" to case studies in literary reception. After all, the slow time of history is available to Dane and her readers. She considers how the "first flights" of nineteenth-century novelists were received in their own day and at the present time. Here again, she entices readers into a literary territory that may be new to them, and a contested one at that: the nineteenth-century woman writer. Dane's choice of Victorian novelists allows her to illustrate the effect of hostility on a woman writer's literary production, anticipating Woolf's *A Room of One's Own*. She finds that the sting of gibes like Gilbert and Sullivan's lyrics: "the lady novelist / I don't think she'd be missed" must have held back "women by the dozen" (178).[4] Dane paradoxically concludes that this historical disadvantage accounts for the fact that good "first flights" are often written by women. After all, nineteenth-century women who did finish and publish novels "must have been at the intellectual and emotional bursting point of expression" (178). The essay concludes with discussion of Emily Brontë's *Wuthering Heights*, which Dane

[4] From the aria "As Someday It May Happen," in Gilbert and Sullivan's operetta *The Mikado* (1885). The lady novelist is mentioned in the context of Ko-Ko's creation of a list "Of society offenders who might well be underground / And who never would be missed—who never would be missed!"

believes is widely considered "the greatest novel that any woman ever wrote" (178). She borrows language from Kipling to capture the explosive impact of Brontë's novel on its audiences of 1926 and 1847: "It devastated the habitable earth for the next six months. Imagine, then, what its rage and pulse must have been at the incandescent hour of its birth!" (qtd. in "First Flights" 178).

The essays that address taste collectively illustrate the ease with which Dane addresses diverse readers, not by effacing their differences but through implicit invitations that each imagine the position of someone else in the periodical community. Questions of taste become interesting forays into other readers' personal histories, and then into the history of familiar authors and the popular reception of their books. Both private and shared enjoyment are also featured in the essays discussed below, in which reading pleasure, boosted by conviction or by critical acumen, becomes the basis for active cultural support of misunderstood or struggling authors.

Pleasure and Critical Insight

Reading to pursue one's own inclinations is the key to the great freedom expressed in Dane's book essays. Implicitly and explicitly, the essays observe and celebrate a variety of readers and occasions for reading as well as diverse material conditions in which people read. The serialized essays each present a new occasion for reading and allow Dane now to immerse in a writer's *oeuvre*, now to dip briefly into four or five books spread out on the table. These diverse occasions for reading contrast to the more narrow, approved reading practices that guide the student or the aspirant to culture whom Arnold Bennett addresses in *Literary Taste: How to Form It*. Dane's essays explore forms of enjoyment that include the satisfaction of an appetite, enthrallment, nostalgia, laughter, the pleasure of learning, stimulation of the imagination, and the excitement, or even the unease, of estrangement and discovery. The major spokesman for *Good Housekeeping*'s literary culture between the wars, Dane consistently endorses reading pleasure in a variety of forms; her book essays augment scholarly understanding of the role played by quality magazines in shaping reading practices and taste. Dane validates many forms of reading pleasure in their own right, protecting this "purpose" for reading against the incursion of a culture of advancement that fosters reading to gain others' approval or to become credentialed. But she also orders these various forms of enjoyment so as to illustrate a circuit of responses in which emotional responses or spontaneous reactions such as spine chills spark cognitive responses such as spiritual insight or intellectual debate. Both self-enrichment and the exercise of critical acumen, then, are included in Dane's program for common readers.

As Laura Frost has demonstrated, the modern period was saturated with the discourse of pleasure. Cultural commentators, "leisure theorists," and modernist writers both reaffirmed and reconfigured the ancient hierarchy denigrating immediate and somatic pleasure and valorizing cognitive and difficult pleasure. Reading practices were central to this discourse. It was argued that the more one indulges in the easy, sensual enjoyment of a talkie, a best-selling novel or a mass daily paper, the less willing and the less capable one becomes of engaging higher, more sophisticated faculties, resulting in costs to the individual and leading to societal, especially cultural, degradation. While Frost focuses on modernist writers, tastemakers and middlebrow critics were also highly invested in this hierarchy.

Modernist writers aimed to renovate literary language, but not merely in order to "make it new." Their diverse projects sought to create difficult reading experiences characterized by tension, paradox, and obstacles to pleasure. Frost argues that they did so not merely to suppress immediate pleasure but to assuage "an attraction to those disavowed pleasures." A process was needed; "the modern repudiation of pleasure must be cultivated and learned" (24–5). When we shift our attention from modernist fiction writers to a reading advisor like Clemence Dane, we find that she foregrounds and explicitly models how reading fosters learning. With a recurring opportunity to speak to readers, Dane occasionally takes the opportunity to caution them against immoderate consumption of confections readily dissolved in the mouth, especially shockers and formulaic romance novels. But her sustained tone is confidence, confidence that a rich Western literary heritage can be brought out in her essays—often in generously excerpted passages—for the illustration and enjoyment of linguistic and thematic "difficulty": metaphor, allusion, satire, enigma, spiritual and psychological complexity, and more. And in one of her strongest essays theorizing common reading, "Fragments that Remain," Dane envisions that, far from succumbing to hypnotic, mindless pleasure, common readers will engage in the critical-imaginative activity needed to rescue great books at risk of drowning in the unceasing tide of new publications.

Dane joins the critical consensus of her day that the most rudimentary of pleasures is the gratification of an appetite. She most often expresses this gratification in pejorative terms, comparing readers' craving for sensational novels to eating sweets all day. The literary equivalent of sweets is "false sentiment, sexual slop, meretricious romance encased in hasty ill-wrought sentences and careless wording" ("News from the Country of Hardwork" 47). More favorable, however, are Dane's evocations of material pleasure, wherein reading is only one form of delectable nourishment. This is the case in "Flapdragon" (1924), where, Christmas over, Dane's persona indulges in a much-deserved curl-up on the sofa "with a saucerful of Christmas-dinner relics—devilled almonds and candied cherries for choice—and a book for company, your own sort of book, the book you've been meaning to read this month of Sundays" (49). In addition to these readily accessible kinds of pleasure, Dane posits satisfaction that unfolds over time.

Some essays represent readers' progress from simpler to richer or more complex responses to literature, for example, the passage from childish to mature responses. In "Eighteenth-Century Amazons," Dane slips unobtrusively from the child's pleasure in hearing stories about her mother to the adult's pleasure in learning history:

> Every child demands of its mother—"Tell us what you did when you were little!" It prefers such an account before any fairy tale. I suppose the pleasure one takes in discovering that people a hundred or a thousand years ago did what we do, and liked what we like, is but a development of that attitude. (35)

This movement along a spectrum of responses from private, childish listening to adult passion for history surveys a reader's responses over much of her lifetime. Together, these two levels suggest Dane's two-pronged approach to common reading, in which the common reader's freedom to enjoy a variety of reading moods is counterbalanced with a desirable discipline.

Illustrating this two-pronged approach, "Some Ramblers" (1923) both probes what it means to "wander" and demonstrates its natural conclusion in critical insight. The rambling reader dips in and out of books and experiences appreciation, humor, and discovery. Dane models these experiences and demonstrates their continuity with critical insight. A form of pleasure, critical insight includes classifying a writer or grasping the conventions of a genre, skills that empower the common reader to make connections and critical distinctions between books.

"Some Ramblers" describes an "ever-increasing collection of indispensable books—books that aren't exactly novels, aren't exactly essays, aren't exactly biographies or books of travel, and yet have stolen from each of these ... their peculiar charms" (29). Dane co-opts the title of a pious book on every girl's shelf in the nineties, *Pine Needles and Old Yarns*, and asserts that the rambler author's "business is to bring you a whiff of pine needles, to distract you with old yarns" (29). Such books are good when you are kept in town or haven't slept. "They soothe without boring ... rouse memories instead of passions." Moreover, "you can open such an author at any page and put him down unfinished" (29). Dane thus suggests that readers need not master the books they choose to read, and that different books suit different moods. Indeed, the rambler is so associated with freedom that Dane invites the reader to compare such a book to the freshness and spontaneity of a picnic, "a pocketful of bread and cheese [and] ... the palmful of cold water scooped from the brook that you enjoy as you lie out on the pine needles reading an old yarn." Continuing to imagine this scene, Dane's persona wonders if it is appropriate to say grace before enjoying an outdoor meal. In a humorous comparison of high and humble meals and their book equivalents, Dane argues that ramblers may be as salvific as holy books. Wandering, Dane implies, need not be a species of irresponsibility or irreligion.

In fact, rambling opens both author and reader to valuable insights. Sustaining the mood of open-air enjoyment, Dane turns to a new book, W.H. Hudson's *A Traveller in Little Things*, which she calls "a series of little tales and impressions" (95). *A Traveller* allows her to define the figure of the rambler: "a man of education and humor with a platonic passion either for nature or for his fellows, and very often for both" (29). He enjoys looking, and doesn't want to touch. Dane makes her readers sympathize with or criticize the writer who is first and foremost a human being—before he is a "great" author:

> But the rambler never stops to pick the poppy, never tumbles into the river in a vain attempt to preserve the snowflake from its natural fate. Above all he never runs breathless, gasping, unseeing, unhearing, with cut feet and torn apparel, in a wild endeavour to reach the rainbow's end and mark the spot where the crock of gold lies buried. Which makes him (his one fault) a little inhuman! (29)

Without offering an explicit, didactic principle, Dane distinguishes between romantic and realist treatments of a subject, contrasting passionate people who try to grasp what is ephemeral with those who calmly survey the object in its entirety, delighting in it but respecting its integrity. This rambler author embalms the object for us in their books "as flies are preserved in amber" (29).

The common reader Dane wishes to cultivate begins with spontaneous, fragmentary dipping into a book and enjoys it in whatever way seems best to her, but she need not produce a critical account of it nor make a determination about its fitness for a canon. But Dane does expect critical thinking as one stage of reading for enjoyment. Although she uses neither of these academic terms, Dane teaches readers the distinction between romantic and realist treatments of a subject. The distinctions, in fact, are useful to individual readers, perhaps helping them decide what they like; and to communities of readers, providing a shared understanding as a basis for discussion and judgment.

The Common Reader of Poetry

In "First Flights," as we saw, Dane invites her readers to transcend, if not suppress, the judgments that arise from "custom and association." By contemplating a great Victorian writer's painful reception in her own day, readers realize that expanded and contracted time frames yield different, equally subjective judgments. Dane encourages her readers to locate themselves on a timeline spanning several generations who gather virtually to talk about good books. But in Dane's essays on poetry, the fact of individual readers' sometimes divisive perspectives is compounded by a fractured cultural field that jeopardizes their ability to distinguish between poetry and mere "verse." In "The Poet's Pen" (1925) and "The Poet v. the Talkies" (1929), the common reader's enjoyment is imbricated with critical evaluation and comparison. Making clear the stakes of this two-pronged response to poetry—pleasure and analysis—these essays assign to poetry a crucial role in the health of postwar culture, even while they ponder the decline of poetry reading. Although the high profile of poetry in these two essays is not sustained in Dane's critical *oeuvre*, in these major essays for *Good Housekeeping* Dane adopts a strong critical stand.

In "The Poet's Pen" Dane sets out to encourage the common reading of poetry in a climate of poetic experiment and confusion. She begins with the discouraging observation that "who buys a poetry book, or habitually reads it as a substitute for a novel? One in a hundred? One in a thousand? I know that a good deal more modern verse is read than was read ten years ago; but I said—who reads poetry?" (39). In contrast to "poetry," Dane finds that plenty of verse is being published, including that of our "confirmed sentimentalisers" and our "ruthless rhymers" (39), as well as a "mass of experimental verse."

Dane is well aware that the proverbial plain man in the street finds poetry hard to read. Before and after the First World War readers witnessed a bewildering series of determined rebellions from Victorian poetic traditions, from Pound's translations of obscure Eastern and Western figures, to Eliot's haunting and pan-historical montage of voices in *The Waste Land*, to Edith Sitwell's tightly stacked images and "confusing private allusions" ("Edith Sitwell"). Those who sought guidance, for example in Arnold Bennett's *Literary Taste*, found that reading poetry had become a chore. Bennett seemed ready to dismiss most of his readers before he had fairly started on the task of guiding them: "the very greatest poetry can only be understood and savoured by people who have put themselves through a considerable mental discipline." But poetry must not be shirked! "The formation of literary taste cannot be completed," he warns, "until the fearful prejudice of the average lettered man against the mere form of verse ... has been conquered" (78–9). And by 1925, although the tenets of New Criticism had not yet been consolidated, the new university discipline of English Studies and the influences of Russian formalism and of T.S. Eliot's early essays all were advancing a new discourse on poetry. Together they established the poem as a complex linguistic object whose formal patterns required trained readers to decipher. In light of this climate, Dane's treatment of poetry in "The Poet's Pen" offers an opportunity to compare her guidance to the common reader with these emerging rigorous methods for the analysis of poetry.

At the outset of "The Poet's Pen," Dane seems to concur that poetry is not for the earnest amateur reader. So fragmented is the reading public that the members of one subset, thrown into the heterogenous company of others for a train journey, can only gape at them in incomprehension. The reader of a modern classic novel is "that odd fish, a highbrow; but we are still respectful." The drama reader is positively eccentric, while poetry readers, distinctly creatures of another species, justify our demand that the train guard "rescue us from the propinquity of a lunatic" (39). As Dane turns this satirical mirror to reflect her readers, inviting their laughter, she assures them that they will not be asked to apply Bennett's "tough mental discipline" or approach innovative poetry via a theory and a polemic invented to defend it.[5] "The Poet's Pen" now sets aside the "difficult task" of reading poetry to explore a comic case study in the historical reception of poetry and to illustrate the enjoyment of contemporary poetry.

Dane's satirical sketch of the heterogeneous train passengers concedes that the strangeness of other people's taste is a truth universally acknowledged. Such a universal experience makes sympathy the most natural response to readers suspicious of poetry. So when Dane defines the true poet not as a "cunning technician" (Eliot, "Reflections" 186) but as a "fore-seer" who might guide society through the half-darkness of the postwar years, she signals that "true" poetry belongs to everyone.

If poetry has salvific potential, it is by the same token difficult to evaluate: his very visionary gifts mean the poet is out of step with his time, easily misunderstood. Again Dane sympathizes with her common readers:

> The reader of today knows that the poetry of to-morrow must, in the nature of things, be a remote beauty for him; yet he is so eager to enjoy the new vision, to hear the new sound. The trumpets, he knows, will at any moment ring in Judgment Day and the revelation of the glory of God. Is he to lie asleep? (140)

Unwilling to miss the trumpet of the Judgment Day, the common reader jumps the gun by getting up in the middle of the night. Then she mistakes the midnight frog song for divine melody. But Dane does not fault the modern reader's insufficient schooling in poetry; nor does she point to a cultural decline in serious reading. Instead, she presents two case studies illustrating a recurrent pattern of poets comically elevated or tragically misunderstood in their own day.

Dane relates an amusing anecdote about the partnership of William Blake and popular poet William Hayley, whose *Triumphs of Temper* was so successful that he was offered the laureateship, although his verse was mocked by his peers:

> When [Hayley] commissioned one William Blake to decorate his library for him with medallion portraits of the world's great poets, the list began with Homer, included Dante, Shakespeare, Chaucer, Spenser, and Milton, and ended serenely with Hayley himself: yet Hayley's world guffawed no protest. (39, 140)

[5] In "Reflections on *Vers Libre*," Eliot deplores a climate of hostility to poetic innovation and finds that poets must increasingly resort to "polemic and theory" to defend their poetry.

If the earnest poetry readers of her own day are mistaking a midnight frog song for great poetry, they are in good historical company. Shifting her attention to Blake, Dane unfolds his long suffering under Hayley's patronage, until Blake "was at last stung into retorting, in the blessed secrecy of his notebook, with an epigram that would have sent poor Hayley blushing to his grave if he had read it" (140). By telling the story of William Hayley and Blake, Dane interests her readers in the lives of poets as fallible beings. She does so deliberately to restore this biographical and historical context at a time when poems, "no longer to be confused with the lives or philosophies of their authors" have become "self-contained objects of inquiry" (Baldick, *Criticism* 66).

The need for difficult objects of study on which students must *work* was one reason for the shift in the activity of the critic during this period from the author to the text. But for her part, Dane continues to underscore pleasure. Armed with the wisdom that the enjoyment of poetry requires suspended judgment and a long perspective, readers may appreciate Tennyson—whose poetry was enjoying a resurgence of interest—Thomas Hardy, and Gordon Bottomley. Dane's actual guidance is condensed into a maxim "The habit of reading verse ... is the necessary preliminary to the judgment and enjoyment of poetry" (140). But what likely sent her readers to the poetry shelves of the library was Dane's account of her sensations and feelings as she read Bottomley's dramatic verse. Upon her first reading, so caught up in the drama, she did not notice the language and rhythm: "You do not in the least realise, in the excitement of watching the characters unfold and the plot develop, that it is the beautiful pulse and flow of the lines that is making enjoyment so easy. You are like a swimmer taken out to sea on the tide without realising it" (145). "Only on the second reading," she continues, "does the craft, the singular and skilful management of the words themselves, consciously interest you" and prompt you to "pause in fascinated interest over" individual lines, "until your mere pleasure in the music is once more overwhelmed by the human meaning that underlies the music" (145).

Dane's stories of poets unnoticed, misperceived, and maligned in their own day restore to poetry its place among common folk. However sublime their vision, poets were not exempt from the troublesome business of getting along with others. To make poetry enticing to *Good Housekeeping* readers, Dane puts her money on the reception histories that release her laughing readers to immerse themselves in the enthralling rhythms of good poetry.

The Responsibility of the Common Reader

Dane's essays on modern poetry identify a doubly fractured cultural field which, on the one hand, has blurred the distinction between poetry and "verse," and, on the other, has allowed the opinions of the highbrow reader to dominate the discussion. Within this cultural climate, Dane's poetry essays tacitly acknowledge, common readers need her support. In contrast, in essays linking reading choices to national literary culture, Dane's rhetoric often takes the form of warnings. In "Quality and Quantity," "A Bunch of Daisies," and "Short Stories," Dane prods her readers decisively, but with good humor. "Quality and Quantity" (1925) finds that best-selling novel readers too often acquiesce in consuming what is dished out to them, while the novelist finds it "hard to deny people chocolates in the hope that, grown hungry, they will ask bread of you instead" (152). The essay ends with Dane recounting a recent trip to the bookstore, only to find a beloved children's book to be out of print. She figures the publisher as Father Time, "reaping down all our tastes and fancies" as his scythe fells "our most delightful flowers that we would fain keep standing, withered as they are, yet a few days longer, leaving us the docks and the nettles to live through our winter instead" (154). This dispiriting vision reveals what happens when readers do not themselves make the determination of what flowers shall stay in print and what nettles can be cut down.

Dane's essays about reading choices locate common reading within a climate of commercialized book production. Most are addressed explicitly to women. Dane finds that women readers both drive the demand for formulaic, insipid romances and are exploited in the commercialized environment. At stake are women's readiness to engage in the public sphere and popular opinion about them. And outlining higher stakes, these essays make clear that the mill churning out magazine short stories and best-sellers jeopardizes the livelihood and the very existence of promising authors, with clear implications for the health of modern literary culture. "Short Stories" and "The Sea and the Sex," both published in 1924, each begin with a critique of contemporary book trends, then fault women readers for the deplorable national trend of "light reading." In "The Sea and the Sex," Dane complains that the moderns have stopped talking about women, "the sex," in favor of sex, the subject of the love stories and sex novels they author. So great is the commercial power of the "love interest" that its inclusion in a novel amounts to an obligation for any but "the greatest of our writers" (48). Yet falling in love and getting married are not the only interesting topics, Dane points out, as great stories of the sea prove. And why should "the stories of the arts, the sciences, the professions, and the trades be left to the technical experts?" she asks. Dane focuses on the demand of women readers as the source of this imbalance. Women are "the chief part of the reading public," she notes, and if, "as I have so often been told by librarian friends, women won't read anything but love-stories," then "it is the women who are making it difficult for any but the rich and famous author to produce the stuff that is in him" (173).

In both "Short Stories" and "The Sea and the Sex," Dane secures her criticism with the help of these "librarian friends," who report to Dane on reading trends. In "Short Stories" the "proprietress of a circulating library" reveals the casual reader's prejudice against volumes of short stories. These readers ask for "'something to last me over the week-end'" (20) and tell her that if they want a short story they will buy a magazine. It would not have been hard for Dane to cite any number of press critiques, satirical or sober, of women's self-indulgent reading. Yet Dane's unnamed librarian friend provides criticism from within the local community of readers, criticism more serious than hearsay, making Dane's warnings to her *Good Housekeeping* readers more personal.

Indeed, an increasingly narrow focus on local, or even her own, readers distinguishes "The Sea and the Sex" from thematically related essays in Dane's corpus. Unconcerned that she may be pointing her finger too directly at women readers, Dane turns her attention to the consequences of women readers' taste on their own futures in the public sphere, futures theoretically secured by their recent enfranchisement:

> It is not a question of our mere literary interest, our whole position is involved. Our long-desired physical and legal freedom, our intellectual independence, this deep-rooted belief of ours that we are intended to move level with our menfolk in a shared existence—all this will avail us little if our choice of reading matter reveals us as Byronic in our view of things as the Pamelas and Amelias we so heartily pity. (173)

Dane strikes a rare, didactic note in this passage, a mark of her feminist mission in this essay: "We should beware of our bookshelves, for our choice of books is bound to betray us. If we read principally sentimentalities and sex-novels, we show pretty plainly where our interest in life begins and ends, and I believe that the world cannot much longer afford to tolerate any human being whose interests are purely personal" (173). At the forefront of Dane's concern is women novel readers' credibility and reputation. But lurking in the shadows of her criticism is the widely discussed "problem" of women's taste in light fiction. Beginning in the Victorian period, women readers, presumed to be more impressionable than male readers, were understood to consume the bulk of published fiction (Flint 12–14). Moreover, vestiges of the belief that reading novels led to daydreaming, time-wasting, and escapism persisted into the twentieth century, as Dane's comments hint. In "The Sea and the Sex" Dane makes clear the links between women's reading and their advancement in the professions and the public sphere.

In addition to the place of women in modern society, Dane worries about the reception of new, promising authors and the health of national literary culture. In "Short Stories," she urges reading whole volumes of short stories, whether individual readers count themselves as writers-in-the-making or as readers plain and simple. Both segments of her audience are likely to impact the success of present-day short-story writers. Dane's thoughts about aspiring writers are prompted by Michael Joseph's *Writing for Profit*, which she reviews in "Short Stories." She admits that "perhaps I am prejudiced against this volume of advice to beginners," adding, "There is no doubt that it is a shrewd book, a sensible book, a book on which to sharpen one's common-sensical faculties *after* the story is written" (102). But if Dane acknowledges the validity of commercial considerations after composition of a story (or one might add, after composition of a book essay for *Good Housekeeping*!), she insists that before it is written, "the golden rule is 'Look in your heart and write!' without stopping to consider whether the publishers and editors are going to pay you in kicks or halfpence" (102).[6]

Writing for Profit was only a recent example of the commercially driven encouragement of young women to write and sell. New young writers appeared almost monthly in *Good Housekeeping*, introduced in glowing editorial sidebars or previews; while ads encouraged readers to "Learn to Write and Earn while you Learn."[7] In fact, the trope of the magazine-reader-turned-writer dates from the eighteenth- and early nineteenth-century periodicals, in which readers "are

[6] Characteristically, Dane expects readers to recognize her unattributed citations of classical literature, in this case one of Sir Philip Sidney's "Astrophil and Stella" sonnets.

[7] "Learn to Write." Ad for The Regent Institute, *Good Housekeeping* vol. 4, no. 6 (February 1924), p. 90.

constantly invited to become writers," Margaret Beetham observes (*A Magazine* 13). In this climate, Dane's goal is to emphasize the short story as a carefully crafted, even difficult, art form. She satirizes an acquaintance who, when he wants something to read, passes over short stories in favor of novels: "the longer the better. It shows the author has taken trouble." This casual opinion leads Dane's persona to vent her evidently pent-up outrage: "Trouble! *Trouble*! Isn't that the most unkindest cut of all? Consider the original bulk of a story as it shapes itself in the mind; consider with what averted eyes a dear sentence has been scored out here, with what wincing determination a choice paragraph deleted there" (20). The paragraph continues in a similar vein for (ironically) about 150 more words, crafting a sympathetic portrait of the short-story writer as a gardener forced to weed out or prune away the very beauties she has been nurturing. The typical would-be writer likewise comes in for a little teasing, with Dane again emphasizing that the craft of the short story is no easy one and can by no means be considered the practice of a novelist merely cutting her teeth on something soft.

Dane rejects the profit-driven approach to the short story: "Here has Mr. Joseph in *Short Story Writing for Profit* spent some two hundred interesting pages in telling the beginner just what the short story should and should not be—and yet—has he quite satisfied us? But then he has hampered himself by that dangerous word 'profit'" (20). Dane introduces the short story instead through a literary definition. A short story is "the brief account of a single incident which acts as a turning point in the development of a character or a group of characters, and by the light of which their personalities can be understood, their past explained and their future predicted by the reader" (20). With the simple advice that "there is no safer school than the work of the big writers" and a list of a dozen great living short-story writers, Dane now addresses both short-story readers and aspiring writers, devoting the second half of her essay to a discussion of great contemporary short stories.[8] To read their authors' volumes of stories is to endorse their substantial achievements and make a bid for their inclusion in the canon of great writers in English. On the other hand, to read short stories only incidentally, as one pages through a magazine, is to allow promising writers to

[8] Dane names Rudyard Kipling, John Galsworthy, H.G. Wells, Arnold Bennett, F.W. Bain, Oliver Onions, Stacy Aumonier, James Stephens, Somerset Maugham, Hugh Walpole, Joseph Conrad, and H.W. [sic] [Henry Major] Tomlinson. She lists not a single woman writer!

be read and then forgotten, their talent "unheralded." For in the current era, young writers are "'little new-lit stars trying to find their places in the uncaring void'" (102).[9] For the sake of these talented writers, it is "a real pity that the general public, by whom the writer lives, should be so friendly to the magazine short story and yet cold shoulder the printed volume" (20). Dane thus seeks to convert "the casual reader" of magazine stories into the "true book lover" (20).

In "A Bunch of Daisies" (1924), Dane is again concerned about the fate of talented writers and about readers' own capacity to read literature, but in this essay she singles out the threat posed by the "overproduction" of books. Like "Quality and Quantity," "A Bunch of Daisies" analyzes the effect on culture of large-scale economic and technological changes in the production and distribution of books. Readers are at once enmeshed in the mechanism and responsible for changing it. Noting the intertwined effects of overproduction on good books (and their authors) and on readers, Dane opines that "the tragedy of this over-production is not only that many a good book, produced with Heaven knows what agony of endeavour, is buried and forgotten under the immense overflows of rubbish, but that the very conception of literature is changing as far as the average reader is concerned" (29).

The injustice of unrealized talent and the sorrow it inspires are of course within the national imaginary, dating back to Gray's *Elegy*. Yet Dane devotes only the first half of her sentence to this tragedy, turning her attention instead to the how and why the "average reader's" conception of literature has changed. Dane blames modern technologies of communication that are turning literature into dictated spoken words. She singles out the typewriter, the dictaphone, and the daily press, not only because these technologies habituate modern ears to spoken rather than literary language, but because they make it easy to write a book. Dane goes one step further than Yeats when he laments "For to articulate sweet sounds together / Is to work harder than" any laborer, for she implies that the creation of art *should* be painstaking:

[9] The allusion is to Kipling's "The Last Term" in *Stalky & Co.*, wherein the school Head reminisces about the early struggles of great men in his circle. He speaks "of great men living, and journals, long dead, founded in their riotous youth; of years when all the planets were little new-lit stars trying to find their places in the uncaring void, and he, the Head, knew them as young men know one another." www.cleavebooks.co.uk/grol/kipling/stalky08.htm

> The mere physical discomforts of the art were once a safeguard, for writing down one's thoughts upon a subject, coherently, beginning at the beginning and arriving in due time at the end, is a laborious business. But typing is easy, and to talk to a short-hand typist easier still. (29)

Dane articulates a version of modernists' notorious rejection of the reputedly debased language of the mass press and their endorsement of less accessible and less ephemeral modes of art. A "crisis in language" arose from the perception that the human utterance was being contaminated by public, journalistic, and clichéd language, argues Ronald Bush (232–3). In book essays substantially devoted to cultural criticism, including "social problem" essays, Dane's work demonstrates the significant extent to which modernist poets and middlebrow journalists shared the same concerns about the effect of mass culture on English literary language. Poets such as T.S. Eliot and Ezra Pound reacted by adopting symbolic, less referential, less transparent poetic strategies, courting a coterie audience, while journalists such as Clemence Dane maintained the periodical's traditional function to educate and influence the public. Dane does so by articulating an activist role for book lovers, or common readers, in which they help steer the direction of contemporary culture toward higher literary standards. Common readers' enjoyment of good books is always bound up with their wide reading, acquaintance with literary conventions, and critical skill.

"A Bunch of Daisies" takes its title from a poem by German poet Christian Hebbel, which Dane quotes at the beginning and the end of her essay, so that the second time, the verse serves as a refrain and furnishes a note of optimism:

> Could but the meadow refrain from wasting its substance in daisies,
> Surely an aloe would spring fifty years hence from its soil [.]

Asking the reader whether she would rather have "A million marguerites every spring or once—once only in your life-time, a flower of paradise" (29), Dane opines that, likely by the law of nature, we can't have both. And the call for ordinary daisies in an unceasing stream seems to be ubiquitous. The column-length ad for The Regent Institute, mentioned above, falls on the second page of "A Bunch of Daisies," ironically confirming Dane's point that "the spirit of the age" is stimulating masses of daisies to flower. "Learn to Write and Earn while you Learn," its heading and subheading promise. More magazine copy is needed! "Hundreds of daily, weekly and monthly publications require the work of outside contributors. It is a striking fact that the supply of brightly written paragraphs, articles, sketches, and short stories does not keep pace with the demand."[10]

Identifying herself as a reviewer, Dane wants to sing the praises of all the deserving writers, but it is an impossible task. Thomas Gray stands behind her, both thematically and linguistically, adding to the rhetorical force of her message. As Dane comes to the end of her essay, she laments the "so many more daisies as yet unhonoured and unsung in the pages of *Good Housekeeping*" (92). But whereas in "Short Stories" Dane suggested turning to books for serious reading, in "A Bunch of Daisies" she calls on readers to help identify the "rare flowers" published every month in magazines. In partnership with the book critic, common readers can take on the role of identifying and singing the praises of these voices at risk of being smothered under the flows of book "rubbish." Readers must also help establish the conditions for an aloe to bloom. A reviewer's summary cannot do justice to these "rare flowers" of books; and their plight is jeopardized by casual and light reading. Dane lingers dramatically on the possible consequence: "Do you ever wonder why the Miltons of our day sit mute, inglorious; if a Blake still sees God from some Lambeth window and cannot sell that vision for a guinea?" (92).[11] Dane concludes the essay with a return to Hebbel's verse. The repetition, and the play on "refrain," recast the poetry as a fervent wish:

> Could but the meadow refrain from wasting its substance in
> daisies,
> Surely an aloe would spring—!

> I wonder if that is true. And if it is, I wonder if our light reading and cheap editions do not in the long run cost us more than we can afford. (92)

In "The Sea and the Sex," "A Bunch of Daisies," "Short Stories," and "Quality and Quantity" Dane makes clear that the practice of wide reading and an understanding of generic conventions holds importance beyond readers' enjoyment of good books. For Dane, there is no question that these skills and dispositions foster a robust literary culture by maintaining one book's intertextual dialogue with numerous others. Yet the cultural conditions of reading in the 1920s put the common reader under particular pressure. The commercialized

[10] "Learn to Write." Ad for The Regent Institute, *Good Housekeeping* vol. 4, no. 6 (February 1924), p. 90.

[11] Blake lived in Lambeth from 1790 and produced much of his creative work there.

environment in which new writers enter the marketplace, the rapid pace of production and multiplication of media, and the consequent overwhelming flood of reading matter, all obligate amateur book lovers—not literary experts alone—to identify and single out for preservation the literature that should endure.

"Fragments that Remain"

Amateur critics rise to this challenge beautifully in "Fragments That Remain" (1926). In this essay, Dane locates high and low forms of the literary fragment within common readers' culture; she engages their curiosity and critical appreciation; and she calls on them to make room in the literary canon for great, but not fully recognized writers.

In "Fragments That Remain" Dane celebrates the fragment and engages in debate about literary snobbery with a critic she admires. The essay foregrounds the enjoyment of books, but its specific purpose is to celebrate the literary fragment and demonstrate its diverse forms. As a critical essay, it defines a genre—and indeed proliferates definitions and examples of it—so as to locate the fragment now in high culture (Marlowe, Coleridge), now in the territory of the common reader and the middlebrow reader. The middlebrow reader is never explicitly named in "Fragments That Remain," but is nonetheless important to the dynamic generated as Dane both approves of and spars with classical scholar and essayist Gilbert Norwood, who writes about snobbery. As she surveys the fragment in its many guises, Dane quotes generously and invites readers to recognize and enjoy its many varieties. One major achievement of the essay is the skill with which Dane elicits sympathy, laughter, reverence, and other responses to fragments or their authors. The common reader is also called upon to recognize her own familiarity with some fragments, such as the biblical parable and the remains of shattered ancient sculpture exhibited in The British Museum. Dane's location of the fragment within public spaces and in the common reader's familiar territory is one way that "Fragments That Remain" contributes to theorization of the common reader in the 1920s. In a second validation of the common reader, Dane connects readers' affection for individual authors and books to their preparation to rescue and keep alive such texts when others have turned to new books. The publication of Conrad's *Suspense* illustrates this cultural dynamic. Dane argues that it is up to common readers to defend the place of such authors and books in literary canons.

"Fragments That Remain" explores multiple concepts of the fragment, a term that acts as a fulcrum by which Dane shifts from questions of authorial production to matters of reader enjoyment. In the course of the essay, Dane considers the fragment as:

- A small, precious part of a whole. Dane discusses famous fragments, such as Sappho's lyrics. She also fills the essay with choice quotations—precious fragments—from beloved books.
- An unfinished or suspended creation.
- A latecomer in a writer's corpus that retrospectively illuminates one or more of their earlier works.
- An epitome.
- A parable, an epitome of a master's teaching.
- "Last fragments": the production of a creator who is failing or dwindling.
- A literary genre that can be imaginatively continued by a reader.

This list conveys something of Dane's exuberant treatment of the fragment. In the course of the essay, in addition to the examples discussed below, Dane touches on Gaskell, Stevenson, James, Meredith, Austen, Scott, Byron, and others. Through such a survey, she illustrates and adds to the tradition of fascination with the literary fragment. Moreover, Dane's playful variety of fragments serves to empower the common reader, especially by indicating how many of these forms already belong to the common reader's culture. Such personal identification was important amidst the modernist vogue for literary fragments and fragmentation. But Dane's treatment of the fragment does not give modernism a monopoly on it. And as she develops her critical celebration of the fragment, she positions herself more explicitly against academic treatment of it.

As we have seen in this chapter, Dane's persona stands at various distances from the common readers she both addresses and constructs. At times she adopts the expert's big-picture view of a literary culture on the brink of a crisis engendered by degraded reading habits. At other times, she is a member of an imagined community of readers ready to call back their common childhood by reading new novels that evoke it. "Fragments that Remain" exemplifies a third role. In this essay, Dane explicitly sets herself apart from shortsighted professional critics and positions herself as a common-reader critic, one whose authority arises from deep familiarity with specific texts. Dane instructs readers in this essay, but her lessons arise organically from generous quotation of literature. As readers savor these passages along with Dane, they experience a direct, accessible pleasure, against modernist readers' experience of Freud's unlust, which Laura Frost characterizes as "gratification attained through tension, obstacles, delay, convolution, and pain" (6). Indeed, Dane's critical treatment of the fragment consistently foregrounds its emotional and cognitive engagement of common readers. For instance, in the central aesthetic question raised by "Fragments that Remain" Dane speculates that fragments such as *Kubla Khan*, Sappho's poetry, and the *Venus de Milo* are exquisite precisely because they leave us pining for the whole that we can only imagine. This hypothesis unifies a discussion of fragments that ranges across media and literary history.

As she surveys fragments ancient and modern, in fine art and in literature, Dane elicits readers' affection, curiosity, laughter, and aesthetic appreciation. The fragment is both incomplete, inspiring pity and curiosity, and precious, often a rare remainder of something valuable that has not survived; and in this guise it elicits affection, desire, and admiration. Dane further illustrates the curiosity and sympathy that lead to critical judgment of a work of art. She considers the fragment that is a work unfinished at an author's death, asking how an author might feel if he could see from his grave that a rival had finished his work. She engages readers' sympathetic imagination in the plight of the author, and in turn illustrates the enjoyable speculation that an unfinished literary work inspires. Dane indicates that such speculation is a form of literary criticism and that it need not be reserved for academic critics; in fact, she begins the essay with a biographical reading of Marlowe's *Faustus* to speculate on the unfinished *Hero and Leander*. She quotes from the conclusion of the play to support her interpretation that "young Marlowe's masterpiece ends in a despairing shriek for more time" (47); then ponders Marlowe as a "dumb shadow" after his death, tortured by watching a friend finish *Hero and Leander*. By engaging readers' sympathetic imagining of the author's feelings, Dane heightens a sense of the vitality of the fragment, which lives on even as its author is abruptly cut off from life and from the power to complete his masterpiece.

More examples of fragments move the conversation from the *oeuvre* of a single writer to the genre of the fragment, bringing Dane into conversation with archaeologists, classicists, and modernists. Curiosity about a writer represents a gateway to broader questions of cultural history and genre. Would a completed *Kubla Khan* be to us like Wordsworth's poetry? "[W]ould the Venus of Milo still be Beauty if she had her arms?" (162). Dane's invocation of Sappho and the *Venus de Milo* intersects with modernist fascination with the fragment. Like modernist writers—and most famously in *The Waste Land*—Dane conceptualizes the fragment as something broken off from an irretrievable whole. The fragment reflected the experience of modernity, from the snatches of landscape viewed from a speeding automobile, to the fragmentation of a once unified reading public, to the juxtaposition of "scraps" on the front page of a daily paper, to the remnants of Sappho's poetry on recently unearthed Egyptian parchment.[12] Yet to invoke the topicality of the fragment, Dane did not need to position herself alongside modernists, for fragments had enjoyed a popular vogue since at least 1896, when Oxford archaeologists working in Egypt discovered a "torrent" of papyri, including fragments of poems by Sappho. Reports of these archaeological discoveries, including "publications and lectures based on them, gripped the public imagination, infiltrating popular novels and music hall songs, newspaper reports, and the Times 'book of the week.'" Museums began to foreground the fragment as they removed neoclassical restorations of ancient Greek sculpture (Goldschmidt). The cultural conversation around fragments, then, cut across disciplines, artistic media, and literary brows.

Dane's literary criticism does not follow the lead of modernism but reflects her immersion in a broader culture. Dane's references to Sappho and to the *Venus de Milo* specifically invoke museum display and reflect substantial public interest in fragments. In "Fragments That Remain," Dane recognizes and endorses this popularity by offering fresh examples and extended definitions of the artistic fragment. Her examples are drawn from shared literary culture, as indicated by "we" in her appraisal of *Kubla Khan*: "We treasure that fragment of a dream as perhaps the most perfect snatch of verse in the language" (47).

As Dane repeatedly stresses the common reader's pleasure in fragments, rather than the fragment's role in modernist aesthetics, she constructs a broad-minded, loyal reader who plays a creative-critical role in the future of literary culture. Two biblical parables, themselves instances of fragments, offer wisdom about the earnest amateur reader's role. The first, The Feeding of the Five Thousand, provides the epigraph to the essay: "And they took up of the fragments that

[12] Hugh Kenner finds that these papyri focalized for classicists and modernists a "renaissance of attention" exemplified in Pound's *Lustra* poems as "an aesthetic of glimpses" (227). Kenner is building on Barbara Charlesworth's discussion in *Dark Passages* (1965) of Arthur Symons's cultivation of an aesthetic of arrested flux.

remained twelve baskets full" (*King James Bible*, Matthew 14.20). Dane returns to this verse at the end of the essay to endorse common readers' reluctance to rush into new "fields," their tendency instead to reap the "fragments that remain" from the previous year's harvest of books. The full verse and the excerpt that titles Dane's essay alike suggest common readers' loyal tendency to recognize as precious what others might discard.[13] Common readers' side-stepping of codified instruction, their freedom to range beyond canonical texts, and their tendency now to immerse themselves in, now to peruse good books, all position them to stand to one side and later to "take up the fragments that remain." As we will see, in "Fragments That Remain," quotation of favorite excerpts—fragments, in fact—is the earnest amateur's principal form of enjoyment within a community of book lovers. If "Fragments That Remain" begins with speculation about writers'—and their literary characters'—fear of premature death, it soon moves on to the enjoyment and the confidence reflected in naming and quoting from beloved books.

The second parable encapsulates Dane's and her readers' esteem for Conrad's posthumously published fragment, *Suspense*. Alluding to the Parable of the Rich Man and Lazarus, Dane maintains that the earnest amateur reader "believes in his rich man, and is thankful for the crumbs that fall." Common readers, she insists, have played a central role in the favorable reception of Conrad's fragment. Only they welcomed his *Rover*, later revealed as a "splendid prelude" to *Suspense*. For while the critics dismissed *The Rover* as a falling-off of Conrad's power, earnest amateurs read *The Rover* and kept Conrad in circulation "until the critics found time to tell the public that he was a great novelist" (163).

A Bone to Pick

In "Fragments that Remain," Dane explicitly positions her audience within a contested and fragmented population of readers. She does so not by defending the middle position of her *Good Housekeeping* audience but by expanding the presumed range of their reading skills and taste. Dane thus challenges the increasing demarcation of "highbrow" from "middlebrow" literature after the First World War. The distinction arose in part from the institutionalization of highbrow

[13] The full verse reads, "And they did all eat, and were filled: and they took up of the fragments that remained twelve baskets full" (Matthew 14.20).

culture within the university and the insinuation that ordinary educated readers could not understand modernist literature.[14] Dane's resistance to the segregation of readers is packaged with humor, a response to cultural debates about taste and reading that scholars have associated with the middlebrow. A middlebrow register of humor and satire defuses cultural anxiety around the attainment of high culture, they find.[15] In fiction or commentary that parodies rather than aspires to high culture, middlebrow humor asserts its own sophistication. Humor is the mode of Dane's tribute to Gilbert Norwood, a well-published classical philologist, whose essay collection *The Wooden Man* she reviews in "Fragments that Remain." Admiring Norwood's book but objecting to some of his premises, Dane extends his satire of literary snobbery.

Norwood's *The Wooden Man* does have something to say about fragments. He supports Dane's theory that it is the fragment's scarcity that makes it precious. But in "Fragments that Remain," Norwood is principally important as a foil to Dane. Against his concern about literary snobbery, her confidence in broadbrow reading is a breath of fresh air; and his list of boring books instigates her quotation of delicious passages from these same books.

In "Too Many Books," Norwood argues that an unrelenting tide of "good books," both new and reissued, locks readers in a perpetual competition to stay ahead of other readers, competition that arises from the social capital of book talk. Since no one can read all these books, individuals thus sort themselves into groups—not by delimiting their taste—but according to their strategy of survival. For example, the typical man in one group

> specializes in the moderns of whom one reads most in the *Times Literary Supplement*. Feverishly he cons the work of all the authors enshrined in that austere mausoleum; feverishly, because he may at any moment be caught napping by some more alert practitioner … . (Norwood 58)

"Too Many Books," first published in *The London Mercury*, squarely addresses the anxiety surrounding cultural legitimacy. Norwood's position as a university professor of Greek and Latin lends credibility to his objection to literary snobbery, an objection

[14] In his discussion of these forces, Ross McKibben further cites the success of modernist literatures that, by departing from recognizable literary traditions, effectively "made the demarcation possible"; and the advent of the Book Society and the Book Guild (477–8).

[15] See Tracy and Hammill.

that cannot be chalked up to sour grapes.[16] Through satirical humor, he also provides his readers a measure of relief. Faye Hammill has identified "pretension" as the primary satiric target of a subset of middlebrow fiction, a satire that these novelists extend to their magazine writing. They "trade in the delineation of social 'types,'" Hammill finds, which was a staple of periodicals such as *Vanity Fair*, *The New Yorker*, *Time and Tide*, and *Punch* (7–8). Both Norwood and Dane are engaged in precisely this kind of critique; their magazine essays correct the notion of an aspirational middlebrow culture, revealing its capacity instead to provide "a vantage point from which high culture, popular culture, and middlebrow culture itself could be critically observed" (Hammill 12).

Dane shares Norwood's antipathy to literary snobbery but refutes, albeit with good humor, his presumption that there is actually consensus about literary value. Even while Norwood laments that "This ignoble competition has ruined taste, for to carry it on we must follow the crowd" (58), he presumes that readers' taste is somewhat uniform. His assumption that all readers find the same books boring, for example, clearly nettles Dane's persona.[17] Norwood even makes a list of such bores and rashly proclaims that those who admire them are "posing." Repositioned in "Fragments that Remain," his opinions only strengthen the bond between common book lovers against the esteemed, but misguided Norwood:

> [R]emarking that "certain entries are obvious" [Professor Norwood] jots down (heaven help him) as prime bores, Marcus Aurelius, Samuel Richardson, "most religious books," *The Faery Queen*, and—yes, it is the truth that that I am telling you—*and*—*The Shaving of Shapgat*. He does! (162)

While Norwood posits a monolithic audience whose taste is known, Dane and her readers know better. Dane uses Norwood to stand in for any number of "expert" attempts to categorize readers and generalize about their taste. She gleefully adopts the mock persona of a humble admirer of the wrong set:

> You see how it would annoy Professor Norwood, holding the view he does about people who read *Pamela* and pretend they enjoy it, if I

[16] During this period, Norwood was Professor of Greek at University College, Cardiff, Wales, from 1908 to 1926; and Professor of Latin at University College, University of Toronto, from 1926 to 1928.

[17] I use the term *persona* when Dane foregrounds and dramatizes the reviewer's feelings and responses.

> dared to praise his *Wooden Man*. Much as I want to, I daren't say to you—this is the most humorous, stimulating and interesting bundle of opinions printed this year, and you simple mustn't miss it! For, apart from my fear of the author's natural annoyance at admiration from the wrong quarter … . (162)

In this polyvocal address, Dane both praises *The Wooden Man* and underscores that Norwood's categories of readers may unhelpfully serve to construct them—and fix individual readers in them—rather than to lead them in the stimulating conversation about books that he recognizes as a great social amenity.

Moreover, the presence of an "adversary" adds zest to the book lovers' usual enjoyment in citing titles and quoting delightful fragments of the books they enjoy. To "prove" how wrong Norwood is about *The Faery Queen*, Dane quotes about ten lines that she characterizes as "the delicious description of the parents of the Thames" (162–3). Next, she regales her readers with a ten-line fragment of "poetic force" from Jeremy Taylor's *Holy Living and Dying*. Such lengthy quotation revives the beloved books whose superabundance, Norwood finds, destines them for death. Dane's middlebrow confidence refutes Norwood's list of boring books but takes a different tack. By sharing delicious bits within the *Good Housekeeping* community of book lovers, she in fact launches the very book conversations Norwood calls for.

The vision of the common reader in "Fragments that Remain"—what some critics fail to understand, Dane explains—is that "most people read because they like reading, and read what they read because it is what they like and for no other reason whatever" (163). There could hardly be a more straightforward definition of the common reader. This unimpeachable idea fuels the confidence of Dane's persona, strengthens the community of common readers against "adversaries," and leads to their exuberant exchange of favorite excerpts. In an adversarial and highly contested cultural field, micro-communities of readers function to defend their taste and keep good books alive.

Chapter 3

The History of Ourselves: Cultural, Rural and Matriarchal Legacies

In her essays on literary, feminist, and rural heritage, Clemence Dane variously construes the past as a creative resource, a form of insurance against the ravages of modernity, or a template for action in present-day Britain. Powerful legacies, these three strands of heritage both reflect and guide collective national identity. When we consider Dane's essays, themselves embedding book reviews, and *Good Housekeeping* more broadly, which both amplified and supplemented Dane's discussion of heritage, we can conceptualize the many-layered, substantial work undertaken in many women's magazines to bring readers into the stream of a wide cultural heritage. Dane's essays provide a case study of a single author's contributions to that effort.

In the interwar period, Britons grappled with ongoing and new forms of instability. The aftermath of the First World War, the decline of British imperial hegemony, the Slump, the spread of suburban and urban areas, and the expansion of mass communication technologies: these had substantial influences on citizens' understanding of how they would build on or depart from the past. In the 1920s, then, the English conceptualized their heritage as a set of natural or cultural goods that were either vulnerable or had been destroyed. Studies documenting these recalibrations of Englishness, many of them focusing on the 1930s and 1940s, point to the importance of symbolic fora of the debate, including myth and collective memory.

Magazines were of course only one of the many media reflecting and transforming Britons' sense of their heritage. In the interwar period, the cinema, literature, amateur photography, and popular travel all circulated the images, myths, and beliefs that construct individuals' sense of collective identity. As this chapter documents, myth and its ability to renew national literatures was of particular interest to Dane and her modernist contemporaries. Yet if myth and archetype suggested that novelty and change would be accommodated in patterns of integrity, many narratives about contemporary England traced a story of irreversible division. Guides to England, travel narratives, and public discourse, for example, found a tension between two Englands: a privileged and a poor. To move between them, writes Peter Lowe, "was to realize that the country was no longer by any measure organic or whole" (5). In varying degrees, the Dane essays discussed in this chapter reflect this loss of a formerly organic whole.

Lowe sets the cultural phenomena in his study against the backdrop of the Slump, the spread of suburbia, and the prospect of a second world war. Like Lowe's study, much of the scholarship examining the reconfiguration of English national identity focuses on the 1930s.[1] In contrast, the Dane essays I have selected were written in and often reviewed books published in the 1920s. My focus on the period immediately after the First World War, which also saw the launch of *Good Housekeeping*, allows me to examine how campaigns for fresh beginnings—new forms of Englishness, new opportunities for women—are negotiated simultaneously with recognition of loss. To provide a thick description of cultural attitudes toward English heritage, I examine Dane's essays, influential sister texts such as *A Room of One's Own*, and *Good Housekeeping* journalism by significant figures such as Storm Jameson, Helena Normanton, and Violet Bonham Carter.

Dane's heritage essays throw into question the moderns' access to the renewal and well-being reflected in narratives of national or human heritage. In "American Primitives" (1924) and "A National Mirror" (1929), the cyclical return of folk heroes, and the rise, fall, and rebirth of national literatures seem to ensure this access. In contrast, Dane's construction of Englishness in essays such as "The Looking Glass of Laughter" and "Fools in the Forest" reflects her ambivalent endorsement of the English "character," her support only for a diminished or satirical Englishness. Dane's book discussions rarely lead her to admire Victorian legacies of progress, expansion, and imperial conquest; instead, she promotes traditions of humor and caricature that deflate British self-aggrandizement. Dane's ambivalence is still more pronounced in essays about England's recent rural or political history: these reveal the

[1] Important studies of English national identity in this period include those by Jed Esty, Ina Habermann, John Taylor, and Judy Giles and Tim Middleton.

struggle and costs of preserving a common good. "The Consort Crown" (1927), for example, recounts women's campaign for access to higher education and to the public sphere, embedding it in a history of women in the Western world. As Dane reads it, that history originates in strength and ends in triumph, bookended by the feminist elements in the Old Testament and the founding of Girton College in 1869. Yet for thousands of years in between, English women have been denied access to the public sphere. Three essays about England's rural past, "The English Eden" (1928), "A Hidden Orchis" (1929), and "Jefferies of the Fields" (1927) likewise present a mixed picture. In "Jefferies of the Fields," Dane recognizes Richard Jefferies as a genius whose books bring back the texture of daily life in rural nineteenth-century England; but in "The English Eden," any relationship to England's rural past is freighted with the irony of the moderns' destruction of the very thing they love. Finally, in "A Hidden Orchis," Dane hails the books of Gertrude Bone—their language, hand-crafted paper, and illustrations—for their preservation of the speech and sensibility of rural people. But she also worries that these rarified books might be neglected in the marketplace and ultimately pass out of memory.

Accounts of women's experience tend to reflect this uncertain balance between loss and triumph, diminishment and expansion. As the chapter turns from Dane's to *Good Housekeeping*'s treatment of heritage, we will see that the magazine often emphasized the expansion and triumph side of this equation. Women's experience of private life underwent important but often overlooked changes in this period, and, indeed, cultural and social historians have demonstrated that middle-class women's lives illuminate changes in interwar English identity more generally. Alison Light argues that the period turned away from masculine and imperial rhetorics and adopted an Englishness "more inward-looking, more domestic and more private" (8), while Judy Giles contends that to grasp interwar changes to English identity we must examine the private worlds of women, whose responses were shaped by public discourses about domesticity (*The Parlour and the Suburb* 4). Yet, as we will see, Dane and other *Good Housekeeping* journalists turn outward to foreground female and feminist activism in the public sphere, such as Caitríona Beaumont documents.

In this chapter, examples of *Good Housekeeping*'s treatment of heritage by Storm Jameson, Helena Normanton, Margaret Wintringham, and others illustrate considerable consistency in *Good Housekeeping*'s authorial and editorial codes.[2] Although the journalists were not collaborating, each made a contribution to a corps of "women in the public eye, known for their sound grasp of their subject ... who can lead women."[3] Each offers insight into the history of British women's private lives so as to pave the way for their confident transition into expanded—domestic and public—roles. They establish critical distance from some legacies, such as Victorian society, while they fully endorse others, such as the conception of women's new role as "national housekeepers." A third approach to their readers' many-faceted heritage is represented by articles that urge women to be more active citizens, through voting and political protest, in order to carry out Britain's "birthright of liberty" on a global scale. In these stories of national identity, we see the *Good Housekeeping* journalists' shared conviction that English history can be mined for the material that can shape modern women's central roles in public and private life.

English Literary Heritage

In "Monuments" (1925) Dane describes a small public of book lovers that "has lately been much concerned over the alleged decay of the novel," leading to a flurry of little-magazine symposia on new trends in the novel. For her part, Dane derides the "folly of believing that the English novel can die one hour before the English nation dies. Is not one the photograph-album history of the other?" (59). In contrast to many experimental modernists of the period, Dane does not believe innovation to be incompatible with the continuity of traditions. In Dane's conception of literary heritage, long-standing traditions will nourish new forms in the modern period, as they do in every period. Hers is an optimism born of the long view, especially her attunement to the force of archetypes that continually renew literary traditions. Dane's attitude in "Monuments" is not the mockery of highbrow pretension that has been associated with an interwar middlebrow stance.[4] Rather, Dane locates herself both inside and

[2] Matthew Philpott's designation of "social codes" is a useful way to discern patterns of interaction between "the wide network of actors involved in the creation, circulation and reception of the journal and include editorial personnel, contributor networks, and readership" (3).

[3] "The Reason for *Good Housekeeping*."

[4] See Faye Hammill, who identifies a trend in middlebrow texts that "mock those who seek distinction through deliberate eccentricity, intellectual posturing, bogus bohemianism, and social climbing" (8).

outside the diverse group of critics who are worried about the longevity of the novel, a positioning that affords both conciliation and distance. Avoiding any cultural labels for this group, she implicitly includes herself when she identifies them as "a small, strange, but enduring section of the community that generally considers the reading of books the most fascinating occupation that life can offer" (59). But she distances herself from their belief that the English novel is in crisis. "Monuments" is characteristic of Dane's essays on literary heritage, in which we find conciliation and the espousal of laughter as strategies to reunite cultural factions.

Indeed, when Englishness is the topic, Dane is most ready to endorse books that deflate the English with satire and parody. In "The Looking Glass of Laughter," Dane's subject is the English readiness to laugh at themselves. She acknowledges differences "in the mirrors that our humorists hold up to us" and expresses her appreciation for Max Beerbohm's recent *New Things and Old*. Beerbohm's mirror has "queer little flecks and flaws behind its surface, so that, looking at yourself, you perceive as it were a smut on your nose, and your mouth acquires a foolish twist ... A cruel little looking-glass is this of 'Max': and yet how witty, how devastatingly lifelike, how inexpressibly funny" (98). Literary heritage functions to consolidate, confirm, and widen readers' sense of an imagined community of Englishmen. At the same time, the metaphor of the looking-glass in which the English are made to view themselves suggests the inherent instability of English character, always seen in reflection, always generated by and as a challenge to one or another formulation of Englishness.

In "Fools in the Forest," discussed below, and in "The Looking Glass of Laughter," Dane refers with a mixture of pride and irony to the English character. If she refers to an English virtue or a global British accomplishment, she steps to one side of it. For example, she finds that the English tell the truth, but with "a veiling gesture" ("Fools" 71). When speaking directly about the special inheritance of English literature, she under-delivers: "Books that are merely rambling monologues on life and a hobby have always been a special manifestation, a special triumph of English literature" ("Fools" 148). And when an outsider criticizes their society, the English do not defend themselves, but instead revel in the presented caricature, by definition unstable. In the face of this criticism,

> [The English] quote neither our literature nor our laws, our past, our present or our future place in the history of the world's growth in refutation. Not we! We wait until the tirade finishes and then, still

> agreeing—oh, agreeing heartily—we dissolve into helpless tearful laughter at the amazing portrait held up to us. For the English, above every nation, adores caricature, and the more deftly our eccentricities are hit off the more we enjoy it. ("Looking Glass" 45)

Dane's pride in British global achievements is guarded; she alludes to these contributions in the very process of illustrating the English tendency *not to* boast, in fact, to exchange self-mockery for self-inflation. By choosing books in which Englishness is gently mocked, Dane affiliates herself with the period's tendency to question whether there was still any core to Englishness.[5] Thus, faced with his interlocutor's refusal to defend Englishness, the "average foreigner" is apt to tear his hair out. "How can he understand us when he has not yet grasped the fact that we do not pretend to understand ourselves?" (45).

English nationalism in this period was increasingly associated with what J.A. Hobson, in his influential *Imperialism*, called "an overflow of nationalism into imperial channels" (10) that, by fostering hostile nationalisms in both colonized nations and competing empires, crushed all hope of internationalism and "humane cosmopolitanism" (8). Like many of her contemporaries, Dane expresses unease at an English nationalism that took the form of self-aggrandizement; where she celebrates an English literary heritage, she carefully delimits its "uniqueness." English literature may owe its character to its humor, says Dane, but "every other quality that has made our literature our prime glory the literature of other nations can match" (45).

World Literary Heritage

In the essays discussed in this chapter subsection, while English literature continues to play a role, Dane explores a wider, human heritage transmitted to her readers through myth, archetype, and the Bible. In "Rolling Stones," "Fools in the Forest," "The Twelve Best Books for Women," "American Primitives," and "A National Mirror," Dane treats literature as the repository and the engine for the archetypal patterns that reveal human instincts and psychology. "Rolling Stones" (1927) is typical. A rolling stone may gather no moss, Dane says, but it leads an adventurous life. She muses on famous literary stones, which invite comparisons across world myth:

[5] Jed Esty demonstrates that early twentieth-century critiques of imperialism figured its fissuring effect on an English identity.

> Think—David's murderous pebble is somewhere in the world still, though Goliath's bones and David's bones are powder: and somewhere in the sea lies the stone that the roc dropped on Sinbad's ship.[6] I have seen the stone that, so they say, Polyphemus flung after Ulysses: it's not unlike the Old Harry Rock at Swanage ... (57)

Condensed into two paragraphs, Dane's survey of legendary stones also includes their role in the fortunes of Cronos, Odin, Hansel and Gretel, and the protagonists of Sir Walter Scott's *Anne of Geierstein*. And then there are the human beings we call rolling stones, archetypal figures to be found in any nation and any era,

> who abhor settling down into a predestined hollow, who stifle under the beautiful mosses of habit and possessions, who seek blows and wounds and pain as other men seek shelter, peace and quiet, whose instinct is not to gather moss but to get their corners rubbed off, as if they knew by instinct that, not in withdrawal from life but in contact with life, lies their preservation. (147)

Dane praises St. John Ervine's new novel, *The Wayward Man*, a "brilliant study of unchanging types," for its representation of "the unending struggle between the forces that preserve life and the forces that change and continue life ... It is the story of humanity epitomized in the story of a Rolling Stone" (148).

This negotiation between preservation and change is central to modernist and middlebrow narratives of modernity alike. Particularly influential was T.S. Eliot's "Ulysses, Order, Myth." Eliot recognizes that in *Ulysses*, Joyce adopts appropriate "styles and symbols" to develop a parallel between contemporary Dublin and ancient Greece. Joyce's mythic method has for Eliot "the importance of a scientific discovery," an insight and set of procedures for use by scientist-artists coming afterward, allowing the "immense panorama of futility and anarchy which is contemporary history" to become comprehensible as it is brought into relation with the past (483). Like her contemporary modernist critics, Dane believes that authors' skillful attention to the age-old patterns beneath modern experiences will make their books central to literary canons. Thus, when we look for Dane's conception of Englishness, we find that it is often formulated in terms

[6] Dane alludes to the Middle Eastern *Sinbad the Sailor* stories, seventeenth- and eighteenth-century additions to the fourteenth-century *One Thousand and One Nights*. In the episode Dane references, the eponymous hero and his mariners find and eat the chick from a broken roc's egg. The giant, angry parent rocs retaliate by dropping giant boulders on the mariners' ship.

Figure 3.1 In "Rolling Stones," Dane treats literature as a repository and engine for archetypal patterns. Illustration by Norah McGuinness, courtesy of Hearst Magazines UK.

of diminishment: conjoined to self-satire, as in "The Looking Glass of Laughter," or yoked to haplessness, as in "Books that are merely rambling monologues on life and a hobby" in "Fools in the Forest" (148). Yet when we consider Dane's corpus of *Good Housekeeping* book essays, we observe that, setting aside her brief, frequent reference to Shakespeare, Dane infrequently devotes an essay to a literary heritage that is specifically English, except when a body of literature records an English pastoralism. More characteristic is Dane's easy passage from English traits to the universal human experiences that she believes will refuel modern literature.

"The Twelve Best Books for Women" (1923) presents a good example of Dane's readiness to balance the relative claims of English and of world literature in readers' literary heritage. The essay naming the "twelve" or the "hundred" best books for (children, women, summer reading, etc.) was already formulaic when Dane was invited to write "The Twelve Best Books." Since the genre calls for brief critical treatment of each item in a miscellany, Dane's essay provides an opportunity to observe how she balances English and a wider, Western literary heritage. What we find is that English literary culture is referenced in citations that, Dane implies, need no further discussion. The paucity of good translations in England arises from "our insular tradition" (19); Shakespeare takes "the twelfth place, the honoured place" on the list; and Dane includes on her list *The Last Chronicles of Barset* so that readers may benefit from Trollope's "unique insight into the heart and soul of the Englishwoman" (106). It is interesting, then, that only in her discussion of the Bible does Dane develop her conception of literary heritage:

> A woman who knows her Bible is an educated human being. She has absorbed great literature; she has learned the trick, or shall we say the simplicity, of pure and harmonious speech—speech suited equally to the mountain-tops and the domesticities of life. She has imaginatively shared in almost every variety of common and uncommon human experience. Love and life, hate and death, time and eternity, she has it all under her hand; and in what other single volume can she find such a portrait-gallery of her fellows? From Eve onward the Bible is lit as by torches with the tales of its women ... the types are eternal. (104, 106)

The literary heritage preserved in the Bible offers women an immeasurable preparation for life. As well, there is a critical principle illustrated here that is central to Dane's body of criticism. Dane's treatment of an English literary heritage often takes the form of a string of titles that cursorily suggest that "books have a way of influencing one another" (Woolf, *A Room of One's Own* 109). The frequency with which Dane squeezes into her essays such condensed, synedochic evocations of book groupings suggests her conviction that we experience a literary heritage through the pleasures of intertextual dialogues.

"American Primitives" and "A National Mirror"

Like Woolf, Eliot, Yeats, and other modernists, Dane sought in myth and archetype a buried, residual, but still articulate heritage connecting modernity to an ancient human past. In "American Primitives" (1924), she posits the cyclical rise and fall of national literatures, which are created through the collaboration across time, in relay fashion, of ordinary storytellers and writers of genius. She correlates this collective literary production with the rise and fall of nations: the decline of a nation engenders the renewal of folk literature, itself the seed of great literature. The folk literature is created by "actors and rememberers and inventors" (70) who gather material, vivify it with local features, and infuse the legend with Romance, "the eternal story of themselves when they lived at the foot of the rainbow only a field away" (70). In this phase of the cycle, the folk material is dynamic and continually animated with the imagination and concrete experience of each storyteller: "As the story flew over the country, the gossips as they told it would add almost unconsciously new touches, new details out of their own actual experience" (70). Then along comes an exceptional artist, who isolates some "fragmentary episode" and crafts it into what is later recognized as a masterpiece (70). Literature is thus an organism whose vitality and continued life depend on a series of supra-personal human forces and cyclical processes.

Dane's vision reflects the late Victorian and early twentieth-century surge of theoretical interest in myth and folk culture. The notion of a cyclical or evolutionary folk culture that she sketches in "Things That Go Bump in the Night," discussed in Chapter 1, and "American Primitives" bears some affinity with E.B. Tylor's cultural history of man. Tylor's Darwinian model posited that customs "dwindle from solemn ritual into mere pageant and pastime" and myths persist in the form of fairy tales (qtd. in Nash 171).[7] The influential figures Andrew Lang, a founder of the Folk-Lore Society, and Sir James Frazer in his monumental *Golden Bough*, also furnished abundant examples of "primitive" beliefs and customs embedded in living folk rituals, fairy tales, and mythical motifs (Nash 171).

"American Primitives" remarkably develops a complete theory of the power of folk material to oversee the vitality, and even the progress of a nation's literature, outside the agency of any institution, hierarchy, or organized program. Such an insight lays the ground for Dane to present the American pulps as a rich corpus of cultural material that satisfies its audience, evades critical notice, and contributes to a future masterpiece. Dane confesses that twice a month an Anglo-American friend brings her a certain American pulp, and she describes her consumption of it, lavishing considerable attention on the entire bibliographic code of the magazine. As in "A Hidden

[7] According to Nash, by hypothesizing the evolution of human thought, Tylor provided a key impetus for the Darwinian approach to mythology studies (170).

Orchis," discussed below, the pulp represents a prelapsarian phase of print serials, before the critical mediation of the reader–author relationship:

> The critic ... dismisses such books as light illiterature and the authors as mere amusement-mongerers who will get no help from him ... And so, authors and public, those much-chaperoned lovers, are for once left alone with each other. (185)

Even the ads are relegated to the back of the magazine, forbidden to interfere with the reader's complete immersion in the story. With direct access to the goods, Dane returns twice a month for the same, reliably satisfying experience: vivid illustrations and a thrilling adventure. She devours:

> [a] fat magazine with a red sun on the cover and a cowboy crouching behind a boulder or gazing through blue slits of eyes at the horizon, or mastering a rearing—pinto, is it, or cayuse?—whose distended nostrils match in colour the—the bloody orb which hangs, somewhere between the letterpress and the list of authors, flooding the desert with day! (184)

The seamless fluidity of illustrations and text contributes to the persona's unmediated immersion in the story. In this vision of a folk pulp literature that largely evades commercial mechanisms and the influence of critics, Dane emphasizes that, more purely and more organically, folk literature thrives on the partnership of storytellers and readers.

Dane once again treats the power of folk material in "A National Mirror" (1929), where she theorizes the reflective power of nationalistic heroes:

> The human creature likes to discover his own image everywhere reflected. He sees a man in the moon and talks of Dame Nature, Mother Earth and Father Ocean. He sees his own nation in his mind as a person—Brittania or John Bull—rather than as an ant-heap of undistinguishable millions. So strong is this instinct that in matters of literature it may be said that the greatest books and plays necessarily mirror a whole nation as well as an individual. (71)

For example, Dane continues, Goethe's Faust has greater power than Marlowe's because Goethe's Faust "reflects a nation," not merely a type of human being (71). "A National Mirror," however, is concerned not merely with the characteristics of successful nationalist literature, but particularly with the function of its heroes in countries that have suffered repeated attacks from powerful neighbor states. Focusing on Charles de Coster's *Tyl Ulenspiegel*, Dane argues that the nationalist tale—and in De Coster's case, the adaptation of such tales to new times—can both record the nation's suffering and loss and strengthen its readers.

De Coster's novel, Dane explains, adapts the medieval legend of Till so that it reflects the sixteenth-century revolt of the Low Countries against Philip II of Spain. For Dane, *Ulenspiegel* also reflects recent European history, especially Belgium's particular vulnerability in the Great War. After providing a thumbnail sketch of the Low Countries, Dane explains that this history is necessary to understand "the peculiar force of the blow which wrecked the country in 1914" (162). By adapting the legend of Till to the sixteenth-century Dutch War of Independence, Dane argues, De Coster pinpoints the climax of colonial aggression against the Netherlands, the moment that brought about the "awakening, through suffering of a whole nation to conscious life" (162).

Dane's ideas resonate with contemporary theories about the role played by trauma and the memory of conflict in national commemorations and rituals. Jan Assmann argues that collective memory is "a projection on the part of the collective that wishes to remember and of the individual who remembers in order to belong" (7). This function of the hero's story to transmit collective memory may provide a partial explanation for the enduring attraction of *Till Ulenspiegel*, a story of recurrent trials and oppression.

Dane believes in the unhappy power of *Till Ulenspiegel* in 1928 to foreground the recurrent pattern of stronger European actors tyrannizing over weaker ones. But ultimately, her interest is in the power of literature to renew itself. Against the defensive position of historical people to endure what befalls them, literature is offensive, biding its time until it can create something new and powerful: "it is the salvation of literature that there is always time to wait until the [author] and the moment arrive; for great literature depends on such legends, and always new legends are being formed" (71). These legends link generations, perhaps even centuries of citizens, allowing them to imagine beyond a nation's suffering to a unified nation at peace. They do so through immersion in the story of an immortalized hero, who may once have been a historical person, but who:

> must pass from fact into tradition, from tradition into folk-tale, and even into nursery rhyme before his second life, his immortality

> begins: before, that is, the national poet or storyteller arrives to re-create him. (71)

Dane's "A National Mirror" shows that literature offers nothing so static as a simple reflection of a nation's history. A literary heritage is passed along to each new generation not to confirm their national identity, but as a vehicle for its reshaping.

"The Consort Crown"

Whereas in "A National Mirror" Dane engages readers' interest in the theory and examples of national folk legends, in "The Consort Crown" (1927) she *creates* such a nationalistic narrative, one that has been largely hidden from the English because it is the history of strong women.

In "The Consort Crown" Dane locates the origin of English feminism in ancient texts, including *The Theogony* and the *Old Testament*, whose stories of female generative power and resilience are available for recovery. She also establishes the history of English feminism as a national heritage, anchored in the nineteenth century by Poet Laureate Alfred, Lord Tennyson and by male-female collaboration in the campaign for women's rights. Ancient and recent histories of feminine strength are brought together in Dane's allegorical treatment of "giants."

"The Consort Crown" tells the long history of female "giants," culminating in the founding of Girton, as outlined in Lady Stephen's *Emily Davies and Girton College*, which Dane reviews. But before turning to the history of great eighteenth-century and Victorian women, Dane delineates a wider human heritage, a transhistorical and literary pattern illustrating the societal reception of visionary genius. The recent feminist legacy and the recurrent archetypal pattern mutually inform and support one another, even as Dane implies that the nineteenth-century campaign for women's rights broke the ancient pattern of persecuting genius.

The universal psychology of the giant and his society furnishes the framework for Dane's wide-ranging survey. Across history and literature, the story repeats itself. At first welcomed, the giant hangs about even after his job is finished, for he "cannot be persuaded to let ill alone" (134). Like Gulliver among the Lilliputians, his outsized virtues and vices inevitably bring him into conflict with his contemporaries. He is soon resented, then persecuted or even executed, by smaller human beings. Dane's literary and historical survey brings out the connections between such disparate figures as Joan of Arc, Galileo, Gulliver, the Italian poet Torquat Tasso, and the protagonist of *The Giant of Oldborne*, one of the books Dane reviews.[8] The allegory generalizes the societal tension between big and small and does not single out for blame any sex, religion, or nation. Allegory then supports and illuminates the peculiarly English iteration of the pattern, to which the concept of the "consort crown" must be added.

Dane takes the title of her essay from Charlotte Brontë's *Shirley*, in which the eponymous protagonist identifies Eve as the source of women's superhuman strength, vitality, and procreative power. She wore "the consort crown of creation," Shirley decrees. For Dane, the consort crown not only symbolizes the revisionary, feminist legacy of Eve; it also refers to the many strong women behind the achievements of "great men." For example, Dane's review of Mrs. Hester Thrale's letters, which had recently been edited by Brimley Johnson, concludes that "power slept in her," and she "stepped in at the eleventh hour to rescue her husband from bankruptcy" (136–7).[9] In addition to Mrs. Thrale, Dane points to Mary Mitford, Frances Trollope, Aphra Behn, and Queen Victoria herself. Each of these women proved a "knight errant" who could "take over a man's job and support her husband, home and family" (136).

In "The Consort Crown," myth and history are permeated with stories of tension between visionary, problem-solving geniuses and their human societies. Dane deftly sketches the pattern that pervades "every ancient religion": the worship of the god—pure idea—and the worship of giants who are "the idea in action." At first, giants satisfy the human wish in their own and in later days to retain and perceive the divine idea even after the god has departed. But, perversely, ordinary human beings soon resent the giants: "For giants are a nuisance: they are always saving their nation, as Gulliver saved the queen's palace, tactlessly!" (132).

Brontë's Shirley is one such giant. Defending her truancy from the Sunday church service, she disputes Milton's vision of Eve: "Milton tried to see the first woman; but, Cary, he saw her not ... I would

[8] *The Spectator* review of this new novel by John Owen reads in part, "A gentle tale of last century about a rustic hero whose enormous height was at once a tragedy and his means of livelihood as 'freak' in a travelling show" (Review 30).

[9] In 1772 Henry Thrale was nearly bankrupted by his scheme for brewing beer without malt or hops. The family was in debt to the tune of £130,000 (£13 million today). Hester Thrale raised money from her mother and other friends and cleared the debt in nine years. She then took an active role in managing the Brewery ("Henry Thrale").

beg to remind him that the first men of the earth were Titans, and that Eve was their mother" (Brontë).[10] The local vicar similarly misconstrues Eve, so Shirley documents her fiercely held convictions by drawing on Hesiod's creation myths:

> I say, there were giants on the earth in those days[11]—giants that strove to scale heaven. The first woman's breast that heaved with life on this world yielded the daring which could contend with Omnipotence, the strength which could bear a thousand years of bondage, the vitality which could feed that vulture death through uncounted ages, the unexhausted life and uncorrupted excellence, sisters to immortality, which, after millenniums of crimes, struggles, and woes, could conceive and bring forth a Messiah. The first woman was heaven-born. Vast was the heart whence gushed the well-spring of the blood of nations, and grand the undegenerate head where rested the consort crown of creation. (qtd. in "The Consort Crown" 35)

In Shirley's vision, Eve both wields a vast procreative force and—contra *Genesis* and Milton—is the source of "uncorrupted excellence," which, in spite of "millenniums of crimes, struggles, and woes, could conceive and bring forth a Messiah."

Yet Shirley does not change the minds and hearts of her community, and in fact Caroline complains that Shirley's head is filled with "a hash of Scripture and mythology" and enjoins Shirley to go into church (Brontë). Dane thus reads Shirley as one more in a succession of visionary, but unrecognized "giantesses." And by incorporating Shirley's speech as the epigraph to her own essay, Dane uses her to foil the narrative of feminist triumph she will tell later in the essay, in which, after several centuries of humanity's persecution of giants, a group of women and men, all just a little larger than ordinary, no longer seem threatening to smaller human beings; and collaborate to realize their shared vision of education for women. Emphasizing the cooperation rather than the antagonism of the two sexes (and setting up a dialogue with the soon-to-be-published *A Room of One's Own*), Dane even nominates Tennyson as the precursor to the visionaries who realized Girton. *The Princess*, says Dane, is a dream of a woman's university. "[I]t took a good many practical sober men and women, giants but not gods, to turn his dream into ... Girton

[10] In Hesiod's *The Theogony*, human beings were created by the Titans, gods that preceded the Olympians. Brontë may also have known Keats's *Hyperion* (1818), an unfinished poem based on the Greek myth of the defeat of the Titans.

[11] Shirley is quoting Genesis 6.4. Dane's generous quotation of *Shirley* (1849), the epigraph to "The Consort Crown," extends beyond this passage.

College!" (134, 136).[12] Dane thus sketches a legacy of British feminism by selecting a few high points in the nineteenth century: *Shirley*, *The Princess*, and Girton.

Published in 1927 "The Consort Crown" shares many of the concerns and rhetorical strategies of the decade's landmark work of feminist theory, *A Room of One's Own* (1929). The two writers' reconstruction of unrecognized female power suggests that they drew on the circulating discourses of mythologists, historians like Eileen Power, and classical scholars such as Jane Ellen Harrison. Newly published life writing by or about women further informed both writers. For example, in 1928, *Good Housekeeping* inaugurated "Bonnet and Shawl" profiles of notable "Victorian wives." Biographer Philip Guedalla began his series with a portrait of Mary Anne Disraeli; subsequent articles featured Emily Palmerston, Jane Carlyle, Catherine Gladstone, and Emily Tennyson (Guedalla, "Mary Anne Disraeli" 14).[13]

Dane and Woolf both bring to light a legacy of feminine genius and call on Britons to continue it. "[G]enius of a sort must have existed among women as it must have existed among the working classes," Woolf writes; "Now and again an Emily Brontë or a Robert Burns blazes out and proves its presence" (*A Room of One's Own* 49). Dane and Woolf both invite us to see this unrecognized genius in the figures of insane or tortured women who crop up in literature and history:

> When, however, one reads of a witch being ducked, of a woman possessed by devils, of a wise woman selling herbs, or even of a very remarkable man who had a mother, then I think we are on the track of a lost novelist, a suppressed poet, of some mute and inglorious Jane Austen, some Emily Brontë who dashed her brains out on the moor or mopped and mowed about the highways crazed with the torture that her gift had put her to. (*A Room of One's Own* 49)

Like Woolf, Brontë and Dane identify giant, powerful mothers who have been forgotten or misconstrued. Dane looks to Charlotte Brontë as a precursor whose protagonist Shirley furnishes a vision of female creative genius; while Dane herself supplies the more mundane but valuable labor of building a typology of giantesses, women who have been misunderstood, tortured, and executed as witches or freaks.

[12] Dane quotes from section V, a letter from the princess to her brother explaining why she plans not to marry, choosing instead to live and study in an all-women university.

[13] The subtitle for "Emily Tennyson" reads "Perfect Woman, and Poet Laureate's Perfect Wife" (36–7).

In turn, this recognition allows Dane to populate a historical survey that establishes the continual presence of "giantesses." In delineating a legacy of exceptional creative women, both Dane and Woolf avoid replicating the patriarchal model of a single genius towering above his society. Thus, while Dane identifies creative geniuses like Emily Brontë who, with "her god within her breast," "half immortal," did not need to bother about her reception (134), she then acknowledges Victorian women writers "not of genius but of immense capacity who found their work in using a pen," including Eliot, Gaskell, Frances Trollope, and Charlotte and Anne Brontë (134). And Dane gives more detailed consideration to the gifts and ordinary human psychology of other giantesses, whose gender made them special targets of resentment; for if humanity has always hated giants, "consider its feelings when Victorian earth (of all ages!) began to produce giantesses also!" (134).

For both Dane and Woolf, the continual historical presence of exceptional women implies a legacy to be passed on to young women. Woolf tells her audience of young women that there is work to be done. If a Judith Shakespeare is ever to be born, it will be because these women have established "the habit of freedom and the courage to write exactly what we think." Only then can a great writer emerge, "drawing her life from the lives of the unknown who were her forerunners" (114). Dane's essay likewise inscribes a filial partnership forged by mothers' bequests and daughters' indebtedness. She extends Brontë's concept of the consort crown to signify not just the exceptional women, but their determination "that the women of the time to come should be trained to wear it worthily" (134). Woolf and Dane construe a female modernity, then, that did not call on modern women to transcend their unemancipated mothers, but, rather, to recognize the established templates these forerunners had already made ready for their use. Identifying Eve as the source of female strength, Brontë emphasizes origins; Dane and Woolf, legacy. Dane, additionally, defines a peculiarly British sense of what it means to wear "the consort crown"; she outlines a history of "knight errant" women who save their families from ruin, and shows how men return the favor in the story of Girton College.

The great Victorian women Dane invokes make individual contributions and illustrate a tradition of British women's strength. Although these women did not have the rights and freedoms of their modern counterparts, they proved their power as wives and consorts. Mrs. Thrale, a forerunner to the Victorian giants, illustrates how "power slept" in these giantesses until it was needed. She inaugurates a knight errant tradition that includes Aphra Behn, Mary Mitford, and Frances Trollope, who rescue their families by producing and selling their writing, in each case stepping into the role of breadwinner after profligate or unfortunate fathers or husbands led their families into financial ruin. These women "proved how a woman could play knight errant, take over a man's job and support her husband, home and family" (136).

Dane's focus on these "knight errants" working for the common good suggests another important similarity between "The Consort Crown" and *A Room of One's Own*. Both Dane and Woolf, each speaking to aspiring young women, affirm the importance of resolving the era's accentuated sex antagonism. Each writer seeks a vehicle in which to unfold her argument dispassionately, avoiding the "red light of emotion," both in the writer and her audience, that the recent, bitter fight for women's rights would arouse.[14] Just as Woolf mixes fact with fiction to blunt the force of her critique, Dane uses allegory to psychologize the reception of "giants," displacing and disguising inflammatory content in a fairy tale mode. Indeed, Dane does not even allude to the recent feminist history occasioned by the publication of *Emily Davies and Girton College* until, tracing the unmistakable historical and literary patterns of the allegory, she has established her readers' sympathy for giants of either gender and can count on them to join her in condemning their persecution. Holding recent history in reserve, Dane frames the essay with two moments of feminist triumph, *Shirley* and Girton.

For Woolf, the resolution of sex antagonism remains a hope only. For Dane, however, Girton represents the evidence and the promise of concord and cooperation between the sexes. Thus, if skillful and supportive wives wear the "consort crown" in the first books Dane reviews, it is passed on to men when Dane turns her attention to *Emily Davies and Girton College*. The men who worked alongside women in the campaign for women's rights played a crucial role, Dane emphasizes. For Lady Stephen's research gives the lie to the often-repeated wisdom that any strong Victorian woman could walk around the barriers erected against her self-realization and contribution. Instead, Stephen documents the extent

[14] The fictional protagonist in *A Room of One's Own* discovers that she cannot learn any facts from the tomes of opinions about women that avalanche her in the Reading Room of the British Museum, for they are written in "the red light of emotion" (32–3).

and absurdity of those obstacles. Dane wishes that "the amazing part played by men in the emancipation of women" was more emphasized in the Girton history. Nonetheless, it is Girton's legacy to women that Dane stresses at the end of "The Consort Crown." *Emily Davies and Girton College* tells "the history of our mothers, not of the flesh but of the spirit. If we are free, independent, happy women to-day, it is the doing of these giant mothers of ours who 'Put aside To-day / ... And with toil of their To-day / Bought for us To-morrow'" (Kipling, "A School Song," qtd. in "The Consort Crown" 137).

As Dane represents it, the heritage of strong women is largely irrational, illustrating others' resentment, suspicion, and the desire to exclude difference. But most of the texts Dane cites—*The Princess*, Elizabeth Haldane's *George Eliot and Her Times*, *Emily Davies and Girton College*—enable her to document a recent and specifically British heritage. Although these examples of literature and history tell a mixed story of irrational and rational forces, they ultimately uncover the enlightened views that drove the cross-gendered, successful campaign for women's rights. Girton College, Dane tells her readers, is "but a symbol of the whole process by which the freedom, education, health, citizenship and independence were given to the women of England" (137). And none of these rights and freedoms would have come about if it were not for Victorian "giants" and "giantesses." Dane reinforces this point in the last sentence of her essay when she speaks of "the debt of modern woman to the Victorian giants as well as the Victorian giantesses" (138).

Victorian Giantesses in *Good Housekeeping*

The picture of strong British women that Dane establishes in "The Consort Crown" is enhanced by a journalistic climate in *Good Housekeeping* that schooled readers in the accomplishments of their giant fore-mothers. When Dane makes a transition in "The Consort Crown" from Victorian women writers to "giantesses of another kind," she describes a field of female accomplishment that *Good Housekeeping* covered regularly. These were "executants, the administrators, reformers, pioneers" (134). When Clemence Dane wrote about Victorian giantesses, when Helena Normanton profiled Josephine Butler, and when Maude M. Jeffery documented the pioneering work and influence of Octavia Hill, they neither rebelled against these figures nor looked back at them in nostalgia.[15] Instead, they were backdating modernity to the mid-nineteenth century, making the case that these giantesses in crinolines set the patterns that have been in use by their younger counterparts ever since.

The staggered franchise for British women added to this journalistic self-consciousness about the opportunity, beginning in 1928, for women on the threshold of the extended suffrage to benefit from the wisdom of older women. Within *Good Housekeeping*, Helena Normanton (1882–1957), Violet Bonham Carter (1887–1969), and Clemence Dane (1888–1965), all discussed in Chapter 5, were only a few of the journalists who filled this role.

Seeing Rural England

> People ... are beginning to understand that rural England is, and has always been, as important as the towns, and that scattered up and down the land are places not only beautiful in themselves, but full of the associations of the past. Each has played its part in the making of England as we know it to-day, and each has some story to tell, if we can only learn to read. (Pulbrook, *The English Countryside* v)

In the first decades of the twentieth century, a new interest in Britons' rural heritage took diverse forms. Nostalgic desire for a supposedly simple, rural way of life had been a by-product of Victorian industrial strain, but in the wake of the Boer War, a new "little Englandism" took hold. Its proponents sought to inculcate a "patriotism" purged of the imperialist spirit dominant in the nineteenth century (Weiner 200–1). They defined this patriotism as "the particular love of England, free of any desire to expand beyond the borders of the English nation" (Weiner 202). E.C. Pulbrook, two of whose books Dane reviews in "The English Eden," champions this vision of a "little England." In *The English Countryside*, Pulbrook

[15] Normanton's profile appears in the April 1928 issue of *Good Housekeeping*; and Hill is featured in Jeffery's "Estate Management as a Career for Women" in the December 1923 issue. Octavia Hill (1838–1912) "leader of the British open-space movement," was also a housing reformer "whose methods of housing-project management were imitated in Great Britain, on the Continent, and in the United States." She established the first of her housing projects in a slum area of St. Marylebone borough, London. After direction of more housing projects, she trained other women to manage mass housing while under the employment of the Ecclesiastical Commissioners (Britannica, "Octavia Hill").

suggests that the country, "full of the associations of the past," is the bedrock of national identity. And in contending that Britons must "learn to read" the story of each rural place, Pulbrook sounds a note that resonates in much of the interwar literature supporting the "discovery" of rural England (v). After the First World War, a more far-reaching discourse centered on the perception that rural England was disappearing, giving rise to efforts to preserve and document it. These diverse campaigns took the form of books, photographs, exhibitions, and voluntary movements such as the Council for the Preservation of Rural England. Clemence Dane's most important contributions to the literature of a disappearing England are her critical essays "Jefferies of the Fields" (1927), "The English Eden" (1928), and "A Hidden Orchis" (1929).

English suburbs grew on an "unprecedented scale" in the interwar period; "over four million houses were built in Britain between the wars," most in suburbs. Even the span of a single year like 1927–8 saw something like 38,000 acres of land developed for housing (Matless 57). "The English Eden" reflects David Matless's description of the suburb as a "contentious English landscape" (57). Dane envisions new little houses backing into the green:

> Little ugly houses, tethered by the abominable tram-lines and railway-lines, back as far from the town as they can, always backing into the green till, as the moors and fields are peppered over with bricks and mortar, the lanes turn into roads and the roads into boulevards and racing tracks, and the national craving for "the country" slowly but inevitably destroys that which it loves. (48)

The scarcity of "green" prompted a search for a rural England that took diverse forms, including exhibits and published collections of photographs, guidebooks, and popular travel literature such as H.V. Morton's *Seeing England* (1926). Photography, by the 1920s a mass phenomenon, especially strengthened the sense of rural England as an imagined community. Ads for Kodak invited amateur photographers to tour old British towns and monuments; their photographs then linked them to other Britons through this common heritage (Taylor 20). The Preservation movement of the 1920s and 1930s was another significant impetus to the popular belief in a rural England that could be saved from destruction.[16]

Dane invokes this rural heritage in "A Hidden Orchis," "Jefferies of the Fields," and "The English Eden." Each looks back to a time

[16] For detailed discussions of the influential and savvy Council for the Preservation of Rural England, founded in 1926, see Matless 46–7 and Howkins.

before the interwar suburban growth. "Jefferies" does so nostalgically by envisioning, imagining, and reinforcing the continuity between past and present. In contrast, "The English Eden" and "A Hidden Orchis," which celebrates books by Gertrude Bone, gaze with reproving irony on England's shrinking rural space and on the cultural fad to "discover" the country.

"The English Eden"

Readers of "The English Eden" trace the adventures of Dane's persona, who motors into Kent for a day's excursion. The persona is a tourist, which connotes a relatively unreflective mode of vision according to the period's "hierarchy of touring," wherein tourists "set out to confirm what they already know through tour guides and brochures" (Taylor 7).[17] At the same time, Dane the critic speaks to her audience about new books and interleaves quotations striking two distinct chords: literary evocations of England as a garden, and biblical warnings about the fate of those who desecrate a sacred space. The two voices are not fully merged, allowing for the persona's excursion in the country to perform, sometimes ironically, the interwar fad for walking, picnicking, camping in, and touring what Dane calls "country England." Indeed, abetted by the affordability of automobiles and lured by photography, guidebooks, and paeans to "old England," Britons flocked to the country. The *persona's* dramatized experiences in "The English Eden" enable Dane to educate her readers in hierarchically organized ways of seeing, from the tourist's sentimentality to the book lover's apprehension of the "spirit" of rural England. The *critic's* quotations, pointing to classic celebrations of England as a garden, compensate for an England that is "dwindling out of being" while they foster a deeper understanding of rural England. "The English Eden" both evokes and destabilizes a double heritage: rural England and its long literary history. Dane opines that the "dwindling" of rural England will continue, and she retrieves both old and new literary records of it. Simultaneously, through the textual excerpts interleaved in her discussion, she points to ancestral voices prophesying, if not war, the human decimation of rural England.

[17] By comparison, the traveler devotes more time, money, and attention to the activity of the gaze, "a prolonged, contemplative" look that required learning and time (Taylor 13).

The essay persona's excursion illustrates the principle that "the national craving for 'the country' slowly but inevitably destroys that which it loves." She writes, "I was driving the other day not thirty miles from 'Babylon, that great city,' up hill, down dale, round and about the weald of Kent" (49).[18] The reference to Babylon, from Revelation 18.10, recognizes that short-sighted humanity brings ruin to the very places it has built to sustain life, and that remorse and death follow in its wake: "Alas, alas, that great city Babylon, that mighty city! for in one hour is thy judgment come." Humanity's unwillingness to put a stop to the destruction of rural England is underscored again at the end of the essay. "We could stop the dwindling of the English countryside, but we don't," Dane laments (127). She presents St. John's vision in Revelation 9 of locusts coming to torment men. God commands the locusts not to "hurt the grass of the earth, neither any green thing nor any tree" (Revelation 9.4). Dane's final comment in "The English Eden" is "But men are not so wise" (127). God's protection of the plants and gardens on earth implies the same capacity in human beings, but Dane finds that this human heritage is paired with a human lapse of wisdom.

These apocalyptic references point to God's gifts to man and the human responsibility to preserve them. Yet these allusions are part of a broader meditation on death in "The English Eden." As she surveys the literature of rural England, Dane frequently refers to human death, from the deceased eighteenth-century author of the *Guide to Tunbridge Wells* to the rural poor championed in *Elegy Written in a Country Churchyard*. The *Elegy*'s country poor die without reaching their potential. But their spirits continue to invest the landscapes they inhabited. And, in another of the *Elegy*'s mementos to the dead, we can read about their lives in the brief words of tombstone epitaphs. To read Gray's *Elegy* is thus to "stand at sunset in any country churchyard from Cumberland to John o'Groats," Dane tells us (125). In one of its aspects, then, the literary heritage of rural England underscores the brief lives of human beings and the enduring lives of the rural places in which they lived.

But penetrating further in the essay shows us that Dane likens the fates of the individual and the place just as often as she contrasts them. In the central moment of the persona's experience, she

[18] Lynda Nead demonstrates that nineteenth-century London was imagined as a "Victorian Babylon." Both cities "symbolised material wonder and tumultuous destruction ... These great trading centres and capitals of empires were brought down by luxury, sensuality and an excessive indulgence in and worship of the commodity" (3).

glimpses a country burial from her automobile. "[W]e passed that little new allotment of death. An amazing champaign spread beyond it to the hills and a white-robed clergyman and a black group clustered round a grave into which the coffin was being lowered" (49, 124). The countryside quietly persists while the small human figures bury their dead. But "The English Eden" provides abundant evidence that the "amazing champaign" won't long endure. And so the death of a single countryman epitomizes the approaching death of a specific place and the death of the countryside itself. And since literature reflects human experience, Dane and her readers can expect more and more literature of the city, while literary records of rural England inevitably fade from our consciousness. Something of this anticipated loss leads Dane the critic to toy with her power to arrest, if only for a time, her readers' nostalgic immersion in rural literature. How can the reader return to the modern novel of the town, having made himself unfit for it by his orgy on country literature? "How can he then appreciate at their just value—crazy pavements? The sympathetic reviewer should withhold from him for a time even the books he must read sooner or later" (126).

Since readers are ultimately destined for urban literature, literary recreations and records of their pastoral heritage become the more important. One of the texts that Dane selects to sustain and feed readers' appetite for the English Eden is John Gerard's *Herball*, which Dane excerpts for her epigraph. Gerard was a plant enthusiast and early English gardener in London. "In 1596 he compiled a list of the plants growing in his garden. Published in 1597, his celebrated *Herball*, containing more than 1,000 species, became the first plant catalog" (Britannica, "John Gerard"). The *Herball* documents the primary human cultivation of beauty in the form of a garden and the secondary cultivation of a literary garden. The epigraph first points not to the countryside or the gardens of England, but to their construction in imaginative literature:

> Whither did the poets hunt for their sincere delights but into the gardens of Alcinous, of Adonis, and the orchards of the Hesperides? Where did they dream that heaven should be but in the pleasant garden of Elysium? (*The Herball or Generall Historie of Plantes*, 1597, qtd. in "The English Eden" 48)

The *Herball* is both an artifact of English pastoral heritage and an instance of its living continuity: "Substantial portions of the *Herball* were reprinted in 1927 and 1964, and it remains a popular book for those interested in plant remedies" (Britannica, "John Gerard"). It is both a compendium of plants native to and cultivated in Britain and a documentation of the human cultivation of Englishness.

In describing how the automobile shapes her persona's experience of rural England, Dane selected a self-consciously nostalgic pursuit. David Matless identifies a "motoring pastoral" that he traces to H.V. Morton's *Seeing England* (1926), in which "motoring became styled as a modern practice in pursuit of an older England" (97). Dane ironically invokes this motoring pastoral, figuring her reader driving through the country but absorbed in the new culture of motoring and thus failing to see anything of rural England. This motorist "dashes along the perfect road with an eye open for beginners and police traps and women drivers (if he is a man)" (125). Yet he can be forgiven for seeing nothing of the countryside, for, in addition to his preoccupation with the road, his mind is happily furnished with pictures of old English inns.

"It's a pity that familiarity should so often dull one's power to appreciate" (125). Familiarity dulls our vision, while preconceptions distort it. For that reason, Dane applauds the recent inclusion of photographs, prints, and drawings in histories of old England. She welcomes the new *The English Inn, Past and Present*, by A.E. Richardson and H.D. Eberlein, "for in text and illustration the authors have clearly tried to give us not merely the facts but the feel of their subject" (125). The success of this effort means that "The reader with their help can easily picture for himself ... the sort of adventures a journey would have brought him twenty, fifty, a hundred, two hundred years ago" (125). Thus, if the motorist sees little of the modern countryside, the literature documenting older England will allow him to make a connection to it.

As she reviews novels, pictorial essays, and guidebooks, Dane the critic proposes a variety of approaches to re-envisioning England and organizes them in a hierarchy that leads readers from seeing England to loving its spirit.[19] Her review of two books by E.C. Pulbrook enables her to make this transition. Dane praises the "pictures and descriptions" in *The English Countryside* (1915); and, indeed, Pulbrook includes some 126 photographs of rural landscape, only a very few including human beings. Turning next to Pulbrook's *English Country Life and Work* (1922), Dane acknowledges the

[19] As John Taylor demonstrates, both the popularization of photography and the domestication of the English landscape through guidebooks in the 1920s and 1930s not only informed modes of seeing England but consolidated their association with specific socio-economic classes and types of tourists.

importance of understanding the spirit of rural England through its laborers. One should not merely admire the "loveliness of one's own country," but "understand what labour, what love, what hardship and sacrifice has gone to the making of the English garden" (124). Dane also captures something of Pulbrook's project through her inclusion of a catalogue of some thirty-five rural workers, from thresher to dairy maid to innkeeper to priest.

The persona likewise pursues an improving path, teaching Dane's readers that superficial glimpses or second-hand accounts of rural England will not reveal its depth. Like the motorist who needs the apparatus of pictures, the persona is somewhat estranged from the country dwellers she sees from a distance and recognizes that her mode of seeing is not adequate to the depth of their lives. The burial scene foregrounds a more sobering form of inadequate vision, wherein the persona perceives her estrangement from the lived experience of the mourners, whom she endows with something of Wordsworth's knowledge of elemental passions. The white-robed clergyman and the black-clad group are:

> employed with such knowledge upon so accustomed a task, and the village street as you turned to see the last of it, had such an air of patience with life and death, that you wondered, as you lost sight of it round the bend, whether the whole episode was real or a dream, and said, "lost England!" with a lump in the throat. Which last, I suppose, was a sentimentality, for I saw an absurd notice *Public Telephone* in the three-hundred year old window [...] (124)

Dane's persona checks her first response to this scene as an epitome of "lost England" with her admission that it was an instance of sentimentality, a sentimentality humorously undermined by the interposition of modern technology. Then she reflects that "the road that ran through the village was not the sort of track they ran over in the days when Gerarde picked 'the small wild buglosse that grows upon the dry ditch back about Pickadilla'" (124).[20] If a single countryman is the most ephemeral element in the rural landscape, the more enduring countryside is nonetheless not exempt from change. Someone

[20] Dane quotes from chapter 283, "Of Buglosse": "There is another wilde Buglosse which *Dol donaeus* hath by the name of *Buglossa:* it hath a small white root, from which arises a slender stalke some foot and halfe high set with smal rough leaues sinuated or cut in on the edges: the stalkes at the top are diuided into three or foure small branches, bearing small blew floures in rough huskes. ‡ ... The little wilde Buglosse growes vpon the drie ditch bankes about Pickadilla, and almost euelry where. ‡" Gerard's minute attention to each feature of the plant is, of course, not possible for the motoring tourist of "The English Eden."

familiar with the historical and literary records of such places, for example the *Herball*, can always go further back, to a more remote past and a more bucolic time than this village in 1928.

Books and language have always already mediated our perception of rural England, Dane tells us. We see it through any number of constructions, particularly the myth of a bucolic, essential, and unchanged "lost England." Dane establishes this point from the beginning of "The English Eden" as she considers both the vowel and consonant sounds in "pavement" and "country." While the word "pavement" concentrates pleasant vowel and consonant sounds, we don't associate it with experiences that reinforce these sounds: "the best beauty it can call up is wet London asphalt, pewter black with golden dapples of light." The opposite is true for "country." When not overwhelmed by pleasant associations, it is "a harsh, grunting, dull-vowelled lump of a word." But "talk of 'the country,' 'living in the country,' ... or 'the English countryside,' and how that ugly word grows and glows and is transformed into a word that Adam and Eve might have used!" (48). Just as language does, literature mediates our vision, as Dane's persona finds when she chases "the sunset down roads and lanes edged with Kipling's 'early English woodland,' all aflare in the autumnal bonfire" (49).

Rural Modernity in *Good Housekeeping*

"The English Eden" is remarkable for its frequent shifts among the many perspectives from which to see the "dwindling of the English countryside" (127): that of the tourist, the literary critic, the guide, and the photographer. To these contemporary perspectives Dane adds the cultural influences of biblical and literary historical texts. Through this design, "The English Eden" consistently challenges the idea that we can fix any single picture of rural England. Within *Good Housekeeping*, there were few voices who supported this effort. "The focus of the women's magazines and women's pages was overwhelmingly metropolitan," notes Nicola Verdon (88), and *Good Housekeeping* did not regularly feature articles on rural women and their particular concerns. Mrs. C.F.G. [Lucy] Masterman's "Those Horrid Tourists!," appearing in Volume 2, is thus of particular interest. Like "The English Eden," it foregrounds the opposition between country and city attitudes and queries the picture of the "tripper's" inadequate understanding of the country. Dane counterbalances the tourist persona with the literary critic: while the tourist remains excluded from country folks' deeper grasp of life and death, Dane the critic finds true modes of seeing rural England in books such as Pulbrook's *English Country Life and Work*. Masterman likewise looks beyond the assumption that the lives of rural people preserve the tranquil qualities of rural England. Masterman's article takes the form of a dialogue, presented both discursively and dramatically. The dramatized report of a conversation with her neighboring country "gentlefolk" enables her to challenge two contemporary stereotypes: that rural people lead peaceful, tranquil lives, undisturbed by the rhythms of modernity; and that the "trippers"—though generally armed with cameras—were uniformly vulgar, insensitive, and disrespectful of inhabitants of the rural neighborhoods they visited. Before closing, Masterman sees fit to offer brief criticisms of the harmful habits of urban visitors to the country, and concedes that "No one who has ever observed the hurried, machine-run life of big cities can fail to be convinced that occasional contact with a quieter, less sophisticated world is necessary for mental and physical health" (64).[21] Although this remark does not capture the thrust of Masterman's article, *Good Housekeeping* used it as the caption to the photo for the first-page spread of bicyclists and picnickers on a country road; its somewhat predictable and relatively uncontroversial statement—as Masterman would have it, "no one ... can fail to be convinced"—might be found in a dozen other articles touting the benefits of a visit to the country. The editorial voice here softens the hard edges of Masterman's revelations of rural isolation and even self-destruction.

"Jefferies of the Fields" and "A Hidden Orchis"

In "The English Eden" Dane undertakes the experiment of seeing England through a variety of cultural lenses: the Old Testament, Renaissance horticulture, and contemporary guides to "old England." With "Jefferies of the Fields" (1927) and "A Hidden Orchis" (1929) she concentrates on the literary heritage of rural England, with particular attention to books that capture the "spirit" of rural England, the lived experience of its dwellers. She singles out two writers, Richard Jefferies and Gertrude Bone, whose fiction, essays, and life writing at once preserve the natural beauty of England and faithfully

[21] Lucy Masterman was a poet, editor, biographer, and the wife of politician and writer Charles Masterman, best known for his 1909 *The Condition of England*.

render the sensibility and the speech of its countrymen. Yet the cultural heritage that these two writers seem to hold in place for their readers is rendered unstable by Dane's own modern sensibility, especially her awareness that most postwar readers will not experience the past as continuous with the present.

In "Jefferies of the Fields" Dane promises that the *oeuvre* of Richard Jefferies will keep readers in touch with their own and with great writers' perceptions and feelings about the country. Awakened early by birdsong one summer morning, Dane's persona reflects that "as the centuries go by," Britons become more and more out of sync with the natural diurnal cycle and, still lying in bed, she makes a mental list of neighborhood birds and their songs. While waiting for the "lull of daylight," she casts about for a book sympathetic to her mood. She considers Jane Austen, "that refuge from every form of boredom," but sets her aside: "I think she loved the country, but her love scarcely gets into her books" (73). The persona is very specific about the sort of book she needs. It is decidedly *not* a book that will transport her into the mind and heart of the writer, but rather, one that will "tell me soberly and believably exactly what all the birds are saying in their unknown tongues" (73). Happily, Dane finds in her stack of books for review a new reprint of Richard Jefferies's spiritual autobiography, *The Story of My Heart*.[22]

Yet the persona soon lifts her eyes from the page to think about Jefferies's short life and his long literary legacy—or so she hopes: "thirty-nine years of disappointment and bitter poverty," yet he will "outlive the greatest names of their age as its hills must outlive the very Rome" (188). She begins to theorize about what makes a writer live for future generations of readers. These meditations on short and long durations are characteristic of "Jefferies of the Fields," which repeatedly voices awareness of diverse temporalities, moving on different planes and superficially incompatible with one another: the past brought into the present; the past cut off from the moderns, and the future of Jefferies's reception. No orderly system of uniform time can capture these uneven and mercurial temporalities.

Dane's juxtaposition of multiple, subjectively experienced times makes "Jefferies of the Fields" unmistakably modern even while these competing temporalities render unstable her readers' access to

[22] Richard Jefferies (1848–1887), naturalist, essayist, and novelist. His success as a periodical writer of rural sketches began with a 4,000-word letter to *The Times* about the Wiltshire agricultural laborer and his lot. In the last years of his life he suffered from tuberculosis and poverty (Britannica, "Richard Jefferies").

the literary heritage that Jeffery represents.[23] She delights in the many quotidian "trifles" that "bridge the centuries and make us know, as if they were a thing of yesterday, what our fathers did in their days and in the old time before them!" (183). Such writing creates a satisfying continuity between past and present, so as to lengthen the duration of the present. But while the details of everyday life recorded in literature bring the past into the present, much the way a gramophone record of a voice would do, the speed at which modernity brings change has the opposite effect of making Jefferies's world recede:

> Forty years have already so shifted our centre of life and our views about everything under the sun, have so altered the very shape and contours of thousand-year-old towns and countrysides, that Jefferies is already a telescope through which we view the past. (188)

In addition to illustrating the past brought near, and the past withdrawing from modern, perhaps urban dwellers, Dane identifies a third temporality, the timeline of Jefferies's literary legacy. The moderns are distant from his Victorian England, but Jefferies is "still too near" to be properly evaluated in the literary canon. His critics have been prejudiced against his origins in journalism or have seen no more deeply than the "minute observance" of Jefferies's writing. But the elongated time of literary reception, Dane predicts, will center Jefferies in the canon.

"A New View of Old Beauty"

> For it is a curious fact that all poetry, all tale, all song, endures in the long run by favour of the facts stored up in it. Imagination can soar like Icarus, but a time inevitably comes when its dreams and its passions shrivel up in the indifferent noon of a later day. ("Jefferies of the Fields" 188)

As dreams shrivel in daylight, sound evaporates in time, and rural England dwindles in space. The perception that all experience is transient led the moderns to ask "what lasts?" This question resonates twofold in "Jefferies of the Fields," wherein Dane ponders the degree to which literature can preserve and transmit the past and

[23] For an extensive treatment of the philosophical, literary, scientific, and societal debates about the conceptualization of public and private time in the late nineteenth and early twentieth centuries, see Stephen Kern.

inquires into the endurance of a writer in the memory of generations of readers. Dane argues that literary records of material experience will continue to make us thrill with the likeness of our predecessors to ourselves. Our literary heritage is vital in this nearly literal sense. Conversely, the ways that modernity has "so shifted our centre of life and our views" make it likely that we will perceive, but no longer share, "the spirit that glows through the minute observance" for which Jefferies is admired (188).

"Jefferies of the Fields" and "A Hidden Orchis" reflect the late Victorian technologies that seemed to enable users to preserve the past and savor it in the present. In the former essay, Dane selects three writers—Dickens, Hardy, and Jefferies—who "between them have preserved for all the years to come a century of England" (188). In the latter, Dane commends the entire *oeuvre* of Gertrude Bone. Like Richard Jefferies's books, Bone's novels and essays document the natural beauty of England through close observation and careful expression of it. Bone also preserves the countryman's speech and emotion, which Dane demonstrates by quoting from the "Preface and Apology" for Bone's 1904 *Provincial Tales.*[24] Bone theorizes that "the average person" speaks "an entirely derived and imparted language." But under the pressure of a crisis or a strong passion, the "ignorant poor" are forced to "find for themselves an expression as nearly as possible derived from their actual sensations," and in these moments they often attain "to a dignified and moving language to be sought for in vain among people of an easier speech." In *Provincial Tales* therefore, like a naturalist photographing the vibrant colors of rarely seen creatures, Bone hopes to "gather such moments as when, breaking under the strength of feeling from their accustomed reticence, narrow and unenlightened natures become thus impassioned and expressive" (Bone v–vii).

Stephen Kern observes that the camera and the phonograph, the latter invented in 1877, enabled people to "bring the past into the present" (38) and even to curate historical memory. In the last decade of the nineteenth century, photographic record societies in Great Britain collected and deposited in the British Museum photographs of interest, while other societies formed to preserve or restore architectural structures and places of natural beauty (Kern 38–9). The institutional preservation of a national heritage, then, was well established at the turn of the century. While written records do not

[24] D.H. Lawrence recorded appreciation for *Provincial Tales* (1904), while Virginia Woolf favorably reviewed Bone's *Women of the Country* (1913) in the *TLS*.

carry the auditory precision of a recording or the visual detail of a photograph or film, they nonetheless can transport the past into the reader's present in ways similar to these media. In "Jefferies of the Fields," through multi-faceted references to time, Dane makes this case. Just as photography and film seemed to preserve the past accurately and with abundant detail, literature, Dane argues, makes Jefferies's bygone world vividly present: "His people live and move with an intensity that is startling. They are so brilliantly real in every detail of their lives that they are like pebbles seen under water, realer than we had realized real people could be" (190). The faithful record of daily life recorded is one of two strands of the case Dane makes for literature's supreme fitness to preserve the past.

As we have seen, Dane's view that literature may preserve a record of the material past aligns her with other early twentieth-century preservation initiatives. But literature can go beyond this documentary function, Dane emphasizes. It can also open up an English literary heritage of love for the country, as Dane illustrates when listing the many writers who could be classified under this rubric. And a writer of genius, as Dane argues is the case for Richard Jefferies, goes still further. He sees and feels intensely, and through the exactitude of his writing, teaches his audience to do the same. Thus Jefferies "makes us see for the first time something we have always known, who gives us, that is, a new view of old beauty" (190).

In "Jefferies of the Fields," Dane's conception of literary heritage is less like an edifice to which successive writers will add and more like an electrical circuit that will send signals to future readers. The links Dane values most are links of feeling, and what turns her against the lukewarm current of Jefferies's critical reception is the conviction that, with each new generation, some human beings will experience his vision and his feelings. The English literary history of the country already illustrates this model: "In the year of Jefferies' birth, a dying girl in a Yorkshire parsonage was writing her last confession of faith and her last poem," as though she were passing the torch to Jefferies. Emily Brontë loved "every leaf, every breath, every stick and stone of her countryside," Dane continues. "Is it folly to wonder if between those two souls, both so young, one arriving and one departing, there passed some message concerning their mutual passion?" (192).

Dane's cautious optimism in "Jefferies of the Fields" contrasts to her pessimism in "A Hidden Orchis." Gertrude Bone appears to sidestep the mass technologies of the marketplace, printing limited editions of her books on handmade paper that are illustrated by her son Stephen. She lingers in a pre-industrial time, Dane implies. Shielding her books from a modernity emblematized by commerce, Bone is already cut off from most of "us." Whereas Jefferies's books teach readers how to extend a precious past, Bone's warn readers that this heritage may already be out of reach.

Bone's talent "droops in the marketplace of modern literature": both the subject and the craft of the books are holdovers from the past. Dane finds that "the booklet is not unlike its own title: it has delicate flower pictures in it drawn by Stephen Bone: its print is beautiful: you like handling it as you like handling a jade carving" (39). Crafted with handmade paper and illustrations or wood cuts, Bone's books seem to evade modern technologies of mass reproduction and circulation.[25] Bone's books were available in trade editions, yet Dane implies that they are unlikely to thrive in a book market where successful competition demands a degree of standardization. Dane hints, too, that Bone's pastoral modernity may be exempt from commodification. Yet, argues Elizabeth Outka, it was precisely nostalgia, including images of England's rural, peaceful past, that was for sale in the early twentieth century.

Despite this valuable preservation of English heritage, Dane hints that their rarified nature is likely to make Bone's books neglected and then become altogether extinct. "It is inevitable that the hidden orchis should become a rarity and then a legend and then a name, and then pass out of remembrance altogether" (118). Bone has her place, "though she is not of our age or of our day." Continuing in a more sinister vein, Dane links the spread of suburbs and cities to the rise of destruction at the hands of a "mob." Bone "lives among sights that most of us reach only to destroy, and hears sounds that cease at the advent of our mob. We cannot help ourselves: we are many, and England is small" (118).[26] Not surprisingly, Dane is reluctant to leave her readers with the suggestion that they are included in "our mob," so she evokes their mournful contemplation of modern London: "Once there were nightingales in St. Martin's Fields ... This we tell each other wistfully when we look at modern London." And she predicts that the same fate awaits modern England, as it becomes "overrun and destroyed by its own children" (118). In the context of

[25] Some of Bone's books, including *The Hidden Orchis*, were produced in trade and limited editions by the Medici Society. The latter were typically limited to fifty, printed on handmade paper and signed, sometimes by illustrator Stephen Bone, Gertrude's son.

[26] In *Culture and Society*, Raymond Williams sketches the history of the word "mob." A "mob" could arise in "unregulated industrialism." A new word for "mob" in the period was "masses" (229).

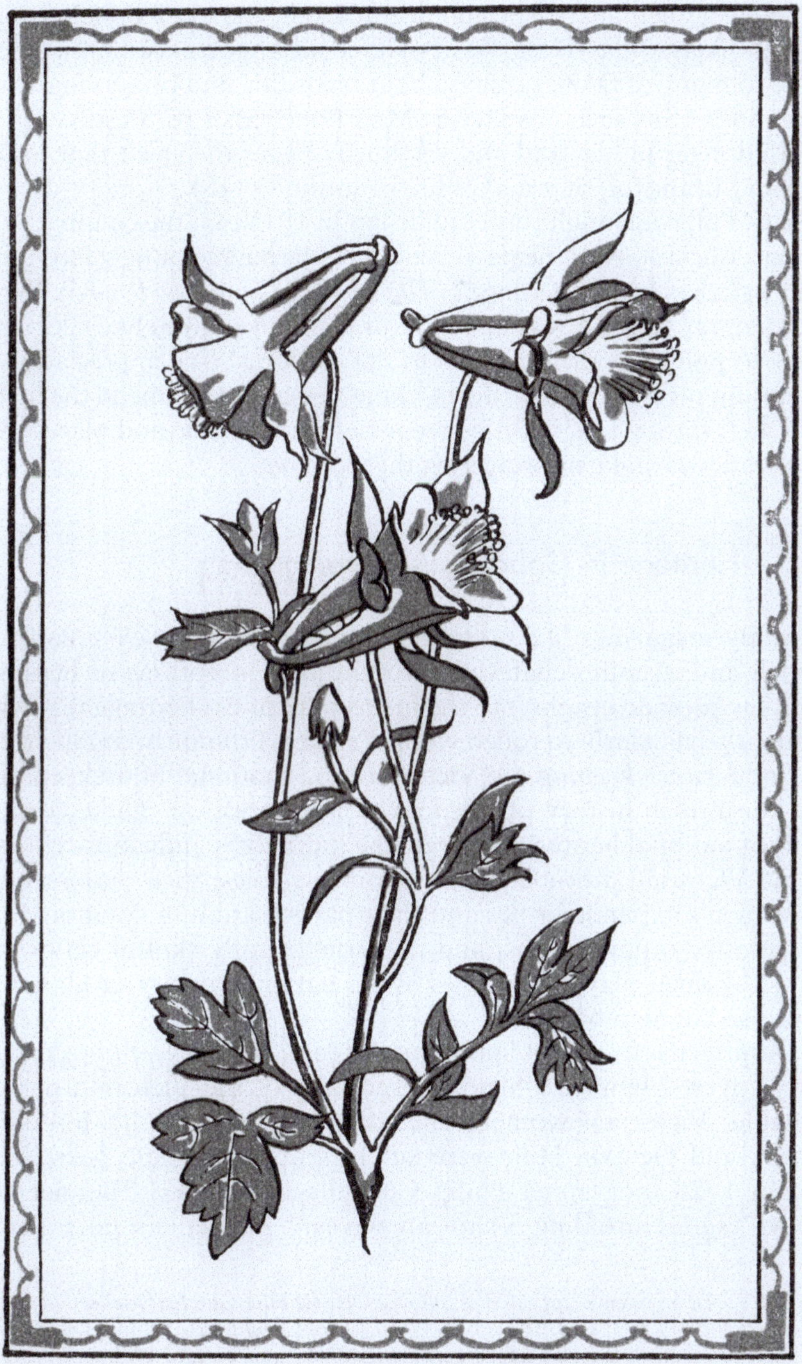

Figure 3.2 Illustration by Stephen Bone for *A Hidden Orchis*, by Gertrude Bone. Courtesy of The Medici Society Ltd.

this environmental and societal degradation, Gertrude Bone's books, though likely to be overlooked, assume an importance that is applicable to many of Dane's essays about recording and preserving "Lost England": "But such a writer as Mrs. Bone exists to preserve for us a little longer in her frail and yet sturdy pages the spirit that makes England beautiful, that makes life beautiful" (118).

E.C. Pulbrook might say confidently in 1915 that the country, "full of the associations of the past," could be the source of new interest in "our priceless [rural] heritage" (*The English Countryside* v–vi). But in the interwar years, it was up to cultural commentators like Clemence Dane to point out the obstacles to the moderns' true appreciation of it. Joining preservationist efforts, Dane's essays recommend the literature that, through its sensitive record of rural people and places, will give readers a stake in protecting this heritage.

Heritage in *Good Housekeeping*

Monthly magazines like *Good Housekeeping* were well-situated to launch and sustain debates about multiple conceptions of heritage, and they provide insight into the forms of national heritage that were thought particularly to touch women's lives. Prominent among these in *Good Housekeeping* are Victorianism, "national housekeeping," and the British history of freedom from oppression. These conceptions of national heritage illustrate the journalists' judicious criticism of the Victorian attitude toward women's roles; their endorsement of women's expanded roles and their participation in voluntary and cooperative organizations; and their rhetorically skillful claim that British women played key roles in the nation's history of liberating oppressed human beings.

Despite its focus on modernity, *Good Housekeeping* consistently covered women's history, especially of the Victorian period. Notable Victorian women, including Gertrude Bell, Josephine Butler, and Octavia Hill, were subjects of journalistic portraits;[27] and in 1928 biographer Philip Guedalla launched a "Bonnet and Shawl" series profiling Victorian wives.[28] Guedalla's portraits in

[27] These Victorian women appeared as follows: Octavia Hill, *Good Housekeeping* vol. 4, no. 6 (February 1924); Gertrude Bell, *Good Housekeeping* vol. 12, no. 4 (December 1927); Josephine Butler, *Good Housekeeping* vol. 13, no. 2 (April 1928).

[28] The portrait subjects were Mary Ann Disraeli, Emily Palmerston, Jane Welsh Carlyle, Emily Tennyson, Catherine Gladstone, and Mary Arnold (the last to appear in *Good Housekeeping*).

particular revealed the hidden side of Victorian women's strength, as Dane had done in "The Consort Crown." Yet while profiles of individual Victorian women evoke readers' admiration for their vitality and accomplishments, articles about Victorian society and culture often adopt a more mixed attitude toward Victorian heritage. In "News from the Country of Hardwork" (1924), although Clemence Dane uses "stuffiness" to segue from Victorian drawing rooms to Victorian *mores*, her review of J.H. Badley's history of the Bedales boarding school proves that it was an enlightened and pioneering experiment in co-education, one that encouraged young people to "form their beliefs and ideals for themselves" (138).[29] Ambivalence about Victorianism also marked Storm Jameson's "What Has Become of Victorian Vitality?" (1928), whose title belied Jameson's delineation of a Victorian girl's regimented life. As she reads the diary of a ten-year-old, privately-educated daughter of a Victorian shipowner, Jameson notes the ironic gap between the girl's sensibility and the material she was to learn. "The passion of *Phèdre* came strangely from between her firm little lips," Jameson muses, "and not a scarlet bow on the tartan dress trembled as passion swelled to anguish in verse of an unearthly and un-English beauty ... What strange and incomprehensible visions, like foreign birds in a northern land, could it have set among her placid thoughts?" (49). Jameson wonders at the lack of an informed rationale for the educational program designed by the diarist's father, amounting to a highly programmed life that was never questioned. These instances of critical distance from Victorian societal practices aligned well with *Good Housekeeping*'s overall mission to support women in their full, modern lives. To the extent that an overall ethos can be gleaned, the *Good Housekeeping* journalists collectively offer frank criticism, praise where due, and recognition of the limited aspects of Victorian heritage that can be built upon or extended into the modern era.

The extension of British women's housekeeping skills to their anticipated "national housekeeping" represented one such recuperation of a recognized heritage. The phrase first appears in the second issue of *Good Housekeeping*, where Barbara Wootton urges that "Every woman to be a good citizen must extend the interest she feels in her own housekeeping to the nation's housekeeping.

[29] Founded in 1893 by John Haden Badley, Bedales's model of co-education was considered an important educational experiment.

The responsibility of the vote faces women today" (49).[30] In *The Women's Side* (1926), Clemence Dane similarly invokes "national housekeeping" to call for women's active engagement in political matters and the public sphere. In the "Foreword" to this collection of her feminist essays, Dane characterizes the essays as "words of provocation" particularly directed at women who may forget that they must "take their share of national housekeeping" so that their own lives will not be threatened by "laws, wars, strikes and revolutions—outside their control" (v). But it is in its coverage of the Women's Institute movement—in two full-length articles as well as a Table of Contents teaser—that *Good Housekeeping* devoted more sustained attention to a British women's heritage of "national housekeeping."[31] "What Makes a *Home-Maker*?" (1922) and "How the Women's Institutes Came into Being" (1925) both provide a history of the movement and explain its current activity and particular service to women in rural areas. In the 1925 article, Phyllis Gibbons emphasizes the expansion of members' simple housekeeping skills, this time through an ethos of cooperative learning, so that from the informal beginning of the Institutes when "three women from outlying districts called upon a fourth to see how she bottled her fruit, and to have a cup of her famous tea" (14), the members now organize a robust series of lectures and demonstrations that include village history, folklore, home handicrafts, and local government. Pride in the power of this heritage to reverberate beyond their own homes can be gleaned from Gibbons's citation of its motto, "For Home and Country," and her clarification that the women join "to work for the good of all" (14). In the earlier "What Makes a *Home-Maker*?" Margaret Wintringham, identified as "the first Englishwoman to enter Parliament," likewise drew an analogy between "good housekeepers" and "good national housekeepers."[32] Noting the importance of the members' self-governance, Wintringham concludes her article with a vision of women's growing competence, their sphere of influence expanding from home, to parish, to village, to district,

[30] The term "national housekeeping" has been astutely analyzed by Delap, Beaumont, and also Wood in "Housekeeping, Citizenship, and Nationhood in *Good Housekeeping* and *Modern Home*."

[31] Among the period's initiatives to preserve rural England, voluntary movements like the Women's Institutes sought to sustain "the distinctiveness of rural life ... via its transformation" (Matless 70).

[32] Margaret Wintringham (1879–1955) won her late husband's seat in Louth, Lincolnshire in 1921, becoming the first female Liberal MP. The editorial identification of Wintringham is from the Table of Contents for Volume 2, Number 1, p. 2.

to county, and finally to country—"for is not their motto 'For Home and Country'?" (83).

Not surprisingly in the period that follows the First World War and women's partial enfranchisement, liberty and freedom from oppression are among the most frequent evocations of British heritage in *Good Housekeeping*. Recognition of Britain's "birthright of liberty" figures in numerous articles by feminist journalists Violet Bonham Carter, Helena Normanton, Clemence Dane, and others. The most rhetorically powerful of these articles include a call to action. For example, in "Petty Tyrannies" (1925), Clemence Dane cites a recent, employer-imposed prohibition against nurses shingling their hair, and after detailing additional "petty tyrannies" endured by citizens, finds that her compatriots often acquiesce rather than stand up for their rights. "Are we English of to-day losing our most precious characteristic, our passion for individuality and independence?" she asks. "To leave the improvement of a bad state of things to the next man with a 'Somebody ought to do something!' is to belong to the herd, to think as the herd, to deny ourselves our birthright of independence" (13). Dane's twofold rhetorical work to arouse concern about a threatened heritage and to call on citizens to bolster it is characteristic of *Good Housekeeping*'s treatment of the British "birthright of liberty."

Bonham Carter and Normanton invoke a specifically feminine legacy to rouse their readers. In "The Last Battle" (1922), Bonham Carter advocates for the extension of the franchise to young women and invokes Mary Wollstonecraft as a precursor to contemporary feminists. *A Vindication of the Rights of Women* "burst like a bombshell on an age in which even Rousseau, that apostle of freedom and champion of the abstract rights of humanity, expressed the opinion that women ought to have but little liberty" (13). Yet while feminist activism remained important after the First World War, journalists like Helena Normanton also made clear women's humanitarian heritage, especially in the British history of abolitionism. In "Waters of Babylon" (1930), Normanton deplores the prevalence of global slavery even while she marks the 100th anniversary of the abolition of slavery in British dominions. She calls on Britain to "secure her own glorious birth-right of freedom for all mankind" (58) and on Englishwomen to "stir up the England of Freedom" by "voice, pen and vote" (148). Invoking her readers' grandmothers, Normanton underscores English *women*'s distinct heritage of support for abolition:

> Our grandmothers drank their beverages and ate their food unsweetened rather than use slave sugar, and dressed in woollen homespun rather than wear garments made of slave-grown cotton. They served their food on china decorated with anti-slavery mottoes and illustrations as a form of propaganda to their guests. (148)

Adhering to a vision of British women's housekeeping skills, Normanton economically illustrates the uncommon history and political application of those skills on a global scale.

While not a systematic review, my survey of *Good Housekeeping*'s treatment of heritage in the 1920s suggests that it commissioned articles representing a threatened or merely obscured heritage that could guide women's negotiation of modernity. Dane and her *Good Housekeeping* counterparts share the conviction that modernity is supported by history. Like the telescope in Dane's "Jefferies of the Fields," the *Good Housekeeping* journalists extend and then shorten the historical span needed to illuminate modernity, framing and reframing historical material. These heritage narratives in some instances reassure readers that cyclical patterns and collective agency will override the turbulence of the modern era, while at other times they serve to spur readers to correct the course of modernity. A hidden heritage of female strength needs only to be recovered for their readers' use.

Chapter 4

The Boundary Stones of Belief

Clemence Dane's contributions to *Good Housekeeping* include a remarkable series of essays about belief. These essays include literary criticism and "social problem essays," as they were categorized in the magazine's indexes. Collectively, they document Dane's repeated affirmation that spiritual belief in the age of skepticism is alive, though sometimes under threat; they provide guidance for citizens amidst the profound changes in the aftermath of the First World War; and they illustrate the power of literature to record and renew the human spiritual imagination. In these essays Dane prepares women and men to negotiate modernity by engaging their spiritual, ethical, and imaginative faculties.

In addition to their support of spiritual experience, both orthodox and unorthodox, Dane's essays about belief contribute to the literary criticism of the postwar period. Her essays on myth constitute a modest, but significant body of archetypal criticism that precedes the mid-century critical movement in myth criticism. Literary historian Chris Baldick singles out Jungian psychologist Maud Bodkin's *Archetypal Patterns in Poetry* (1934), a "much-noticed work on recurring 'timeless' motifs and themes in world literature" as an early contribution, but finds that "myth criticism, or the interpretation of literature in terms of perennial motifs and themes, had made little significant headway before the Second World War" (*Criticism and Literary Theory* 69, 134). The Dane essays discussed in this chapter reveal that quality magazines like *Good Housekeeping* have been overlooked forums of sustained critical discussion, including myth criticism, that engaged and enlightened common readers.

Moreover, Dane reflects the documented global outlook of the period. Her surveys of religious myth set British texts within Western and world canons so as to render the historical and global magnitude of human spirituality. She was in good company. The 1890s and early twentieth century saw marked hunger for greater understanding of "the meaning of life and the spiritual dimensions of the universe" from Britons who no longer identified with Christian observance and who sought answers from both Western and Eastern religions (Owen 4–5).[1] As a Christian literary critic, Dane holds the double consciousness that Michael Bell argues characterizes mythopoeic modernist writing, recognizing that her "deepest commitments and beliefs are a world view ... which cannot be transcendentally grounded or privileged over other world views" (1). Yet Dane's global literary surveys like "Children of Light," "The Mother Night," and "Cities of God," though they recognize the relativity of each belief system, seek less to individualize and compare sacred traditions than to establish resemblances and recurring archetypes, as if she is sketching the entirety of belief through her humanist endorsement of mythopoeia. Dane illustrates what recent scholarship recognizes as the postwar global world view that inflected the lived experience of ordinary Britons, through the phenomena of immigration, travel, and the new media. Producers of and audiences for anthropological fieldwork records, travel memoirs, newspapers, radio broadcasts, and film, Britons constituted an international community, argues Michael North (15–17).[2] These media brought distant parts of the globe near as they were captured on screen and in newspapers.

If Dane's essays are informed by a global world view, they are also supported by the predominantly British contributors to *Good Housekeeping*. This chapter will argue that *Good Housekeeping* supported religious practice by regularly featuring the voices of well-respected authorities on spiritual questions.

During and after the First World War, there was widespread concern about the decline of Christianity, often measured by dwindling numbers of churchgoers. Writing for *Good Housekeeping*, the Reverend Reginald John Campbell typified and summarized the clergy's search for the source of this decline. From the working class to the intellectual middle classes, the public seemed to agree that churches were failing to make religion relevant to their congregations. Campbell observed that "One can scarcely pick up a newspaper or magazine which does not contain some criticism of the churches for their inefficiency and dullness, or some attack upon

[1] Owen's monograph documents the strength and vibrancy of fin-de-siècle mysticism, occultism, and "mystery traditions of all kinds" (4).

[2] North identifies limitations to and expands Raymond Williams's conception of the international communities formed by expatriate writers in metropolitan Europe.

them for not being able to adapt themselves better to modern conditions and supply what the public wants" (14). Joining this public debate, *Good Housekeeping* invited prominent religious figures, including Campbell, a "world-famous preacher"[3] and the "famous woman preacher" A. Maude Royden, to probe the decline of religion in contemporary society.[4] Each spoke from a position of authority and analyzed changes in "civilisation" from an intellectual standpoint. Each linked the health of civilization to the restoration of religious belief. Royden identified renewed interest in religion and attributed it to the war, which had "shaken us all so badly that, to many, the one desirable thing seems to be something that we can hold on to. Either it is a Church or it is a Book" (20). But what the public most wanted, Royden believed, was honest examination of religious and societal problems. Young audiences were flocking to the theater to see George Bernard Shaw's *Saint Joan* because they sought "a religious problem of universal interest discussed in a spirit of honesty both moral and intellectual" (126). More foreboding than Royden, Campbell spoke of a revolutionary change in civilization that "has come suddenly, explosively, portentously" (88). He deplored the moral and spiritual composition of "modern man," whose self-appointed business is to harness the natural resources of the world for his own benefit. The mechanical advances making possible this mastery over nature directly correlate with the moderns' "unhealthy spiritual state ... We have not time to find our souls, and there are many of us who doubt whether we have any souls to find" (90). A stakeholder in these questions of the moderns' moral and spiritual state, Dane argues in one of her earliest articles for *Good Housekeeping*, that civilization can only "advance" in a climate of intellectual honesty in which citizens can find or reconceive of God. Unless twentieth-century citizens do so, she warns her audience, "we have failed in the purpose of our racial, as well as of our individual life" ("This Century's Religion" 74).

Beginning in 1928, *Good Housekeeping* ran two series of articles by cultural icon Bruce Barton, the first, episodes in the biography of Jesus Christ; and the second, retellings of biblical

[3] The editors used this epithet in the Table of Contents blurb for Campbell's article. Reginald John Campbell (1867–1956) was a British Congregationalist and Anglican divine.

[4] Editorial byline for "Religion in Modern Fiction and on the Stage," by A. Maude Royden, p. 20.

stories featuring children.[5] These series undoubtedly appealed to a wider *Good Housekeeping* audience than the cultural criticism of Campbell, Dane, and Royden. Both series told the stories of biblical characters in modern prose that highlighted the dramatic, often political tension of their societies. Both featured full-page color illustrations for each installment. Each series—and the two running sequentially—engaged and re-engaged readers' attention over a period of months. Between 1923 and 1925, then, as represented by Campbell, Dane, and Royden, *Good Housekeeping* deepened its coverage of difficult spiritual problems facing British society. With Barton's *Man of Galilee* and *Children of the Bible* series, the magazine popularized and deepened readers' familiarity with the remarkable protagonists of the Old and New Testaments.

As this chapter will demonstrate, Dane participates in and extends the early 1920s' debates about the role of religion to shore up an unstable society. She examines the gaps between religious dogma and spiritual hunger, and like Campbell and Royden, while respecting the privacy of individual faith, she makes the important link between spiritual faith and social mores. Yet Dane's exploration of spirituality goes beyond religious belief. She reflects the modern period's exploration of the whole spectrum of spiritual experience, from visionary dreams to fairy belief. Indeed, Dane's essays express what recent scholarship recognizes as a long-standing tension between doctrinal ideas and "residual beliefs in magic, reincarnation, and astrology, among other beliefs" (Viswanathan 467).[6] Often what interests Dane is not the individual features of these phenomena, but their collective evidence of human "instinctive recognition of life outside our life, of lives behind us and lives to come" ("Faerylands Forlorn" 150). Dane may scoff at but she is also fascinated by the modern trend to disguise spiritual instinct as intellectual experimentation. The moderns hunger for fairy tales, but profess that "We don't believe in them, not we! ... But we are always ready to run an eye over an essay on thought transference, or the account of a séance" ("First Flights" 175).

[5] Bruce Barton (1886–1967) was an advertising man and best-selling religious writer, best known for *The Man Nobody Knows* (1925), in which Barton dubbed Jesus the "founder of modern business."

[6] In a call for the development of literary histories that more accurately track the development of secular literature, Viswanathan synthesizes research that refutes the model of a simple opposition between early modern religious literature and post-Enlightenment secular literature. In the "secular age," in fact, "religious belief is contested by the alternative (even heterodox) knowledge systems it had suppressed or marginalized" (468).

Dane's strengths as a literary critic are manifested in her attention to the formal modes of religious literature. The historical tableaux that provide the framework of her essays lead her inevitably to contemporary literature. Dane reads modern dilemmas in the terms of biblical and other mythic patterns; each age invents or refines the age-old forms and modes—verse, parable, comedy, irony, paradox—for the expression of religious yearning, spiritual power, and human conflict. In Dane's book essays, moral and philosophical debates about spirituality and modernity are mediated by literature. For Dane, the Bible is the foundational text in Britain not because of the religious dogma it yields, but because its great variety of literary forms gives each reader a concrete foothold in spiritual insight. From proverbs to parables, biblical literary forms endure or can be renewed with each generation. In "Children of Light" (1927) Dane maintains that "a truth perfectly expressed never degenerates into a mere wise saw" (41). It is the form that protects the insight and enlightens those who turn to it in any era. Other biblical forms, such as the archetype, can be identified in modern literature while gaining power from affiliation with previous expressions of the type. In a lay sermon delivered during the Second World War, Dane was to say that "The Bible has done more than any other legacy to shape British character, fulfil British speech, and influence British literature" ("Britain's Heritage"). Nor does the Bible enjoy an exclusive purchase on spiritually potent form. Indeed, in "The Sixth Commandment," Dane calls for writers to recognize the capacity of drama and the novel to lend magnitude to serious subjects. These forms have the best chance of combatting the daily press's spellbinding influence on readers and its tendency to trivialize or even bypass the moral dimensions of human crises. Dane's literary criticism calls for drama and the novel to restore "the sense of size" to moral and spiritual subjects (204).

"The Boundary Stones of Belief" begins with discussion of three foundational essays on the topics of faith, hope, and belief: "This Century's Religion," "The Mother Night," and "Children of Light." Each addresses a distinctly modern need, and each does so by setting modern spiritual questions within a long span of history. Although each essay foregrounds religious conflict, each affirms the authority of the people to determine the course of spiritual life in Britain. These foundational essays confirm the security of religious worship within the history of civilizations and demonstrate how it has been encoded in and protected by literary forms.

"This Century's Religion"

In "This Century's Religion" (1923), Dane tells "the story of religion" from an evolutionary anthropological perspective and reassures her readers that the twentieth century is not the "godless one" that we are often warned about (10). Dane's stance is both authoritative and reassuring. Often viewed in this essay through an evolutionary lens, history provides an authoritative framework for Dane's pronouncements; and in turn, history reassures her readers that the moderns, like earlier phases of civilization, are on track to add to the concept of God.

"This Century's Religion" is Dane's most unreservedly religious essay for *Good Housekeeping*. It provides a fascinating window onto Dane's early contributions for *Good Housekeeping*, preceding her book essays, in which her opinions are not mediated by her discussion of literary texts. Instead, Dane delineates a long arc of history leading from ancient civilizations to contemporary culture. "This Century's Religion," for instance, describes the racial imperative of all civilizations to construct a God. The bygone centuries have, in turn, found God to stand for "Power, Life, Law, Wisdom, and Love" (76). And in the aftermath of the First World War, with more hopefulness than complacency, Dane finds that "comparing the ideals of each age in turn, we can surely say, humbly and thankfully, that we have progressed upon our way" (10). Yet alongside the model of evolutionary progress toward an ever "greater" God, Dane upholds a God who is relative to each civilization, who must have "immediate and real connection with the needs and problems and interests of our twentieth-century existence" (74). Religion must make itself relevant to society.

The Story of Religion

In arguing that the "realisation of god is the supreme experience of man and nation alike" Dane may risk alienating some readers. But Dane's editors and Dane herself avoid this pitfall. An inset editorial on the first-page spread refers to Dane's "profoundly thoughtful and stimulating article," presenting it as an intellectual and cultural contribution (10). And Dane herself steers clear of dogmatism by acknowledging that the twentieth century has suspended the "strict observance of the customs of the sect into which we are born" but that religion itself is not "dead" (10). "This Century's Religion" acknowledges that the search for God, the "attempt of the created to unveil their Creator" (10), engenders conflict, but emphasizes that it is an enduringly human experience:

> [E]xperience, individual, racial, and human, is always the same in type as it is always different in detail ... The child, the family, the pre-pre-palaeolithic man, each stands at the same portal of experience, each profoundly convinced that no hand but his has ever gripped the knocker before ... And the questions that it asks are always the same—"Who am I? Who made me? Whither do I go?" (10)

The realization of God is an experience of "overwhelming importance" to each individual yet is so universal that it constitutes "the story of the world." And Dane hints that it is individual conviction that sows the seeds of human conflict. "It is his personal prize, his unique possession. He has discovered God, and he will not give up his discovery, his religion, for anything the world can offer him" (10).

All civilizations reveal that strife marks the human search for God. Biblical accounts include stories of triumph, of the Holy Spirit filling human beings, as well as stories of division and "confusion" exemplified in the Tower of Babel of Genesis. The discovery of God runs side by side "with the inevitable conclusion of self-absorbed humanity that other people's gods are an abomination" (10). Dane finds evidence of humanity's impulse to divide themselves from one another in sects and creeds. Institutional religion, Dane believes, reflects and exacerbates this "confusion." Out of touch with their flocks, the clergy retreat to academic and increasingly irrelevant positions, while each sect denounces "those who disagree with them" (74).

The Contemporary Search for God

Given the evidence that religion lies at the center of human histories of conflict, how can Dane spur religious inquiry in 1923? She returns to her premise that individual, racial, and human experience move in lock step. She invites her readers to envision themselves as the innermost of a series of Russian nesting dolls: "The history of a man or woman is the history in little of a civilization, and the history of a civilization is the history in little of mankind" (10). Dane's paraphrase of the nineteenth-century scientific concept that "ontogeny recapitulates philogeny" confers an unmitigated authority on the pattern that she finds repeated throughout the history of the human race. In Dane's later *Good Housekeeping* essays about spiritual belief, she endorses the moderns' range of spiritual beliefs and practices. But in "This Century's Religion," she yokes the individual's successful identity formation to their construction of God and aligns the health of the nation with its active search for God. "In realising God a man realises himself; he separates himself from the mass of life, the mass of thought; he becomes an identity" (10); and "though it has taken countless generations to give us our idea of God, unless we can add to it, we have failed in the purpose of our racial, as well as of our individual life" (74). Dane's alignment of the individual and the human race results in a mirror-like mutual reflection of human beings and the God they construct. Each level—racial, national, and individual—supports, confirms, and even seems to guarantee the others.

Thus, in the last section of her essay, Dane's project is to characterize God in 1923. She mediates between an older and a younger generation's attitudes as she offers a series of signs that the human construction of God is alive and well.

> The decline in power of the sects, their alternation between fretful apology and impotent denunciation of those who disagree with them, the indifference of the young to popular religion, the neglect of the Bible as an infallible guide, the growing feeling among all classes that the churches' standard of right and wrong is an academic one that has daily less and less to do with common-sense rectitude, the intense interest in spiritualism, psychoanalysis, "fancy religions," and all the other spiritualities of the hour, goes to prove, I think, not that we are forgetting God, not that we are dispensing with religion, but that our conception of both is once more in the melting-pot. (74)

The list of cultural symptoms in this long sentence acknowledges a diversity of feelings across generations and social classes, while the mounting rhythm of Dane's clauses leads triumphantly to the "melting pot" that unites believers. Additionally, Dane has space to express disapprobation ("the neglect of the Bible as an infallible guide") and to criticize the clergy's demand for fidelity in creeds and their antagonism of the sects from one another. And in another mediating device, Dane introduces the perspective of a twenty-three-old who stands metonymically for Britons' spiritual histories and for their religious outlook in 1923. This "charming girl of twenty-three or so" says she hasn't read much on the topic of religion "since I was eighteen, and I was an atheist then," but she expresses interest in

William James's *Pragmatism* since he is the brother of Henry James (74). Dane's young interlocutor illustrates that

> we have outgrown the God of our racial childhood, all through the Victorian age we have been "atheists at eighteen" and now, in our twenties, we are ready to be interested in religion again, so long as it is a "Brother of Henry James!"—so long, that is, as we can prove it to have immediate and real connection with the needs and problems and interests of our twentieth-century existence. (74)

In aligning all Britons, no matter their class or age, with the spirit of the twenty-three-year-old century embodied by the young flapper, Dane acknowledges the rupture of the moderns from the past. Each citizen enjoys a "youthful sense of emancipation from the trammels of doctrine," and therefore it might come as a shock to them that "we are as much 'in religion' as if we were sitting in church" (74). And she endorses the relativity of modernity: "It is hard to remember that when we hear the word 'God' in our forefathers', even in our fathers' mouths, that they do not mean what we do" (74). Dane's rhetoric suggests that Britons are emancipating themselves from a confining past, and her diction echoes the novelty, fluidity and fragmented experience of the modern construal of God: "we are beginning, in oddest disconnected ways, to define to ourselves what the quality is that we seek in our God" and "Odd little straws they are that show the road our God is taking" (76).

"Odd little straws," however, are unlikely to inspire the twentieth-century construction of God that Dane believes is imperative to national healing in the aftermath of the First World War. She rouses her audience with a series of challenges: "[O]n the threshold of a new age, have we no quality to add to the immense conception? Have we exhausted the Inexhaustible? ... Have we indeed set a bound to the possibilities of the Mystery that made us?" (74). What, Dane asks, will this postwar God look like? Combatants return from "the horrors of the war" convinced that God is not merciful. Will Cruelty be the divine attribute that the twentieth century contributes to the historical conception of God? Paradoxically, though, she finds that "the nation as a whole has recovered its belief in a future life, and it is admitted on all hands that it is the war, the war alone, that has restored it" (76). For Dane, this is the hopeful sign that the twentieth-century contribution to the ongoing construction of God will add to his goodness, fulfilling Dane's assumption of humanity's continual progress. She turns once more to the confidence of youth and emphasizes its readiness to laugh, an index of what the twentieth-century

God might be. At one time, for instance, games on Sunday would have been a sign of godlessness. Yet, Dane observes, "the youth of the nation goes forward serenely to its Sunday football and its Sunday tennis ... Its conscience is obviously clear" (76). "It laughs and is sure" that God doesn't mind. "Is not this a twisted, humorous straw? ... How do we modern people contrive to believe and be irreverent at one and the same time?" (76). Dane muses that the twentieth century may well "add the heavenly attribute of Laughter to our conception of the Divine" (76).

"The Mother Night"

Like "This Century's Religion," "The Mother Night" (1925) explores authoritative threats to popular expressions of religious belief. And just as the former essay concluded with the hopeful image of confident youth incorporating laughter into their conception of God, so does "The Mother Night" emphasize the power of popular cultural forms to encode and protect the people's expression of faith.

In "The Mother Night," appearing in the Christmas issue of *Good Housekeeping*, Dane outlines evidence of pre-Christian worship of seasonal goddesses of peace and goodwill. She also describes the suppression of such worship by the early patriarchs of the Church. This critique of institutionalized Christianity is arguably softened by Dane's location of religious persecution in the past and by her subordination of this theme to the essay's message of peace and goodwill. Yet the publication of Dane's appreciation for the deities also testifies to *Good Housekeeping*'s editorial liberality even as it depended on revenue from advertisements promoting Christmas shopping. For example, in the November number, the editors announce that "To help our readers in Christmas Shopping, this section has been augmented to six pages" (see Figure 4.1). The Christmas number promoted Christmas through fiction, shopping, and gift suggestions, and nonfiction concentrated on Christmas. Rose Macaulay contributed "How to Enjoy Christmas," a wide-ranging satire of Christmas commercial and social customs in Britain. Additionally, "Christmas and the Child," by educational theorist E.E. Kenwrick, and "Religion in Modern Fiction and on the Stage," by the prominent (Anglican) preacher and feminist Maude Royden, represented particularly authoritative contributions to this Christmas issue of *Good Housekeeping*. In an issue overwhelmingly oriented to commercial, social, and Christian perspectives on Christmas, then,

CONTENTS for NOVEMBER

The Christmas Number

OF GOOD HOUSEKEEPING will express the season's greetings with a galaxy of brilliant contributions. These include the opening instalment of a masterly new novel by Hugh Walpole, and fiction and articles from such distinguished writers as I. A. R. Wylie, W. Somerset Maugham, Gene Stratton-Porter, J. E. Buckrose, Maude Royden, Rose Macaulay, Frank Swinnerton, St. John Ervine, Mrs. Sidgwick, Clemence Dane, etc.

SPECIALLY attractive are eighteen pages in colour, including a delightful new serial for little folk. To help our readers in Christmas Shopping, this Section has been augmented to six pages. And the eight-page Cookery Section, with selected seasonable recipes, will be a veritable delight to housewives.

TO come back to workaday November. Miss Frances Louise Stevenson, private secretary to Mr. Lloyd George, in an article that is of special interest to the great army of self-supporting women, counsels: "If your work does not make you happy, it is not the right work, no matter how much money it may bring you. . . . When you have found the right work, you will find that it will prove to be not work at all, but pleasure."

ATTENTION is specially invited to the announcement on page 23, regarding the extension of the Furnishing and Decorating Section. To the selection of fiction and articles Barry Pain, E. M. Delafield, Gene Stratton-Porter, J. E. Buckrose, Frank Rutter, St. John Ervine, Percy A. Scholes, and Clemence Dane bring distinction.

GOOD HOUSEKEEPING NOVEMBER 1925 VOL. VIII. No. 3.
Rates of Subscription, 17s. 6d. per annum, post free to any address in the United Kingdom or Abroad.
Registered at the General Post Office for transmission by Canadian Magazine Post.
Published monthly by the Proprietors, the National Magazine Co., Ltd., of 153 Queen Victoria Street, London, E.C.4, and printed by Hazell, Watson & Viney, Ld., London and Aylesbury
The Editor will not hold himself responsible for the safety of any MSS., but when stamps are enclosed he will make every effort to ensure the safe return of rejected MSS.
The Editor begs to inform the readers of "Good Housekeeping" that the characters in the stories in this number are purely imaginary, and that no reference or allusion is intended to apply to any living person or persons

Figure 4.1 Table of Contents for November 1925. Courtesy of Hearst Magazines UK.

Dane's "Mother Night" questioned Christianity's monopoly in the minds and hearts of British citizens.

Like an archaeologist, Dane's approach in "The Mother Night" is to unearth the fragments of a buried and trampled belief in powerful goddesses. Drawing on a variety of sources, Dane argues that the ancient Egyptians, Romans, and early Europeans all worshipped maternal deities, often nature divinities. Moreover, her sources tell her, many early Europeans kept a vigil, a "mother night," in honor of a deity who traveled the land on the 25th of December, accompanied by children. Dane quotes Jacob Grimm's *Teutonic Mythology*, perhaps reading James Stallybrass's translation of the fourth edition (1882): "whatever name they bore, [these deities] were born of a common idea, were thought of chiefly as divine mothers who travel round and visit houses" to teach the human race spinning, weaving, tending hearth, sowing, and reaping. "These labours bring with them peace and quiet in the land," adds Grimm (qtd. in "The Mother Night" 114).[7]

At one level, Dane's essay functions to illustrate a comparative approach to myth, much as Sir James Frazer had in *The Golden Bough*.[8] Frazer's monumental study found archetypes common to many "primitive" religions, whose influence extended into twentieth-century culture. But while Frazer posited an *evolutionary* model in which humans' superstitious belief in magic was superseded by enlightened belief in science, Dane seeks to *recover* the pacific and pastoral elements of the goddesses and to trace the role of the clergy in debasing them. But she must also show that the force of the deities has been so suppressed across the centuries that it is present only as a residue in the moderns. She makes this case both in textual criticism and in cultural commentary.

[7] In addition to Grimm, Dane may have been familiar with nineteenth-century scholarship theorizing a single great Goddess behind the goddesses of ancient Greece (Hutton 92–3); and she may have read twentieth-century classical anthropologist Jane Ellen Harrison, a key member of the Cambridge School of Anthropology. In *Themis: A Study of the Social Origins of Greek Religion* (1912) Harrison argued that "the dominant Earth Goddess of the pre-Greeks reflected a matrilineal social organization" (Arlen 169). Ronald Hutton adds that Harrison "posited the previous existence of a peaceful and intensely creative woman-centred civilisation, in which humans, living in harmony with nature and their own emotions, worshipped a single female deity" (93).

[8] The twelve volumes of Frazer's expanded third edition appeared between 1906–15. Britons' sense of historical and religious relativism, however, began in the Victorian period, which brought to their attention evolutionary theory, archaeological evidence of ancient religions, and the study of comparative religions. See Richard Altick, *Victorian People and Ideas* 99–101.

It is this second approach that opens the essay. Dane illustrates the legacy of buried, or only furtively expressed, feeling in the opening of "The Mother Night," which contrasts American and English attitudes toward the concept of a Mother's Day. In these conversational paragraphs, Dane's persona, intrigued by these cultural differences, expresses relief that Britons decline to celebrate a Mother's Day. In fact, she claims that their reluctance to express strong feelings publicly amounts to a national trait. Dane does not make explicit the connection between this reticence and a history of clerical suppression of fervent goddess worship—the scholarly topic of the essay—but many of her readers will. With the passage of the centuries, the discouragement, and even punishment, of expression have led to the dwindling of communal expressions of belief such as carols and ballads; readers can find them only when they have been collected by anthologists and folklorists.[9] But if the English do not want *publicly* to express their feelings about mothers, *furtive* expression enjoys long-standing tradition. The celebration of the Mother's Night proves that such feelings exist and find covert expression annually, Dane claims: "we have ... at least a Mother's night that we celebrate yearly, quietly, furtively, under cover of a great Christian festival" (15). Throughout "The Mother Night," Dane balances criticism of the historical debasement of the maternal deities with consoling evidence that a residue of feeling and belief is passed on, and after thousands of years still finds channels for expression.

Donning the hat of erudite critic, one of many she wears in the course of her tenure at *Good Housekeeping*, Dane supplies many examples of the abiding force of these deities. She quotes from major authors like Goethe and Matthew Arnold, as well as from folk ballads and historians; and she singles out Pre-Raphaelite Holman Hunt's *The Triumph of the Innocents* (1883–4) for the austere, chiseled quality of its Mary during the Holy Family's Flight into Egypt. Hunt paints an "older inherited conception of the divine Mother" that may provide a clue to the switch of allegiance from the pagan to the Christian mother. Hunt depicted "the Mother who took the long journey into Egypt with only the spirits of the innocents as a guard and a defence" (114). "It must have been no hard wrench of faith," Dane opines, to begin worshipping a Mother whose unwavering

[9] Such anthologies, including *The English and Scottish Popular Ballads*, edited by Francis James Child, and *The Oxford Book of English Verse: 1250–1900*, edited by Arthur Quiller-Couch, are among Dane's sources for the verses and hymns she features.

faith carried such high stakes and whose triumph over adversity must have seemed miraculous.

The range of Dane's examples of deity worship demonstrates the pervasive persistence of the maternal goddesses in the Western and Christian imagination. The *Good Housekeeping* editors teased Dane's essay as "storied fantasy," but clearly Dane did not want the survival of these goddesses to seem either her own fantasy or a feminist tributary to a religious mainstream. Instead, "The Mother Night" presents the twofold history, on the one hand, of persecuted believers and, on the other, of persistent, if furtively held, belief. The first source Dane cites, the English monk and historian the Venerable Bede, refers obliquely to events and figures that comprised the mothers' night.[10] Bede reports that:

> The ancient peoples of the Angli began the year on the 25th of December when we now celebrate the birthday of the Lord: and the very night which is now holy to us, they called in their tongue "modra necht," that is, the mothers' night. (qtd. in "The Mother Night" 15)

Bede surmises that the festival was so called "by reason of the ceremonies which on that night-long vigil they performed" (15, quoting Bede). Dane emphasizes the significance of Bede's reticence:

> But there is not a word of what the ceremonies were: no names of the mothers beyond, elsewhere, a casual reference to a March goddess and an Easter goddess. Heathen "divine mothers" were not suitable for discussion by a good churchman of the eighth century: they were a little too near and alive still in the woods, and the swamps, and the fountains, and the hill-tops for that. (15, 114)

Dane accounts for this minimal commentary by pointing to what a good churchman of the eighth century *could not say*. Bede is like the first fragment yielded in an archaeological dig, and Dane needs to unearth more pieces to re-compose the story of this pre-Christian belief. She turns to Goethe's *Faust*, which reflects both the Mothers' sublimity and their debasement in Christianity. Before Faust can return to earth in the Golden Age, he must visit "the Mothers," goddesses "enthroned sublime in solitude" (Goethe). Faust is later "haunted by them in their degraded shapes as 'the four grey hags,'

[10] Bede the historian (~672–735) was an English monk in the medieval Anglo-Saxon kingdom of Northumbria and author of *The Ecclesiastical History of the English People* (~731).

Want, *Guilt*, *Need*, and *Care* before he can be received by the Mother herself" (114).

Dane's most direct criticism of the Church comes in a few sentences of allusion to witch-hunts and persecution. She references "accounts of the fierce persecution of wise and beautiful heathenisms ... images defaced, the books burned, the lovely legends mutilated" because of "clerical zeal" and "fanaticism" (115).[11] Dane follows this "clerical zeal" no further; her dominant theme in "The Mother Night," after all, is the peace and goodwill that informs Christmas. Yet it is clear that she mourns the passage of an early phase of Christianity that was informed by maternal goddesses and infused with nature. She concludes the essay by quoting three quatrains from an anonymous carol of the fifteenth century.[12] The carol celebrates the birth of Jesus to a matchless "Mother and maiden," and it does so by enfolding the mother in the pastoral elements of the dew, grass, flower, and spray and depicting the stillness of the infant's coming to her there:

> He came al so still
> There his mother was
> As dew in April
> That falleth on the grass ... .

Having characterized the Mother Night throughout the essay, Dane can conclude by calling the fifteenth-century carol a "song of the Mother Night." Her analysis of the traditional ballad "The Cherry-Tree Carol" similarly illustrates an early Christianity whose deity presided over a beneficent nature.[13] The ballad begins by telling how Jesus, from within Mary's womb, lowers a cherry tree bough so that Mary can reach the fruit she desires. Dane quotes more sorrowful stanzas too, in which the baby Jesus tells of his own death and resurrection. Dane is fascinated by the contrast in these two modes, the first joyfully affirming the God's connection to bountiful nature, and

[11] Dane may specifically have in mind persecution of accused witches, which reached their peak in Europe between 1560 and 1630 (Thurston). Some nineteenth-century interpretations, such as those by Karl Ernst Jarcke in 1828, claimed that victims of early modern witch trials were "members of a previously unknown pan-European pagan religion which had pre-dated Christianity, been persecuted by the Christian Church as a rival religion, and finally driven underground, where it had survived in secret until being revealed in the confessions of those accused in the witch trials" ("The Witch-Cult in Western Europe").

[12] The carol is included in the 1919 edition of *The Oxford Book of English Verse: 1250–1900*, edited by Arthur Quiller-Couch.

[13] "The Cherry-Tree Carol" is included in *The English and Scottish Popular Ballads*.

the second acknowledging that suffering and sacrifice were the price of his ultimate triumph. Dane muses that in the mind of the carol's author, "surely ... some devout Englishman ... stories of the old faith still lingered":

> stories perhaps of the kind mother *Abundia*, ever returning with the spring, at whose tread flowers sprang, who could pluck fruit from blossoming trees, whose passage ensured the harvest. (115)

Dane laments the loss of this early phase of Christianity: "How beautiful such decking out of the new faith with flowers of the old must have been we only realise when we compare the early carols, hymns and stories with the productions of those arid centuries when creed had obscured gospel" (115). As the Church produced creeds for its believers to affirm, it usurped the authority of the people themselves to turn to the primary accounts of the gospels and to interpret them in hymns, carols, and other popular forms.

Dane's invocation of those "arid centuries" and of the "fierce persecution of wise and beautiful heathenisms" (115) turns readers' attention to societal reception of believers, a problem that concerns her in "Faerylands Forlorn," "Children of Light," "Capes of Good Hope," and "Cities of God." The distinctive approach to this topic in "The Mother Night" is to link the treatment of believers to the national trait of reticence. Dane suggests that British reluctance to express feelings publicly has arisen from centuries-old patriarchal suppression of citizens' freedoms.

Perhaps furtive expression has its uses, allowing Dane to insert a critique of the commercialization of Christmas into a magazine replete with advertisements for Christmas gifts, products, and services, under cover of a light-hearted exposé of the English attitude toward the expression of feeling: "We hate having our feelings appealed to publicly, except in the theatre" (15). Nonetheless, the English tolerate the charitable appeals on "flag days," not wanting to grudge the money to a worthy cause. But they make their donations while believing that "a public display of personal emotion is not quite decent" (15). Thus Shakespeare's Coriolanus chose to "mar his fortune" rather than display his wounds to earn the loyalty of the people. Dane continues, "it is the same feeling ... that influences our life-cheated ex-service men" (15). Others should make the charitable appeals on behalf of ex-servicemen without expecting them to display their wounds. A connection to the modern celebration of Christmas is not voiced but is available to the discerning reader: deep feeling—and spiritual belief—convert uneasily to the coin of monetary exchange.

"Children of Light"

In "The Mother Night," Dane examined the role of folk myth both to embody spiritual belief and to provide a subversive account of the historical division between clerical and popular belief. In "Children of Light" (1927) Dane again emphasizes how literary modes—here, irony, paradox, and comedy—at once encode spiritual wisdom and provide the forms for its renewal in each era.

Imaginative modernist writers, observes Pericles Lewis, sought to explore or renovate a range of spiritual experiences, including "borderline states of consciousness, forms of the divided self, the process of conversion, the function of ritual, [and] the magical potential inherent in words" (5). Dane theorized how inherently versatile literary tropes supported such spiritual experimentation. Alongside these modernists, she investigated the capacity of literary forms to keep pace with the period's changing spiritual sensibility. "Children of Light" specifically focuses on the paradox, a vehicle that leads the spiritual quester to arrive at complex truth. Dane also illustrates how other biblical forms, such as the archetype and the parable, help readers negotiate particular kinds of truth. Finally, having demonstrated the power of these forms, Dane explores the role of longer forms—drama and the novel—to do justice to the complexity of the conflict between the children of light and the children of this world.

"Children of Light" explores the "eternal" conflict between the "children of light" and the "children of this world," between those who pursue worldly success and those who, choosing to serve God, sacrifice their own chances of earthly happiness in order to benefit the world they leave behind (41). The recurrence of this archetypal conflict across mythic and literary traditions gives it compelling significance and establishes its continued cultural authority. Dane illustrates this clash by retelling two sacred parables. She then sketches more examples while demonstrating how several literary forms engage readers in discovering the spiritual insight they enfold.

The conflict is expressed in Luke's parable of the unjust steward. In the parable, Jesus tells his disciples about a steward who is accused of wasting the possessions of the rich man for whom he works. Hearing that he will be fired, the steward calls the employer's debtors in and discounts their debts, so that he may later seek shelter in their houses. "And the [rich man] commended the unjust steward, because he had done wisely: for the children of this world are in their generation wiser than the children of light" (Luke 16.8). It is the paradox of the children of light, sketched in verse 8, that interests Dane. Taking a comparative approach to illustrate the parable's truth, Dane moves smoothly from Jesus Christ to AEsir, ancient Norse children of light who battle giants of ice and snow in an Armageddon called Ragnarok. Dane explains the "sacrificial folly" of the AEsir: "*Tyr*, who gave his hand to save his fellows, will fight left-handed ... and *Odin*, who plucked out his eye to buy wisdom, will blunder in the battle, half-blind, and weaponless *Frey* will miss the sword that he exchanged for his love *Gerda*" (41). But although the children of light are ill-prepared for the battle, each of their sacrifices ultimately takes the form of a gift to be used in building a new heaven and a new earth: selflessness, wisdom, and love. The Norse myth provides a second example of the paradox, in Dane's words, that "the sacrificial folly of the children of light is an eternal blessing to humanity, while the wisdom of the children of this world serves its generation only and endures no longer" (41).

If human beings are indeed divided into two camps, with "worldly" people intent on the narrow sphere of their own interests and "enlightened" people dashing about to save the world, it is no wonder that Dane can sketch numerous examples of the contrast between them. Working her way through literary history, she traces the archetype of the children of light from original, venerable sources to contemporary expressions of it. Her heterogeneous examples, often supported by quotation, include Blake, Joan of Arc, St. Francis, Don Quixote, and Matthew Arnold's *Thyrsis*, among others. Analysis of Plato's *Apology* establishes the faith that poets are divinely inspired but have no "knowledge" as Socrates looks for it. But Dane lavishes most praise on two contemporary writers who give the archetype particular relevance in modernity: Hugh Walpole in *Harmer John* and George Bernard Shaw, whose crowning achievement in *Saint Joan* retrospectively illuminates many precursors in his dramatic *oeuvre*. Shaw's work proves the ongoing importance of the paradox: "It is indeed a remarkable thing," Dane opines, "that, in an age which in life and literature worships material and intellectual success," that is, an age in which the values of the children of this world prevail, "one of the acutest minds of the time should have been constantly preoccupied with this problem of the children of light" (165).

Throughout the essay, Dane underscores that beyond the themes and values they express, biblical literary forms—parables, aphorisms, paradoxes, etc.—are suited to enlighten and console audiences so as to guide them in their own lives. Dane's emphasis on literary form points to the importance of reading, and not simply prayer and regular Church attendance, in the Christian life. Social historians corroborate the historical importance of Christian reading and the variety of its aims. For much of their history, Britons were schooled in biblical stories and independently read stories of Christian heroes such as Bunyan's *The Pilgrim's Progress*. Linda Colley argues that patriotism strongly motivated such reading from the eighteenth century through the Second World War. The prospect of a Catholic monarchy was only one of a number of national threats that drove Britons to understand their role in a national campaign by reading the Bible, sermons, and popular Christian literature (25–9). And in the nineteenth century specifically, Evangelicalism played a significant role in the continuation and extension of Britons' pious reading:

> [Evangelicals] believed that the grace of God could, and did, descend to the individual man and woman through the printed page. The cultivation of the reading habit was therefore as indispensable as a daily program of prayer and observance of a strict moral code. With the Bible always at the center, there grew up a huge literature of admonition, guidance, and assurance. (Altick, *English Common Reader* 99)

For Dane, the literary form is important beyond its role to encode the wisdom of a particular sacred tradition, since it is the form that enables a truth to find new expression in each era and each culture. Thus, Dane praises the Norse myth: "When our Norse forefathers fashioned their heaven ... they but embodied in a tale their recognition of the eternal strife between two opposed ways of human living and thinking" (41). The tale, Dane tells readers, gives a body to—and thus makes live—an abstract or invisible truth. Dane returns to this point in discussing Hugh Walpole's new novel, *Harmer John*, whose "extraordinary interest for us," she finds, is that he clothes "these dry bones of tradition ... with real flesh and blood, breathing life" (166). Nor does Dane draw her examples of archetypes exclusively from the Bible. In the case of Shaw's drama, for instance, Dane designates the precursors to Saint Joan as eidola.[14]

Continuing to enlighten her readers about the virtues of short biblical forms, Dane tells them that "a truth perfectly expressed never degenerates into a mere wise saw," and therefore it becomes "to minds bewildered by the problems of life, a sort of clinging post, as welcome and necessary as a bollard to a fisherman landing

[14] Dane calls characters from Shaw's plays shadows or eidola, of the type that Shaw perfected in *Saint Joan*.

his boat in rough weather" (41). In "Children of Light," Dane highlights the distinct forms of truth delivered by paradox, comedy, and irony. For instance, the "truth perfectly expressed" that "the children of this world are in their generation wiser than the children of light" is also a paradox. How can it be that the pragmatic children of this world leave no legacy for their civilization, while the "sacrificial folly" of the children of light generates what will become the strengths of that civilization? Like the children of light in this example of a paradox, the form of the paradox yields its gifts only after sustained consideration and often only when historical perspective becomes possible. Indeed, in another dimension of the paradox gradually unfolded in the essay, Dane suggests that, though the children of this world may be busy accruing material goods for themselves alone, we cannot do without them, for they alone know how to communicate truth in the language of their day. In contrast, as Dane's examples from Blake and from Plato's *Apology* illustrate, children of light, those ciphers of divine wisdom, are perpetually charged with disruption, unpardonable offenses, and crimes punishable with death. Dane recalls the examples of St. Anthony and St. Francis. "How, for instance, can the dignity of the Church be maintained when one of its saints holds a service for the fish of the sea, and another insists on preaching to the fowls of the air?" Yet history teaches us to look beyond the judgment of their day: "in this tercentenary we celebrate the folly of St. Francis, not the wisdom of the clerics" (165). The very form of the paradox then, which many of Dane's readers first encountered in worship or in biblical reading, fosters both effortful reading to uncover meaning and patience in the pursuit of truth.

If the Bible is for some readers a source of faith, in Dane's journalism for *Good Housekeeping*, it is above all a rich compendium of literature. Shaw is for Dane an important contemporary playwright not merely because of his perennial interest in the problem of the children of light, but because he crafts dramatic forms that uniquely illuminate such cultural problems. As Dane considers Shaw's treatment of the children of light, she shows how the modes of tragedy, irony, and even comedy accommodate this collision of perspectives and provide compassionate contexts for it.

Dane argues that comedy characterizes the world of Shaw's visionary characters, and is, moreover, "the only possible way in which the type can be fairly and justly represented." That generic designation leads to Dane's insight that Shaw should be compared to Cervantes, not to Shakespeare: Cervantes "drew with the same humor and passion the tragic enthusiast in a comic world, the child of light, lost in the caves." On the other hand, "It was the disintegrating weakness in a man's soul that interested Shakespeare, not the fantastic strength" (166). Embedded in Dane's decisive sentences are insights about the choice of comedy vs. tragedy. In a tragedy, she implies, the world triumphs over the hero, but in a comedy, the reverse is true. Both Shaw and Cervantes, masters of the comic and the ironic, each in his own day, exhibit that "strength of the soul which the most exquisite mockery cannot destroy." Shaw has explored the "unreasonable chronicles of the children of light" and found in them "the substance of things hoped for, the evidence of things not seen" (166).[15] For Dane, Shaw's plays are occasions to teach her readers about such paradoxical literary tropes as the "tragic enthusiast in a comic world."

Dane selects Walpole's new novel *Harmer John* as her final example of a longer form that provides a compassionate context for conflict. The novel presents the collision of a child of light, here, a stranger-savior, and his society. As we saw, Dane emphasizes that the "extraordinary interest *for us*" of *Harmer John* is that Walpole gives modern flesh and blood to the "dry bones of tradition" (166) (my emphasis). Thus, Dane engages readers' interest in the novel through her analysis of its compelling characters and plot even while her diction points to the archetype; the worldly elements of its setting and characters create a bridge to its spiritual truth. What Dane calls Harmer John's "crazy innocence" refers back to the many examples in her essay of the savior's and his society's colliding perspectives. And to describe the hero at the crisis of the novel Dane intertwines biblical references and the diction of social realism. The visionary protagonist

> suffers his temptation in the wilderness: he conquers his devils: he goes his own obstinate unpopular way, opposing to the growing anger, hostility, malice and scorn of the townsfolk his unshaken faith in his dreams ... He has not built New Jerusalem: he has only cleaned, mended and set up again in its place a little lost fountain, the work of a forgotten artist that lay in ruins ... (166)

"Children of Light" exemplifies Dane's skill both to please and instruct. She balances breadth—for example, cataloguing many titles that conform to the archetype—and depth. By listing titles Dane conveys a sense of the recurrence and scope of the archetype

[15] This definition of faith comes from Hebrews 11.1.

and its variants: the visionary, the stranger, the savior. Such lists are counterpointed by her close attention to remarkable modern stories about children of light. These outstanding examples both illustrate and refine the type. And they are necessary for its renewal in modern society, Dane believes.

Ethical Applications

"Cities of God"

"Children of Light," "The Mother Night" and "Cities of God," as well as "Dream Holes," discussed later in the chapter, demonstrate that literature is a record of human belief. Each essay also underscores the conflicts that have shadowed inspiration and conviction. In a lay sermon delivered in the midst of the Second World War, Dane spoke about the Bible's profound legacy to shape British character, speech, and literature. But, she added, "never has there been a legacy so costly. It has been preserved [only through] the toil, the wars, the civil strife of millions" ("Britain's Heritage"). Dane's understanding of the historical intertwining of faith and conflict is reflected in these essays' humanistic attention to the visionary individual whose conviction transforms the very society that persecutes her.

This irony is at the center of "Cities of God" (1926), in which the visionary individual is the utopia builder. In this essay, Dane explores the archetype of the utopia, showing how conceptions of the ideal ordered city animate ancient myth and persist through literary history to the contemporary period. In turn, this significant literary record sheds light on contemporary society. Dane traces the expression in poetry, fiction, life writing, and society of recurrent archetypal elements which mark the history of religious belief and secular cultural debates alike.

In both sacred and secular exemplars, Dane demonstrates, literary utopias are generated by the human capacity to imagine the ideal; yet both strands feature flawed human beings. In a literary survey that ranges through Western literary history—a hallmark of her criticism—Dane considers both utopias and mock utopias. As she illustrates the many variations of the far-sighted city builder, she suggests that this human hero manifests an inherent, or god-given visionary power. Forward-looking Prometheus rebels against societal inequity, creates a better world, and is martyred for his efforts. These archetypal elements link the Greek myth to other figures across sacred traditions. Dane tells the history of the utopia with references to Plato's *Republic* and *Critias*, Thomas More's *Utopia*, Swift's *Gulliver's Travels*, Blake's *Jerusalem*, Samuel Butler's *Erewhon*, Edward Bulwer-Lytton's *The Coming Race*, the utopias of William Morris and of H.G. Wells, and new books such as Gerhart Hauptmann's *The Island of the Great Mother* and Geoffrey Faber's *Elnovia*. But she also demonstrates that the utopian impulse goes beyond literature and art: a history of Atlantis by Lewis Spence, a new edition of the letters of Hannah More, and contemporary societal debate about how to repair or replace Waterloo Bridge all take readers out of the realm of imaginative literature and into contemporary manifestations of the archetype.[16]

Dane offers her own humorous renditions of classical and biblical myth, familiarizing and domesticating its heroes to show that they act on essential human impulses. She references plenty of texts with Christian themes, from Spenser's *The Fairie Queen* to Blake's *Jerusalem*. But to say that she proselytizes would be to miss the point. Rather, Dane's interest is in tying the recurrence of archetypal patterns to religious sensibility. In turn, religious impulses spring from the human imagination. In "Cities of God," a story's imaginative power remains the pre-eminent criterion for judging its success. Most of us, Dane confides, "read the *Critias* oftener than we read the *Republic*. The story of lost Atlantis, the island city that a god built, ensnares the imagination more than the city of God that a man wanted to build" (136). What makes good literature is not its doctrinal strength but its power to fire the imagination. Dane's insight about the primacy of the imagination undergirds the rich continuum in "Cities of God" between sacred and secular texts and makes it one of Dane's most powerful essays about belief.

"Cities of God" frequently reminds readers of the utopia's origins in sacred literature. Dane also brings to the topic the insight that the human vision of the ideal city is always infiltrated by flaws, mockery, and even destructive impulses. As the utopianist tries to penetrate the mysteries of God's creation, his faculty of reason may destabilize the purity of his faith. Thus, in her survey of literary utopias Dane finds that notes of doubt and mockery often infiltrate the perfect land. In an original critical insight, she demonstrates that the mock utopia is already contained within the utopia, on which it comments

[16] Showing structural wear and tear, Waterloo Bridge was closed to traffic in May 1924. For ten years, heated debate about the fate of the bridge pitted advocates of strengthening and repairing it against proponents of constructing a modern bridge to replace it.

ironically. Far from opposing one another, the literary utopia and the mock utopia are disguised twins.

Just as the mock utopia undercuts the utopia, "Cities of God" shows how the drive to build a heavenly city is intertwined with the impulse to destroy a predecessor's edifice. Dane is attentive both to the irony of this dynamic and to the paradox it reflects. Although she does not name or define the term, paradox is clearly central to the experience of religious faith. "What is paradoxical about the mysteries of the faith," explains Catholic Culture, "is that reason cannot fully penetrate their meaning, so that what seems contradictory to reason is profoundly true in terms of faith" ("Paradox"). Dane's focus on paradox in her literary-critical discussion imitates the structure of believers' thought and feeling. One such paradox is that both sacred and secular literature reflects the utopian dream of the perfect city and the reality that such perfection would be inhuman. A myth must seize the imagination of its audience by bringing to it "something human and comprehensible," like the story of lost Atlantis (136). For this reason, Dane retells and domesticates several foundational myths. For example, she imagines a sequel to the story of Adam in which he writes down "the whole story of the sort of food, drink, wife, house and garden that he would really like if God, wind and weather and the wife would let him have his way" (45). Adam is a utopianist, she believes, and his clay side does not rest on the seventh day because the work of his hands "is not so good as the imagination of his heart" (45). The archetype of the celestial city records the human striving to reach the standard of what God has built.

But if it is human to dream of perfection, perfection leaves what is fully human out in the cold. Few authors of utopias realize this, Dane contends, though "Swift does when he feigns that the Houyhnhnms believe Gulliver to be dead because he swoons from grief at leaving them. For they are above grief" (134). While utopianists introduce notes of doubt into their ideal cities, satirists, conversely, betray a covert attraction to the utopian dream: "The beautiful idea bedevils them while they mock, like sour anchorites seduced by a nymph" (138). When we look closely, the satirist and the idealist are not so far apart, a point which illuminates the hold of the utopian idea on the human imagination.

A second paradox is embodied by the Promethean hero, who profoundly transforms but remains outside the community. The citizens benefit from, but have little understanding of, and take little interest in, his enterprise. He is essential to, but isolated from, the city. If Prometheus is the public-spirited urban planner, Epimetheus is the homebody who warms his hands at the hearth fire, gazing at the embers and dreaming of his own golden past. Dane modernizes the love between Pandora and Epimetheus, presenting the ordinary, domestic happiness that is made possible by Prometheus's rebellion even while the married lovers remain ironically unaware of his heroism. In Dane's entertaining retelling of the myth, Pandora chooses Epimetheus because when the gods bring her to Prometheus, he barely notices her, and, indeed, the faraway look in his eyes makes him queer:

> Prometheus—of course I'm very fond of Prometheus—he's your brother after all: and I do know what a lot of trouble he had getting us this fire, and I'm sure I hope it isn't too cold on Caucasus, and that the vulture's beak has worn blunt by now, but Prometheus—well, you know, Prometheus was a queer person. (134)

Their average, married-couple complacency is perhaps that of most households. Yet it is not their domestic story, but the tales of visionary reformers that record and keep alive human belief in the possibility of a better world.

In his own time, however, Prometheus gets a lukewarm reception at best. Dane emphasizes the comedy arising from the discordant perspectives of Prometheus and Epimetheus. And as we find in Dane's essays on myth and history, including "Children of Light," "Dream Holes" and "Faerylands Forlorn," the prophet's words fall on deaf ears and his vision is misconstrued. Dane pursues that preoccupation in "Cities of God." The Promethean hero lives amidst Epimethean married lovers for whom utopia is their own golden past and who take little interest in the heroic deed from which they benefit.

Razers and Reformers

To realize his solitary dream, the lone utopianist often destroys the work of a predecessor. Dane traces this element of the archetype to ancient religious myth. Her references to the biblical celestial city bookend heterogeneous expressions of the archetype within the essay. "Cities of God" begins with the vision of Jerusalem in the Book of Revelation and ends with Dane's invitation to her audience to call London the "Dear City of God."[17] The epigraph and the caption for

[17] The Book of Revelation is significant not only because John describes his vision of Jerusalem, but because, as scholars believe, it treats a contemporary crisis of faith analogous to that experienced by Britons from the late nineteenth century and well into the twentieth century (Britannica, "Revelation to John").

the first-page illustration quote Revelation: "And he carried me away in the spirit to a great and high mountain, and shewed me that great city, the holy Jerusalem, descending out of heaven from God" (*King James Bible*, Revelation 21.10). But Dane promptly reminds readers that alongside this gated city radiant with the glory of God there is "a bye-way to hell ... on the very hillside of the Coelestial City;[18] for the Spirit that delights in destruction is always in shadow-close attendance on the Spirit that dreams of Utopia and the kingdom of heaven" (45). It is these intertwined human impulses—the striving to reach or build a heavenly city and the impulse to destroy an edifice—that interest Dane in "Cities of God."

Writing about Blake's "Jerusalem" (1810), she points out the painful gap between the celestial city of Revelation, in which "there shall be no more death, neither sorrow, nor crying, neither shall there be any more pain" and Blake's infernal industrial London:

> And did the Countenance Divine,
> Shine forth upon our clouded hills?
> And was Jerusalem builded here,
> Among these dark Satanic Mills?

"Cities of God" asks whether cities on earth can be built to cultivate civility and civilization, if not divine peace. Ultimately Dane finds that there is third way to be considered alongside the satirist and the idealist: the reformer who neither seeks to undermine another's creation nor strives for divine perfection. She points out that many utopias and mock utopias, whose practitioners have been predominantly men, are realized only by destroying the efforts of a forerunner. In contrast, women's utopias reform an existing city.

For Dane, Rudyard Kipling's "The Palace" (1903) perfectly illustrates the male way of realizing one's vision by razing the edifice of a predecessor. The speaker, a "King and a Mason," as he prepares to build a palace, comes upon the wreck of a previous king's palace. He proceeds to destroy contemptuously what remains of his predecessor's work. But the creation of his predecessor speaks to him as clearly as if he had risen from the dead:

> ... yet, as we wrenched them apart,
> I read in the razed foundations the heart of that builder's heart.

[18] The quotation draws on language in *The Pilgrim's Progress*, Section VIII. "This is a by-way to hell, a way that hypocrites go in at."

> As he had risen and pleaded, so did I understand
> The form of the dream he had followed in the face of the thing he
> had planned. (13–16)

Each palace builder is likely to suffer the same fate as the speaker's predecessor. We recall that Dane's reading of the celestial city in Revelation included the caution that "the Spirit that delights in destruction is always in shadow-close attendance on the Spirit that dreams of Utopia and the kingdom of heaven" (45). Dane cements this point with a reference to Max Beerbohm's essay "Something Defeasible," in which the essay persona witnesses a little boy construct an elaborate sandcastle, and is on hand later when the incoming sea water dissolves it. What interests Beerbohm is the delight in destruction on the part of all parties. First the onlooking children exult, then the young architect himself exchanges his sobriety for "intense animation." To Beerbohm the "glare of his eyes was less indicative of a dreamer than of a triumphant fiend," and he concludes, "It was the boy's own enthusiasm that made me feel, as never before, how deep-rooted in the human breast the love of destruction, of mere destruction, is." Dane refutes, or at least qualifies, this view. The picture looks very different when we include women's utopias.

In the last part of the essay, two books about women's civilizing work in the world contrast to men's satirical imagination in literature. Dane pivots from male to female utopianists with the comment, "What Gothic cities men build impatiently in their hearts for their gods to dwell in, forgetting the God who chose for His company publicans and sinners!" (138). As we will see, Dane's analysis of utopian destruction vs. utopian reform supports her conviction, obliquely expressed, that Jesus followed the model of reform, coming among ordinary men and women and working in the imperfect world as he found it.

To "remodel and reform," Dane opines, is a "prosaic way" of "Utopianising," less "spectacular" but more "humane" than the "large-gestured" creation of "spacious desolation" before building (45). These reformers should be counted among visionary builders. After observing that women do not seem to write utopias, she offers two examples of women's city building in history and contemporary society. Dane says that as far as she can remember women have never *written* a utopia (138, 140). But sometimes women *build* one. As she turns to women, then, Dane does not work to identify a women's literary tradition of utopias. Nor are women singled out as architects with unique visions. Instead, Dane establishes the importance of women's civic contributions. Her first example is the religious writer and educator of the poor, Hannah More. Dane has recently read a collection of More's letters, edited by R. Brimley Johnson.[19] These give an account of her Promethean efforts to build "cities on an island in her time," including her efforts to set up schools in England. The kind of cities More built, then, would align with Cicero's idea of the divinely sanctioned city governed by "councils and assemblies of men bound together by law."[20] Dane's second example is Emma Cons, whose restoration of the Old Vic was then the subject of a new book by Cicely Hamilton and Lilian Baylis.[21] In bringing this derelict theater back to life, Cons helped remediate the notorious slum district of London. Quoting Kingsley's *Alton Locke*, where the slum is referred to as a "licensed pit of darkness," Dane reminds her readers of the biblical association between slums and hell. Cons followed women's motto of "adapt, modify, improve!" (140). Dane dwells on the resulting benefits to London and to England: "What the Old Vic has done for Londoners and through them is well known." And the story of how it was done inspires pride and humility in the hearts of Cons's compatriots and prompts Dane to inscribe her copy of the book with the motto "Dear City of God." In so doing, she follows a tradition of Ovid and Marcus Aurelius.[22]

The design of "Cities of God" invites readers to draw the contrast between men's destructive methods of utopia and women's reforming approach. In Dane's two accounts of women's efforts to build or renovate communities, the essay turns away from religious myth but not away from the archetype of the utopia. It moves on from imaginative literature to take up historical and present-day heroism that arises from an individual's vision applied to a public good.

Like Dane's foundational essays on the topics of faith, hope, and belief—"This Century's Religion," "Children of Light" and "The Mother Night"—the essays featured in "Ethical Applications" acknowledge threats to human faith, hope, and idealism. Dane continues to explore the classic and modern texts that illuminate the complexity of threats such as the archetypal struggle between the

[19] Hannah More, 1745–1833, was a religious writer, educator of the poor, and participant in the Bluestockings.

[20] Cicero (105–43 BCE) outlines his vision in Scipio's Dream, which figures in his *On the Republic*. According to N. Miller, "Cicero's purpose is to show how public service, the importance of civic life, is a divinely sanctioned activity."

[21] *The Old Vic*, Jonathan Cape, 1926.

[22] See Marcus Aurelius, *Meditations* 4.23.

builder and the razer discussed in "Cities of God." But "Cities of God," "The Sixth Commandment" and "Capes of Good Hope" also reach beyond literature and beyond *Good Housekeeping* readers as they seek to apply ethical principles to societal problems. Each of these essays identifies stakeholders—civic activists, cultural critics, and nonfiction writers—whom Dane then calls on to influence popular conceptions of these problems.

"Capes of Good Hope," "The Sixth Commandment," and the Mass Media

Whereas in "The Mother Night" Dane decried the undue influence of clerical authority in the historical determination of Christianity in Britain, in the twentieth century she identifies a new and troublesome influence over moral standards and spiritual belief: the new mass media. "Capes of Good Hope" (1925) and "The Sixth Commandment" (1926) deplore the distorting influence of print media on citizens' attitudes toward societal and moral problems. In "Capes of Good Hope," mass technology nominally connects people around the globe, but Dane worries that unrelenting news stories of human atrocity estrange comfortable English audiences from distant humanitarian crises. In "The Sixth Commandment," Dane acknowledges that human spiritual energy may be manifested in evil and criticizes the tendency of news media to sensationalize crime. Both essays recognize the capacity of literature to treat moral problems with appropriate magnitude and call on imaginative writers to exert an ethical influence on novel readers and theater audiences.

"Capes of Good Hope" is concerned with unfashionable belief in an era of cynicism. Dane chooses three works of contemporary literature that prompt her to affirm her belief in human goodness. Her evaluation of each text foregrounds her position in a critical minority and outside of critical fashion. She is aware that others may call "sentimental" a novel she calls "beautiful"; that others may find a drama to be cynical, where she finds it hopeful (114). Such books are "like headlands coming into sight after a dreary voyage—green headlands, Capes of Good Hope" (112). "Capes of Good Hope" thus models the persistence of hope and belief even when it means rowing against the tide.

"Capes of Good Hope" is one of a handful of essays in which Dane explicitly situates herself in relation to other critics. She models her efforts to find hope in a predatory world, but is not satisfied with her own peace of mind. She is not writing as a personal essayist but as a cultural critic, and her deep concern is what it would mean for British culture to be dominated by cynicism. Dane looks beyond her *Good Housekeeping* readers first to the professional critical community to gauge their interest in recognizing and praising creative expressions of belief in human goodness. Belief or cynicism are not visitations from the ether but are intentional acts. But, ultimately, Dane calls on the collective power of creative writers. In her single monthly column she can dwell on the virtues of one or two remarkable, hopeful books, but a *series* of such books will be needed to turn the tide of British society toward hope.

As in her other essays about belief, in "Capes of Good Hope" Dane posits a conflict between two prevailing societal outlooks, in this case cynicism and hope. In each of these essays, Dane argues that while only a minority of her contemporaries feel hopeful or believe in human good, the case for belief is strong. Dane gives voice to both outlooks in the course of her book essay, but ultimately affirms hope. She begins, however, by positing that cynicism or apathy are inevitable. She tells an anecdote about her cat catching and killing a beloved wagtail: "For two years a wagtail has strutted and dipped on the lawn under my window with the undulating, incessant motion that he learnt, I suppose, from the ripples of the river hard by. He was the prettiest small friendly thing and—such a good father!" (49). When her cat pounces on the pretty wagtail, Dane is reading "The End of Gordon" in *Eminent Victorians*, which for Dane confirms the truism that sooner or later the cat captures the wagtail.[23]

Strachey not only confirms the truism; he shows that each act of deadly violence begets fresh violence.[24] "How hateful life is, with the cat always lying in wait for the wagtail, and always, always getting him in the end!" Dane concludes (49). But after reading Noël Coward's *The Vortex*, Dane is ashamed of "my cat and wagtail grizzle" and proclaims her thesis that even if one is called a sentimentalist or an idealist, "to cease to believe in the ultimate good end of the cat-and-wagtail tragedy is to die in your soul" (110).

[23] Published in 1918, Lytton Strachey's irreverent portraits of four eminent Victorians revolutionized English biography. Each reflected his view that the biographer should "attack his subject in unexpected places" (vii).

[24] In 1883, the British government had commissioned General Charles George Gordon, former Governor-General of Sudan, to evacuate Egyptian soldiers and civilians during a revolt led by Mohammed Ahmed, the self-proclaimed Mahdi. Against orders, Gordon tried to defend Kartoum against rebel forces led by Mohammed Ahmed. In January 1885, the Mahdi's forces succeeded in capturing Kartoum and executed Gordon. Dane includes the British Empire among the violent parties.

Dane praises Coward for his "courage to refuse to assume the fashionable pose of disillusionment," and, in turn, attends to the fashionable disillusionment that characterizes critical reception of *The Vortex* (110). Dane was led to expect a "hatefully witty, wittily hateful" play that was "the very last word in the topsy-turvying of relationships that the war has made the fashion," but finds nothing of the kind when she reads the play (49). She suggests, in fact, that the currency of the "admiringly catty" reviews coming thick and fast in the papers is that they are in vogue, not that they are critically astute. Indeed, there is little correspondence between Dane's lexicon and that of the cynics. "[A]nyone who cares for the to-morrow of English drama must surely be moved," Dane declares: "For here is a young writer who actually believes in old-fashioned faith and hope and charity—and says so" (49, 110).

Dane's interest in *The Vortex* extends beyond its hopeful outlook. She is impressed that the skillful author of this "box office success" knows how "to make people believe in his 'I believe!'" and that he has many years of playwrighting ahead of him (110). Audiences' enjoyment of the play will make Coward's "I believe!" infectious, Dane opines. And what he believes is "that there is a god in us as well as a beast, and that in the end, though we do not see the end, the god will win" (110). Moreover, just as newspapers prompt disillusionment and even apathy through regular bulletins of human atrocities committed near and far, Dane hopes that she is "watching the beginning of a series" that can counter this trend (110). She argues that the publications of individual young writers who believe in human goodness are promises of more such literature to come. The daily press does not have a monopoly on seriality.

In reviewing Hillaire Belloc's *Mr. Petre*, Dane again turns against critical trends to find spiritual meaning in a portrayal of a cynical contemporary society. Of the books she discusses in "Capes of Good Hope," only Belloc's novel speaks of religious faith—or its absence. And even then, Dane makes the point that she deliberately hears a religious register in what she admits is an "amusing, witty extravaganza." Dane interpolates this religious meaning into Belloc's novel by setting the "august" words of St. John in dialogue with it: "Peace I leave with you: my peace I give unto you: not as the world giveth, give I unto you!" (John 14.27, qtd. in "Capes of Good Hope" 112). This unworldly peace is absent from *Mr. Petre*.

The eponymous protagonist of *Mr. Petre* finds himself pulled into the mill of money-making, even though he "loathes the money and the money-makers, and the world where money is made." He is helplessly caught in the grip of "the holy spirit of business," Dane says, suggesting that the pursuit of material wealth has supplanted the quest for spiritual wealth in modern society. For the steadfast Christian faith of St. George, the patron saint of England, seems to be absent from the modern world. A second reading of the novel elicits Dane's own ethical responses; she even hears Belloc making similar pleas:

> But where nowadays—you hear Mr. Belloc demanding of the unmoved heavens—is St. George to come from? And what, you privately add, when St. George had slain the dragon did St. George do with the money-bags which he undoubtedly found in the dragon's cave? (112).

Dane imagines St. George riding away from the dragon's treasure, "still a poor knight, but one sure of heaven, which is only another word for the peace of God" (112). Belloc leaves open the question of whether Mr. Petre will attain that peace, for as the novel concludes his hero is sounding the question of "how to give big money and not give a curse with it" (111). Whereas Noël Coward in *The Vortex* believed in "faith and hope and charity—and says so!" (110), in the case of *Mr. Petre*, the reader must bring her own belief to the novel. Thus, if after an initial reading of *Mr. Petre* Dane concluded that it was "a flighty trifle meant—surely meant—to amuse for half an hour in the train" (112), upon her second reading she recognizes that Belloc is "obliquely protesting" against a climate of apathy, the "'what's the use of anything, why nothing'" attitude (112). Only her own belief allows her to hear Belloc's oblique one.

As we have seen, in discussing the critical reception of *The Vortex*, Dane called attention to the rapid succession of reviews that quickly formed a critical consensus. And in her review of several more new books, Dane continues her analysis of the power of newspapers and magazines to shape audience responses, a concern shared by many of her peers. In this period of unprecedented high literacy rates, almost everyone read, and what they read were mass circulation daily papers, Sunday papers, and local papers. As Chris Baldick puts it, newspapers and magazines provided the "most regular and most formative relationship between the majority of the population and the written word. Almost everything else that was written, and most of what was read in this period, was in some way shaped by the overwhelming commercial and cultural dominance of these publications" (*The Oxford English Literary History* 17). But it should not be assumed that periodicals' commercial stake precluded their reflexive criticism of their commercial and cultural influence. *Good Housekeeping* provides a case in point. From its fashion pages to the *Good Housekeeping* seal of approval for household products, to advertisements for consumer goods, its imbrication in commerce is clear. Yet as Dane's essays demonstrate, commercial publications like *Good Housekeeping* in the mid-1920s expressed concern about the power of radio, newspapers, and magazines to establish trends and fashions not merely in such highly visible links to the marketplace as ads and fashion pages, but in the voices of journalists and critics.

In "The Sixth Commandment" Dane deplores the newspaper's mediation of societal attitudes, especially its indiscriminate juxtaposition of serious news and entertaining tidbits, which are themselves laid out alongside ads for consumer products. Dane worries in particular about one effect of this mediation on readers, the trivialization of murder. Like a decadent and delectable food, a reported murder crime, says Dane, is "a weakness to which many of us confess, or why should murder trials be better copy even than divorce cases?" (74). In both essays, too, Dane calls for literature to restore to a serious subject its proper proportions. In "The Sixth Commandment," Dane proposes that nonfiction take up the role of sensible and informative communication about homicide, and that imaginative literature help shift the reaction to murder from a sensational thrill to horror. In this spirit she critiques a new nonfiction book by F. Tennyson Jesse, *Murder and its Motives*. Dane believes that Jesse has missed an opportunity to enlighten the public. Instead of detailing "six not very interesting criminals" Dane wishes that Jesse had written "a chapter on the attitude of the community to the whole problem ... It is, after all, the attitude of the public which is the most worth studying" (74). Dane calls for a sociological study, not a lesson in pathology. At the heart of the matter is the question: "Why does murder thrill?," to which Dane adds, "It ought to shock, horrify, disgust or frighten" (74). "The attitude of the public" has been shaped, she hints, not just by mass media but also by misguided playwrights who have failed to follow the Greeks. For the Greeks understood that murder is *obscene*, to be kept off stage. "The Sixth Commandment" calls for nonfiction studies, playwrights, and novelists to arouse shock and horror when they represent murder; that is, to make audiences feel murder's moral force. Eliciting these moral reactions requires tools other than the graphic depiction of blood and gore. Dane makes her case in discussion of Shakespearean tragedy as well as a new novel by Louis Golding, *Day of Atonement*.

"The Sixth Commandment" makes two distinct contributions to the theorization of this moral force. First, Dane recognizes that violent crime grows out of and must be checked by an entire community. Second, Dane connects violence to the manifestation of human spiritual power. As she says after reading *Day of Atonement*, "the breath of a god [is] in every man, or if not a god then a devil's power" (204).

In contrast to her concern with communal responsibility in "The Sixth Commandment," in "Capes of Good Hope," Dane targets the critical community. She reflects on tides of critical fashion that become difficult to resist: each voice that contributes to a growing consensus builds a critical template, making it more difficult for subsequent critics to dissent. In the case of *The Vortex*, a critical fashion acts as a magnet to draw more and more journalists and audiences to subscribe. But in a contrary trend, the repetition of distant humanitarian crises leads audiences to unsubscribe from feelings of concern. Readers overloaded with news of crises on the other side of the globe succumb to apathy, while cynicism becomes a media-fueled fashion. In both these examples, what concerns Dane is that cynicism is fashionable, and that fashion is fueled by communication media.

As Dane turns her attention to newspaper reporting of global events, she identifies three intertwined phenomena that contribute to readers' emotional distance from the urgent human crises they are reading about: first, the daily repetition of such news stories; second, the simultaneous proximity and distance of the crises; and, third, editorial decisions about article length and layout and their oblique judgment about what is important. The most influential cultural critics of the day saw that audience estrangement was at the heart of the mass media experience.[25] Dane observes that the average Briton's awareness of the world is mediated by the morning *Times*, which they consume alongside their eggs and bacon. And she worries that such mediation gives apathy a foothold. She is disturbed by what Michael North describes as the simultaneous nearness of events taking place far away and the emotional distance created by the mediation of the newspaper, film, or radio broadcast (North 15–18).

Newspaper page layout and word count also influence audiences, Dane perceives. How, she asks, does the brief column space devoted

[25] See North 18. As Lippmann put it in *Drift and Mastery*, "We are all of us immigrants in the industrial world, and we have no authority to lean upon ... The evidence is everywhere: the amusements of the city; the jokes that pass for jokes; the blare that stands for beauty, the folklore of Broadway, the feeble and apologetic pulpits, the cruel standards of success, raucous purity" (qtd. in Steel 80).

to the Rif War in Morocco and the greater space allotted to the Epstein *Rima* controversy tacitly communicate an evaluation of their relative importance?[26] Spain and France were the imperial powers trying to crush the indigenous Berber tribes in the Rif, but, Dane implies, it might just as well have been a report of British imperial violence. For *The Times* is "accustomed to reporting atrocities permitted nearer home than Morocco" (111), in spaces meant to "secure English identity," as Simon Gikandi notes (165). Additionally, Dane decries the frequency with which the daily papers are obliged to report atrocities. *The Times* is "accustomed" to reporting such atrocities, and Dane worries that such regular reporting will inure readers to evil. Have readers become so accustomed to reading about atrocities that they merely shrug their shoulders as if to say "It's all in the day's, the world's, work"? (111).[27]

Of course, it is the atrocities themselves that most concern Dane. A journalist like her counterparts at *The Times*, Dane nonetheless takes a critical and not merely reportorial approach. She models the questions that humane citizens must ask: "Why do people commit atrocities? What do they get out of it? Why do we let them do it? As Galsworthy says somewhere, 'What second-hand devil is it that gets into us when we run in packs?'" (111).

Inclusive Circles of Belief

This chapter has demonstrated that Dane defends all forms of spiritual inquiry, believing that the practice of belief is essential to individual health and civic life. The chapter will conclude with an analysis of two essays in which Dane identifies and applauds a range of spiritual activity that extends beyond traditional forms of religious worship. In a study of largely secular literature, "Dream Holes" represents the literary and social mechanisms by which belief is transmitted, transformed, and diversified. And "Faerylands Forlorn" argues that many self-declared skeptics do experience spirit, but channel and rename

[26] The unveiling in May 1925 of Jacob Epstein's sculpture honoring novelist Henry Hudson, a panel representing the character Rima, led to a raging debate about public art in articles and letters in London newspapers. As Caroline Levine argues, the controversy centered on the value of avant-garde art: "Letters to the press repeatedly bewailed Epstein's rejection of traditional artistic styles, and particularly his refusal to imitate nature faithfully."

[27] Dane notices, corroborating North, that one effect of this simultaneous nearness and distance is cynicism. North argues that the new global mobility in the 1920s and the media "both contribute to a greater sophistication, even to cynicism" (North 18).

their convictions as modern pastimes or fields of study. Both essays challenge the post-Enlightenment tendency to dichotomize belief and reason, setting them in antagonistic camps. Instead, each essay conceptualizes an inclusive and expanded circle of believers. Dane's mission in these two essays, then, is to foster belief and tolerance. For Dane, as we saw in "Capes of Good Hope," the exercise of imagination and belief prepares readers to serve as citizens with conviction and hope.

The concerns expressed in "Dream Holes" (1928) sit at the intersection of belief and literature. It asks, "How can literature give us an indirect sense of the divine?" Dane's subject in the essay is human beings' curiosity about the eternal, and she develops a modest genealogy to classify literary movements (realism, Romanticism) and writers according to the strength of writers' desire to perceive the eternal. "Dream Holes" additionally surveys a variety of literary genres that have proven their capacity to render visionary experience, considering the role of poetry, essays, and children's literature to express human beings' yearning to see the eternal.

Dane points out that this human desire has varied tremendously across history and culture. She sketches an allegory of "dream hole literature" to delineate these differences. According to provincial glossaries, "dream holes" are "the openings left in the wall of steeples, towers, barns, &c for the admission of light"(Grose). If the term "dream hole" is not Dane's, the concept of dream hole literature appears to be. The human being in relation to eternal things is like a prisoner in "a windowless tower with two locked doors," Dane's allegory begins. "He knows that he has been brought in through one, and will one day be carried out at the other," she continues. Although the tower is without windows, the builder has afforded a small aperture for the admission of light, "dream holes," as "the country people call them" (33). A dream hole is set so high up that only those who clamber up the tower walls may see outside it. Others in the tower choose merely to sit under the shaft of light admitted by the dream hole. Still others—Dane mentions philistines and realists—interest themselves only in the things of this world and make no attempt to benefit from dream holes.[28]

"Dream Holes" demonstrates that spiritual experience is fundamental to some of the world's great literature, including modern

[28] Dane's introduction of the designation *philistine* exposes the trace of religious strife and contention that continue to stigmatize the philistine. The Philistine was once among those who sought God, but persecution and stigma isolated him from fellow—or alien—believers.

secular literature. Dane's theory of dream hole literature explains how. When we look closely at some of the most radiant passages in poetry and personal essays, we can trace them to writers' desire to keep alive a tradition of ecstatic experience even when they have lost the capacity or the will to perceive the eternal world directly. Literary emulation and friendship have established the pathways by which they have looked indirectly at the divine world, immersing themselves in and reworking the visionary literature of others. "Dream Holes" offers no direct analysis of religion and faith in modern British society, pointing readers instead to the sublimation of spiritual instinct in creative activity.

Much of "Dream Holes" is devoted to writers and artists who look through "a child's dream hole" (132), including Blake, Dickens, Barrie, Ewing, Carroll, Stevenson, Jefferies, Graham, Nesbitt, Kipling, and Masefield. In addition to John Masefield's newly published *The Midnight Folk*, Dane takes particular interest in a new edition of Blake's *Songs of Innocence*, illustrated by a child, Jacynth Parsons. Dane finds unpromising the idea of a child refashioning Blake's own remarkable visual and poetic designs, but her skepticism dissolves when she turns over the pages of the review copy:

> [Parsons's] *Night*, and *Little Boy Lost*, to name only two out of the series, are no reverent feeble reflections of a great artist's thought: they are the young visions of an independent spirit: and very strange and new and beautiful they are. ... there for once the visions of youth are recorded, not by an older man or woman remembering the view from the dream hole, but by the child who is still looking through. (134)

Dane praises Parsons's independence from Blake, yet Blake has inspired these "young visions of an independent spirit." Dane's remarks bring into focus her two major concerns in "Dream Holes": the distinction between direct and indirect spiritual experience; and, related to that, the happy effects of literary influence.

The generative insight supporting "Dream Holes" is that the true range and diversity of human spiritual expression can only be grasped by looking much further than retellings of the Bible or literary explorations of Christian themes. As I have explored Dane's concept of belief in this chapter, I have noted her identification and inclusion of many unconventional spiritual phenomena and practices. Dane's analysis of literary influence is a good example, for it yields a rank of writers and artists who express their yearning for the eternal only indirectly.

Figure 4.2 Illustration by Jacynth Parsons for "Little Boy Found" in *Songs of Innocence*, by William Blake. Courtesy of The Medici Society Ltd.

Some writers, Dane tells readers, do not clamber up to the dream hole but allow their account of this world to be bathed in the light coming through the peep hole to the eternal. Dane includes in this group "wise" essayists, alluding to Montaigne and Bacon, then turns to Charles Lamb, Edmund Gosse, and Max Beerbohm, essayists who "bathe [their] subjects in the queer brightness, like the brightness of the air on a snowy day" (33). Indeed, she credits Gosse with a "radiant transformation" of Lucian of Samostene's take on the story of Helen and Cinyras, which she calls an "arid bit of mockery" (131).

Consideration of literary influence sheds further light on figures in Dane's allegory who opt not to look through the dream hole but to be bathed in the light coming through it. In poets' translations of classical authors and in their poetic tributes to predecessors, Dane finds a record of their desire to locate the eternal world and to recreate its beauty in poetry. Poetic language, she argues, may be the substance that enables writers to sit in the shaft of dream hole light. Dane's most developed example in this category is the literary friendship of Andrew Lang and Edmund Gosse.[29] Dane alludes to Lang's and Gosse's contributions to *English Worthies*, a new series of biographies of Englishmen of "influence and distinction"; Lang edited the series.[30] Dane further quotes from Lang's poem "L'Envoi to E.W.G. [Edmund W. Gosse]," included in *His Friends Old and Young*, in which Lang establishes his poetic link to Gosse through their common indebtedness to Lucian. Dane alludes only partially to this dense fabric of male homosocial bonds and their intellectual benefits when she quotes Lang's verse tribute to Lucian:

> The sage who laughed the world away,
> Who mocked at Gods, and men, and care,
> More sweet of voice than Rabelais,
> And lighter-hearted than Voltaire.

But *Good Housekeeping* readers who retrieved Lang's poem in its entirety would see that it begins with an acknowledgment of Lang's and Gosse's shared poetic vocation: "Each in the self-same field we glean / The field of the Samosatene, / Each something takes and something leaves / And this must choose, and that forego / In Lucian's visionary sheaves, ..." Perhaps missing an opportunity for feminist critique of this male network (and notably in contrast to Virginia Woolf in *A Room of One's Own*), Dane emphasizes instead each writer's mining the work of a predecessor who seemed to hold the key to the quality and texture of an other, eternal world. Woolf demonstrates the exclusion of female students and writers from the mechanisms of literary influence and mentorship. In contrast, Dane focuses on the benefits of male literary friendship to readers who enjoy a resplendent literary production. Both writers are conscious of the age-old homosocial cultural practices, but Dane turns aside from a feminist analysis to suggest the conserving tendencies of a

[29] Gosse and Lang were among the English Parnassians who turned to formal French poetic forms in the afterglow of the Pre-Raphaelite movement. Minor poets of technical proficiency, they were drawn together by their common interests. See Marysa Demoor.

[30] New York: D. Appleton. The first volume, *Charles Darwin*, by Grant Allen, was published in 1885.

literary tradition that, century after century, allows readers indirect access to dream holes.

In "Faerylands Forlorn" (1925), part book essay, part cultural criticism, Dane enjoins her readers to have faith in their convictions. Synthesizing literary and non-literary examples, Dane explores the experience of conviction, societal hostility to believers, and the faithfuls' strategies for concealment. But her most important purpose in this essay is to expand the circle of believers. Many of her readers, she understands, might answer "no" to the question "Has faeryland a definite existence?" (150). But Dane points out that all of us, in our dreams, experience secret places and other worlds, and she enjoins her audience to heed the evidence of their senses and claim the validity of their own experiences: Shouldn't these be the basis of belief in reality?

> For if seeing is believing, if hearing, touching, tasting, tears and laughter are proofs of reality, how can we doubt our dreams? But if reality is not a question of the five senses, then what in the name of Puck and common sense, is reality, and where shall we set up the boundary-stones of belief? (150)

Like the other essays of belief discussed in this chapter, "Faerylands Forlorn" concerns itself with the problem of belief in an age of skepticism. Dane explores the private experience of unconventional belief—the intuitions, visions, and convictions that reality lies just on the other side of the workaday world. She puts new books in dialogue with the literary history of belief in fairies as well as with such critically mainstream visionaries as William Blake and Dorothy Wordsworth. She also assesses societal hostility to untraditional belief, the divide between believers and nonbelievers created by such hostility, and the social marginalization of believers. Dane does not merely ask her readers to reconsider their skepticism about others' belief; she calls them out to identify themselves as believers of one form or another. Frequently describing the experience of "eccentric" or "naïve" believers, she then turns the mirror of her representation back upon her supposedly rational audience. "Faerylands Forlorn" thus enlarges the circle of believers by expanding the concept of belief.

In Dane's view, an individual's intuitions, dreams, and visions, if they are taken for signs of reality, are usually ridiculed by others, leading believers to conceal their convictions. In contrast, public expressions of belief—Dane includes everything from churchgoing to psychoanalytic treatises about the subconscious—are often revered, even though public affirmations of belief may bear little relation to the apprehension of spirit. As we noted earlier in the chapter, there was marked concern in the early twentieth century that traditional forms of worship in Britain were declining.[31] Dane herself holds little stock in public forms of worship. She notes the Victorians' continued adherence to the practice of worship even when belief was absent; and, more broadly, criticizes a tendency for congregations—or theatergoers—to affirm their belief in "loud tones" that on the contrary suggest little connection to their own spiritual lives. But Dane does acknowledge a widespread yearning to locate and perceive spirit, and she draws a distinction between popular movements and private faith. She argues, for example, that one may "mock at 'spiritualism,' and yet believe that the spirit survives" (150).[32] At the same time that she develops this criticism of worship, Dane seeks to expand the circle of self-proclaimed believers and, to that end, invokes a community of undeclared believers.

Archetypes of the Hidden Holy Place

> It is always the same land. Avalon, St. Brandan's Isle, the Middle Land, the Beanstalk Country, the Earthly Paradise, the Land of Youth, the Isle of Apples, the Land of Heart's Desire—what are they but names, such fair fantastic names ... for the Kingdom of Heaven itself. (156)

Dane's conclusion to "Faerylands Forlorn," appearing in slightly shorter form as the epigraph, underscores the universal fascination with a holy land that is elsewhere. "Faerylands Forlorn" explores the related archetypes of the hidden, holy place and the human being who travels to it. First, there is the passage to a designated or hidden place for belief. The lost land is both longed-for and separatist, created because of the antagonism of nonbelievers. This motif acts as a metaphor for Dane's thesis about skepticism, that it conceals belief which continues to live. The importance of this archetype can be gleaned by its presence in literature and in lived experience, in childhood and, more rarely, in adulthood. Thus, in another sense, the land beyond the workaday world is lost upon our passage from

[31] Pericles Lewis makes a more nuanced assessment of this decline. He posits a divide between elite groups who were considering "the spiritual possibilities of life outside a church or synagogue" and the broader culture, which remained traditionally religious (3).

[32] Spiritualism, the belief that the spirits of the dead may communicate with the living, was enormously popular in the 1920s. Edward Cecil wrote for *The Globe* that it was "spreading like wildfire" (qtd. in Staveley-Wadman).

childhood to adulthood. The intuition that reality is greater than the material world we perceive "is a state of mind that all children know, though most forget it as they grow up," says Dane, alluding to Wordsworth's "Intimations of Immortality" (150).

Moreover, the protagonist's passage to another land links childhood reading of fairy tales to biography and society. Dane makes a connection between human encounters with fairies, as recounted in Edith Somerville and Ross Martin's *Irish Memories* (1917); the biblical and Arthurian archetype of the deceased hero who returns "when they have healed them of their grievous wounds"; and postwar forms of grief and consolation: "even to-day the belief in a place of rest for heroes has not utterly died out," says Dane, citing legends that have gathered around Parnell and Kitchener (152). Dane thus invites readers to recognize the evidence that although belief takes many forms, it is alive and well.

As she surveys the body of captivating legends, fiction, and nonfiction about journeys into hidden holy lands, Dane underscores the long-standing dynamic in which believers are trained by nonbelievers to conceal their experiences—or they are punished for failing to do so. On the one hand, she contrasts the "sceptical nowadays" to a simpler era when believers did not suppress their intuitions and spiritual experiences with their rational faculty. On the other hand, her list of examples of human-fairy encounters is substantial and ranges across historical periods, showing the strength and uninterrupted line of belief in the material existence of such beings. The list includes, for example, the legend of the twelfth-century Green Children of Woolpit, the history of Anne Jefferies (1625–1713), imprisoned for refusing to deny her fairy sightings, and the Reverend Robert Kirk's *The Secret Commonwealth of Elves, Fauns, and Fairies*. Folklorist Andrew Lang edited an edition of this tract, whose manuscript is dated 1691 but was most likely not printed until 1815. Both *Irish Memories* and *The Secret Commonwealth* document human voyages into a fairyland, voyagers' messages sent afterwards to their human families, and—what particularly interests Dane—the skepticism or fear of these family members, who therefore ignore the abducted one's plea for help returning from the fairyland.

Lang's edition of *The Secret Commonwealth* suggests that, like Dane, he is unwilling to discredit paranormal experience. He added a subtitle to Kirk's tract, "A Study of Folk-lore & Psychical Research," indicating two modern fields of study that likely shed light on human-fairy encounters. At first glance the approaches of the folklorist and the psychical researcher might appear diametrically opposed.[33] Yet Lang avoids stating that popular beliefs in fairies are *merely* beliefs, opening the door to quasi-scientific approaches that might confirm the reality of the paranormal encounters. His introduction provides the fascinating history of the Reverend Kirk's clerical and spiritual life, which included such theologically sound endeavors as an "Irish" translation of the Bible, and a Psalter in Gaelic (1684). Having thus certified Kirk's scholarly credibility, Lang recounts the report of Kirk's abduction into fairyland, his presumed death, and his subsequent appearance to a relative to give directions about his desired return to human society: "'Say to Duchray, who is my cousin as well as your own, that I am not dead, but a captive in Fairyland; and only one chance remains for my liberation'" ("Introduction" xii). Lang provides the details of Kirk's failure to be restored to society, which he deems "extremely to be regretted, as [Kirk] could now add matter of much importance to his treatise" (xiii). Lang soon explains his own, more scientific interest in Kirk's book:

> Our study of Mr. Kirk's little tractate must have a double aspect. It must be an essay partly on folk-lore, on popular beliefs, their relation to similar beliefs in other parts of the world, and the residuum of fact, preserved by tradition, which they may contain. On the other hand, as mental phenomena are in question—such things as premonitions, hallucinations, abnormal or unusual experiences generally—a criticism of Mr. Kirk must verge on "Psychical Research." (xv–xvi)

While Lang hopes that the two academic disciplines can *illuminate* the fantastic dimensions of Kirk's experience, Dane, in her own essay on the literature of fairy encounters, emphasizes the vulnerability of the human being at the center of these narratives, the individual who is seized with the conviction of a spiritual force not sanctioned by the Church. Attending to the private nature of such belief, she explores the authority of the believer's sensory experience; the believer's self-concealment in the face of societal mockery; and the strength of the conviction that seizes the believer.

Dane turns her readers' attention to people who believe that the workaday world might suddenly "rise and melt and vanish, leaving the real things hidden behind them bare and beautiful" (150). In "Faerylands Forlorn," belief is a form of strength. Dane approaches this strength indirectly, first presenting the believer's self-concealment

[33] The psychical researcher studies the "special mental abilities" or phenomena that "cannot be explained by science" ("Psychical").

in the face of societal mockery of believers. This is the experience of both educated and uneducated people, she claims. Educated people may say nothing about their private experiences, but they likely use their knowledge to "quiet the mind, to soothe its doubts with their instinctive recognition of life outside our life, of lives behind us and lives to come which they must not too explicitly acknowledge lest they be laughed at" (150). Some force transcends the individual life of here and now, Dane contends, and perception of this force is reassuring in an age without a spiritual compass. She also considers "the folk of a less civilised day" and opines that they "took this queer instinct" more simply: "Their reason did not trouble their belief in faery-lands, and some of them—call it what you please, hallucination, illusion, dream, vision, so long as you do not call it necessarily plain lying—some of them went into those lands" (150–2). For the people of this unspecified past, reason did not contravene faith, and thus, pioneers, they could freely make excursions into faerylands.

Dane's contemporaries enjoy no such freedom. And yet, while "Faerylands Forlorn" touches on the persecution of believers, its emphasis is on the tenacity of belief. As Dane depicts it, the strength of intuition or conviction is such that it seizes the believer most often when she is in the midst of nonbelievers, as if to retain its foothold in the believer who is becoming more scarce:[34] "At certain seasons, especially in the country, in open spaces, and in rooms crowded with people, such folk will have a sudden conviction that all on which they are looking may, in the next moment, roll up like a painted curtain"; or they may at other moments, "stretch out a tentative finger and stroke down the empty air, as if the curtain were so fine that it could be ripped at a touch, to let in the glory that is already shining through the invisible mesh" (150).

These passages about glimpses of a glorious world suggest that "Faerylands Forlorn" hopes to enchant doubting readers. In contrast to "Children of Light," Dane devotes relatively scant attention to the pressure of believers to conform to communal or societal standards and lavishes more attention on their apprehension of spirit. She charms her audience with descriptions of the ordinary-extraordinary moments when believers are infused with or even seized by spiritual awareness, and thus she opens up a literary-critical space analogous to the secret holy places documented in literature.

[34] The individual's seizure by a powerful spiritual force describes the experience of Laura in *Lolly Willowes*. Dane mentions Sylvia Townsend Warner's novel in "First Flights" (1926), in which she touches on the topic of fairy tales.

Chapter 5

The Voice of Women

From its launch in 1922, *Good Housekeeping* featured articles about women's citizenship by distinguished female journalists, politicians, barristers, and activists. On the heels of the Representation of the People Act of 1918 granting the franchise to the majority of women over thirty came the Sex Disqualification (Removal) Act of 1919, whereby women could enter the professions, take university degrees, or exercise "any public function." The landscape of opportunities for women was changing dramatically. All of the journalists discussed here: Violet Bonham Carter, Clemence Dane, Helena Normanton, Rebecca West, and Rose Macaulay, contributed multiple essays over the first years of the magazine's run or beyond. These journalists form a periodical community: they use the print space of the magazine to convene writers and readers concerned with women's social, educational, and political progress.[1] Often they are in dialogue with one another as they address the same questions. Between 1922 and 1928, the year in which women over thirty gained the vote, this corps of *Good Housekeeping* journalists debate women's psychological and intellectual preparation to participate in politics; they call out women who retreat from duty; they coach women to run for political office; and they find satisfaction in the evidence of British women's record of sound ethical judgment.

These journalists also come together as a periodical community insofar as they collectively push back against the construction of the "soft" woman newsreader by the daily press, which shaped more and more of its features to appeal to women, a class of citizens it wagered had no interest in lengthy parliamentary speeches or indeed any aspect of the public sphere. Beginning in the late nineteenth

[1] See Beetham on *The Englishwoman's Journal*, begun in 1858 ("Periodicals and the New Media" 235).

century and through the interwar period, the daily papers steadily reduced their coverage of "hard" political news in favor of more human-interest stories delivered in simpler language and shorter blocks of text. Initially editors aimed to reach the "average" reader with no advanced education. But the trend toward "soft" news continued and increasingly courted the woman reader. *The Daily Mirror*, launched in 1903, had inaugurated a "woman's page" addressing domestic and other "feminine" concerns; and as the chief spenders of the household budget, women readers were crucial to newspapers' advertising revenue. Illustrated advertising and other graphics also transformed the daily papers in the first decades of the century (Bingham 26–32; LeMahieu 9–20). In "The Dictatorship of the Lay-Out Man" (1938), Holbrook Jackson complained that the verbal text was now subjugated to "the control of the layout man" so that "consecutive reading of more than five hundred words" was impossible even for "readers with enough concentration for the task" (qtd. in LeMahieu 265). He attributed this demotion of the printed word to the increasing influence of women readers "and other feminine concerns on newspapers" (265). Firmly linking women readers to a preference for illustration over verbal text, he hinted that reading the daily papers emasculated men: "when men think pictorially they unsex themselves" (qtd. in LeMahieu 265). This misogynist viewpoint was not new. As Karin Littau points out, since the emergence of mass culture, women readers had been pathologized, charged with a tendency to "indiscriminately and biblio-manically *devour* literature for cheap thrills or vulgar sentiments rather than use it for moral betterment or the refinement of mind" (156).

What *Good Housekeeping* and the daily newspaper of the interwar period have in common is the paramount importance of the woman reader and the imperative to retain the advertisers targeting her. But the monthly magazine and the newspaper differ markedly in their treatment of the verbal text. The largely uninterrupted columns of print and longer articles in *Good Housekeeping* presume an educated woman reader with plenty of power for concentrated reading, well beyond "consecutive reading of more than five hundred words." Nonetheless, the first issues of *Good Housekeeping* both confirm and challenge the suspicion that women readers took little interest in politics or in civic and national issues. They admonish "apathetic" women who have not taken their share of "national housekeeping" by exercising their new responsibility to vote; and they encourage hesitant women to serve on juries or to take up careers in politics.[2] But these betrayals of doubt are few in comparison with articles that indicate the journalists' confidence in women's capacity for political contributions. These essays, replete with political "verbal text," provide both fact and opinion about women as voters, public speakers, members of parliament, and diplomats. Moreover, journalists such as Helena Normanton sought to remind *Good Housekeeping* readers of British women's activist history.[3] In so doing, she located women's political engagement in noble traditions that needed to be protected or revived by contemporary women.

In this chapter, citizenship means women's preparation to fulfill civic responsibilities and exercise new privileges in the public sphere: to engage in civic and national debate, to vote, to serve on juries, or to hold elected office or other leadership positions. Each female journalist discussed here established her own terrain and her own voice with respect to these topics. Politician Violet Bonham Carter, daughter of the former prime minister Henry Asquith, coaches women as they enter the political fray. Barrister and historian Helena Normanton provides evidence of illogical and inequitable patriarchal law, explains legal opportunities for women to increase their participation in the political sphere, and furnishes the surprising history of women's past participation. Novelist and playwright Clemence Dane serves as a humanist and literary expert, frequently advocating for the role of imagination to address contemporary civic and ethical questions. As she underscores more ethereal or spiritual citizen qualities in "Sex and the Business Woman" and "Golden Opinions," Dane's approach is quite different from Helena Normanton's well-constructed and evidenced-based arguments. Likewise, Bonham Carter warns that public opinion must keep pace or even run in advance of legal rights. Both Dane and Bonham Carter thus emphasize the individual, spiritual, and cultural changes that must undergird women's citizenship. The voice of Rebecca West is a special case: she had earlier established her methods of satire and critical attack in articles for the *Clarion* and *The New Freewoman*. To *Good Housekeeping* she brings the experience, outlook, and confidence that prompt her to reach beyond women readers to critique the political, economic, and ideological systems

[2] See for example Helena Normanton, "The Woman Juror," and Constance Williams, "Political Work as a Profession for Women."

[3] Feminist periodical scholars have demonstrated the importance of periodical communities to women's political activism from the mid-nineteenth century forward. See Tusan, and Beetham, "Periodicals," on The Langham Place Circle.

in which they are enmeshed. Like Dane, West argues that informed citizenship depends on a culture of reading, especially including fact and opinion. If West's satire armed women against exploitation, the satire of Rose Macaulay in her series of "problem" essays offered comic relief to the many serious treatments of modern women in *Good Housekeeping*. Essays like "Problems for the Citizen," for instance, foiled magazine essays that sought to empower women by representing the civic sphere as an amorphous, faceless bureaucracy liable to bring out the worst in human agents.

From Apathy to Political Conscience

In *Women Making News*, Michelle Tusan demonstrates the crucial role played by the woman- owned and -run activist press in forming women's political subjectivity in the nineteenth and early twentieth centuries. The audience for mainstream women's magazines like *Good Housekeeping* was broader, yet *Good Housekeeping* shows that in some cases these quality periodicals continued the work of shaping women's political subjectivity in the decade following the passage of The Representation of the People Act of 1918. *Good Housekeeping*'s coverage of women's new suffrage was extensive in the first years following the magazine's launch in the UK. Even the first volume included articles by suffragist Millicent Garrett Fawcett and by political worker Constance Williams. How to inculcate in women themselves a sense of their political identity was needed, judging from the journalists invited to write on these topics. Helena Normanton, the first female barrister to practice in England, was among these. For at least the first decade of her regular column, Normanton wrote persistently on the history of British women's political subjectivity and the urgent need for their political engagement after women's partial franchise of 1918, when women's legal rights significantly trailed behind those of men.[4] In "How Women Won the Vote" (1929), even as she celebrates the activists who drove the landmark political emancipation of women, Normanton points the finger at those women of the militant days who did not participate "because they were aloof, apathetic, and unimaginative" (99). Her criticism is also a call to women to recognize the responsibility of their franchise.

[4] In 1931, Normanton began a new series for *Good Housekeeping*, *The World as It Passes*.

Women and Peace

internationally. The women of the civilised nations, if they are articulate, will never permit a great war for the sake of the beautiful eyes of the Oil Barons or Copper Kings!

These three possible causes of difference, and there are no others between England and America, can be settled, and will be settled, if public opinion so demands. And that women can leaven public opinion sufficiently for this purpose is beyond question.

One of the most hopeful of recent developments, in which I have played a small part, has been the action of a section of Representatives at Washington, headed by Congressman Frederick Britten, in demanding direct negotiations between American Elected Representatives and British Members of Parliament for the free and frank discussion of the outstanding causes of difference. This action has been welcomed by the great majority of British Members of Parliament of all parties. At this time of writing the probabilities of such a meeting are hopeful. The results cannot but be beneficial and might well be decisive in the cause of peace. But there is great opposition from the vested interests. Professional diplomats, Cabinet Ministers, executives, the permanent members of the Civil Services, would not be human if they did not resent such short-circuiting of their ancient functions and prerogatives. The suggestion that direct conversations should take place between elected representatives is revolutionary. But the situation, and the dangers that may arise from it, justify departures from established precedent. Women must certainly be members of this proposed conference on both sides of the table. Steps have already been taken to this end. The influence of American and British women behind the proposal and in support of the historic meeting when it takes place will be of incalculable value. I have specially referred to this matter because it is a sphere in which women can make their influence felt immediately, and with the greatest effect.

I have no doubt about the general attitude of women in these matters. They are as patriotic, in the best sense, as men. But they will come with a new outlook to our councils and approach these great problems from a fresh mental angle.

The history of the last twenty years and the present state of international relationships show how much these are needed.

Our Publications

Good Housekeeping Diary and Household Account Book

Edited by D. D. Cottington Taylor. A twelve months' complete guide for the woman of every class. Bound in various shades of cloth and leather and packed in cardboard boxes, size 4¾ in. × 6½ in.

Cloth Edition in box **3*s*. 9*d*.** net, post free 4*s*. 3*d*. net.
Leather Edition in box **5*s*.** net, post free 5*s*. 6*d*. net.

Good Housekeeping Menu and Recipe Book

By D. D. Cottington Taylor. A well-thought-out and exhaustive collection of menus and recipes for the middle-class housewife.

Price **2*s*. 6*d*.**, or 2*s*. 9½*d*. including postage.

Good Housekeeping Cookery Book

By Florence B. Jack. Recipes of every kind for every occasion and to suit every purse.

Price **2*s*. 6*d*.**, or 2*s*. 9½*d*. including postage.

Good Housekeeping Invalid Cookery Book

By Florence B. Jack. These tested and thoroughly reliable recipes are published with a common-sense introduction on invalid cookery by the author.

Price **2*s*. 6*d*.**, or 2*s*. 9½*d*. including postage.

Good Housekeeping Dictionary of Facts

Over 400 household hints for saving the time, money, and energy of the housewife have been collected and arranged in a handy form for quick reference.

Price **1*s*.**, or 1*s*. 2*d*. including postage.

Good Housekeeping Sweet Making Book

Over one hundred tested sweet and candy recipes.

Price **1*s*.**, or 1*s*. 2*d*. including postage.

Good Housekeeping Cookery Folios

The Bride's Primer of Cookery: The making of Jams, Jellies, and Marmalades, Pickles and Chutneys, Fruit Bottling. *Food and Health:* A reprint of the lectures and demonstrations given at the Institute on Food Values and Diet. *Pies and Pastry Making.*

Price **6*d*.** each, or 7½*d*. including postage.

Good Housekeeping Service Folios

Laundrywork, Parts I & II; Upholstery; Household Cleaning; Home Repairs and Decorations.

Price **6*d*.** each, or 7½*d*. including postage.

Good Housekeeping Furnishing Folio

Outline of Furnishing containing 28 Colour Schemes, also Wall Treatments, Types of Flooring, etc.

Price **6*d*.**, or 7½*d*. including postage.

A Primer of Personal Loveliness

The care of the complexion, hair, hands and figure. Health-building rhythmic exercises.

Price **6*d*.**, or 7½*d*. including postage.

Obtainable from "Good Housekeeping," 153 Queen Victoria Street, E.C.4

94 All advertisements in GOOD HOUSEKEEPING are guaranteed.

Figure 5.1 While feminist journalists like Bonham Carter, Dane, Normanton, and West urged women's political engagement after the partial franchise of 1918, *Good Housekeeping*'s in-house titles catered to the practical housewife. April 1929. Courtesy of Hearst Magazines UK.

Women's apathy remained a marked concern in the early years of *Good Housekeeping*. In "Political Work as a Profession for Women" (1922), Constance Williams deems that the "average woman is still somewhat indifferent to political matters" (117); and in "The Political Future of Women" (1922), Violet Bonham Carter warns that, in contrast to judgments that women's political opinions are immoderate, most women exist "in a state of complete apathy regarding politics and the significance of politics in the lives of women" (11). The vote would not automatically transform women into politically engaged and well-informed citizens: "You cannot turn a woman into a 'citizen' by passing an Act of Parliament. You might just as well mutter a spell over her. We must take other steps to bring her politically into action" (12).[5] Bonham Carter's frank criticism was remarkable for its direct challenge to *Good Housekeeping* readers, women in the prosperous middle classes. She was especially caustic when comparing working-class women to "West End" women. While the working-class woman is "intimately aware of the fluctuations in wages and prices, of housing conditions, of the effect of temperance legislation," and while "great facts like strikes and unemployment hit her with tragic force," to "the woman of means and leisure these conditions and events often have no significance or existence. She may, or may not, read about them in the papers. Even if she does, it is a toss-up whether or not they awaken in her any interest or any sense of responsibility whatsoever" (12). As we will see, Bonham Carter, Rebecca West, and Clemence Dane gave reading—news, opinion, and literature—a central place in woman's preparation for citizenship.

Bonham Carter expressed her critical opinions about women's preparation in the first pages of "The Political Future of Women," but in the concluding pages predicted women's assets as elected representatives. She argues that while "the power of seeing out over the edge of one's own life to a wide impersonal horizon is very rare," woman's traditional role of caretaker already equips her with many of the dispositions and skills needed in citizenship and in politics specifically (12). In a metaphor commonly deployed to foster women's political subjectivity, Bonham Carter invokes the concept of citizenship as "national housekeeping" to address the question of whether politics make a good career for women. Lucy Delap dates the metaphor of the state as the home from the end of the nineteenth century

[5] Writing for *Time and Tide*, Rebecca West framed the problem of women's "anemic" political engagement a bit differently, as we will see below in this chapter.

and situates it in the context of Edwardian liberal governments' increased responsibility for "an increasing range of 'domestic' tasks, such as the feeding of school children, the collection of rubbish, and widows pensions" (146). In these ways, the state could seem analogous to the home or the family. Feminist activists sought to "capitalise on this developing role for the state which was widely seen as requiring women's input, to argue for women's citizenship rights" (146–7).[6] The metaphor continued to gain currency after women won those rights. For Bonham Carter, active citizenship could be considered an extension of what was already women's special domain: "It involves, after all, doing for one's country what one has always done for one's home, its housekeeping, its finance, the care of its children and the direction of their education and health" (12). As Delap sums up the message embedded in the national housekeeping metaphor, "Domestic interests did not necessarily limit women's political outlook, but could be viewed as a gateway to the wider political world" (148). Indeed, Bonham Carter makes clear that women politicians should not be confined to domestic questions and should impress upon women the importance of foreign policy and international relations, "our direct responsibility for them, and their immediate and intimate reaction on our lives here at home" (110).

Education for the Woman Citizen

In "Sex and the Business Woman" (1926), Dane theorizes that women's lack of education has rationalized women's inequality to men. Education, she says, has been an Eden arbitrarily denied to women. In Dane's view, overcoming prejudice against educated women, and education itself, are the keys to women's recent emancipation. With the help of novelistic "evidence" from Jane Austen and Fanny Burney, Dane locates that prejudice in the past. On the contrary, says Violet Bonham Carter, debates about how women should be educated are still very active. In "The Dilemma of Woman's Education," which appeared in the first volume of *Good Housekeeping*, Bonham Carter warns that "the term 'educated woman' is still a stigma" that conjures up "a rather inhuman figure, someone a little drily and drearily efficient" (12). She thus

[6] For further discussion of "national housekeeping," see Chapter 3; Wood, "Housekeeping, Citizenship, and Nationhood" 219–20; and Deen, "Cultivating Citizen Readers" 103–4.

identifies women's education as a cause for activism. Before women can be effective leaders in public or in domestic life, they will need to "exorcise this bogy" of the educated woman.

Bonham Carter and Dane explicitly address the kind of education women will need. Both use the watershed moment of women's enfranchisement to advocate for women's liberal education, the liberation of her mind from ignorance and prejudice, through education. Bonham Carter sees the domestic woman as a haven for an education that is no longer available to professional men and women.[7] These professionals will need to be narrowly educated—become specialists—to prepare for fierce competition in professional arenas. Nor will those entering the professions have the luxury of cultivating their individuality, for the professions require conventionality. In contrast to professional women, domestic women should be educated so as to gain "a wide perspective" ("The Dilemma" 12). Bonham Carter pinpoints domestic women's "transmissive function. It is one of the laws of her essentially generous nature that there is nothing she possesses which she does not share and pass on" (12). Above all, Bonham Carter desires, for herself and other women, an education that trains her to "mobilize" and "command" her faculties at will, in order to make of them "obedient and more or less accurate instruments which we can wield at our pleasure" (12). Similarly, Dane urges that education should lead the learner to "a full and free and noble expression of itself, rather than a cramped, haphazard, and tentative one" ("The Educational Value of Acting in Schools" 79).[8] Neither writer seeks to have women follow the university curricula of their male counterparts. Bonham Carter judges that freedom from traditional education will position women advantageously for elected office, to which they can bring "the invaluable asset of an open and unencumbered mind, free from the toils of tradition" ("The Political Future of Women" 110). Dane denigrates "learning by rote," and lobbies for educational programs that accustom the mind "to rely on itself, think for itself, and judge for itself" (79).[9] In keeping with her para-curricular approach to education, discussed in Chapter 1, Dane repeatedly emphasizes the distinction between book

[7] Bonham Carter here presumes, as Fiona Hackney also finds, that even while magazines like *Modern Woman* courted professionally minded women, formal and informal marriage bars meant that "the prevailing idea that a 'woman's place' was in the home persisted" ("Getting a Living" 110).

[8] Dane slightly adapted the essay for *The Women's Side.*

[9] Dane makes a similar case in "News from the Country of Hardwork," discussed below.

learning and education. The actor eschews textbooks and classrooms in favor of experiential education: "Human experience is his book to read" (79).

Just as "national housekeeping" implied women's special fitness to provide judgment about the direction of the nation, so the broad, self-directed education advocated by Dane and Bonham Carter marked out women's distinctive domain with respect to men. Both writers held out the hope that in their public roles, women would use such unofficial skills as imagination, compassion, and a sense of beauty. In one of her first essays for *Good Housekeeping*, "The Educational Value of Acting in Schools," Dane argues that the trained imagination, empowering the individual to understand all the states of the human soul, holds the key to democratic advances in education and culture. And the best way to develop and apply the imagination is to take up acting. The actor understands all manner of human beings and expresses this knowledge to "the man in the street." The actor is indeed "the only historian" to whom he will listen (79).

"The Educational Value of Acting in Schools" describes what and how the actor learns and demonstrates how her training leads to success, not just in theaters, but in public life. The actor must "know and express—that is, learn to understand—all the confused and suppressed impulses, good, bad, and indifferent, of the human animal" (79). This kind of imagination is "the secret of all success" in civic and political spheres, a belief Dane underscores through the examples of the statesman and the general, whose work entails putting themselves in the place of an opponent (80). Nor is such leadership confined to the privileged few who have benefitted from an elite education. Literature provides abundant examples of common folk whose imagination brings success to a group enterprise. Dane turns to the "unlettered fisherman" of an 1897 Kipling novel for an example:

> Do you remember the description in *Captains Courageous* of the captain of the *We're Here* preparing for a fishing campaign?
>
> > So Disko Troop thought of recent weather and gales, currents, food supplies, and other domestic arrangements from the point of view of a twenty-pound cod—*was in fact for an hour a cod himself* and looked remarkably like one!
>
> There you have it in a nutshell! Why was the unlettered fisherman the acknowledged leader of all the deep-sea fishing fleet? Because he,

> even on so humble and unthrilling a matter as cod fishing, took care to use his imagination. (80)[10]

"The Educational Value of Acting in Schools" makes clear, then, how the actor-citizen can contribute to her community or nation.[11] Far more than an essay about curricula for children, "The Educational Value of Acting in Schools" advocates for a broad, liberal education for women in terms that resonate with Violet Bonham Carter's journalism for *Good Housekeeping*. In fact, Dane included a revised version of "Educational Value" in her 1926 collection of essays, *The Women's Side*. Female citizens are the explicit audience for this volume, whose preface admonishes newly enfranchised readers who have not yet engaged with questions of national importance and who remain sunk in apathy. Thus the "Preface" to *The Women's Side* repurposes the wisdom of "Educational Value" for women readers. In Chapter 1, I argued that this guidance democratizes education by validating the magazine and book reading taking place outside the precincts of a university. Although the 1922 "Educational Value" precedes Dane's book essays for *Good Housekeeping*, Dane has already developed this vision of democratic access to education, as is clear in her claim that "the man in the street" will accept history lessons only from the theater actor (79).

Dane does, however, lobby for acting to gain the status of a scholastic curriculum. Elsewhere in her *oeuvre*, Dane likewise endorses pioneering and experimental initiatives in education, such as the co-educational pioneer, Bedales, that promote self-directed learning and independent thinking. Such experiments are the focus of "News from the Country of Hardwork" (1924). Here, in the context of praise for H.G. Wells's *The Story of a Great Schoolmaster*, Dane hails educational leaders "all over England [who] ... believe that in education (not book learning) lies the salvation of the country" (139). This distinction between "education" and "book learning" appears again in "Golden Opinions," discussed later in this chapter, where it plays a key role in Dane's advice to women that they preserve their difference from men, and, specifically, that they choose books to foster qualities not taught in academic institutions. Peace of

[10] In an approach that distinguishes her from the other female journalists for *Good Housekeeping*, even when Dane is speaking to her readers about public or national matters, she characteristically turns to a shared literary heritage, and often to fiction or drama, for "evidence" of the real-world principles she is discussing.

[11] The *Good Housekeeping* version of the essay acknowledges the young person's desire to be a good Christian; the *Women's Side* version recasts that desire as "being a good citizen and doing your duty" (100–1).

mind and soul heads the list of these qualities. "Golden Opinions" urges women to cultivate peace in themselves, for of all the "equipment which modern woman is forced to acquire," this is "the only one which is indispensable, and the only one which cannot be taught in the schools" (52).

Helena Normanton and Agents of Change

In their representations of the ideal woman citizen, Dane, Bonham Carter, and Normanton sought more than independent thinking and an empathetic imagination. They expected female citizens to use their voices to contribute to public fora. Violet Bonham Carter's "Public Speaking: Part I" and Dane's "The Educational Value of Acting in Schools" both theorize the importance of such contributions. Both essays depict a professional woman who holds sway over others in a political context, and in this way they implicitly illustrate the continuity between journalism and public appearance. Their vision of how the skills of public speaking or performance can increase the ordinary citizen's power in a community makes these two essays of particular interest here. In both roles the power of the professional woman resides in her ability to hold an audience captive and to move them. In effect, the journalist shares the secrets of her own trade.[12] Periodical scholars have noticed a wide variety of such mirroring techniques, which they link to the function of the periodical as an imagined community.[13] Bonham Carter's and Dane's mirroring techniques reinforce this periodical community, itself a training ground for the civic arena in which the woman citizen is expected to act. The community functions to circulate information and to stimulate debate, and it fosters readers' more active political engagement by inviting them to see themselves in the public roles described by the woman journalist.

Invoking the continuity between their journalism and the activities of public speaking or acting, Bonham Carter and Dane identify fora in which women can exercise influential voices. Members of the *Good Housekeeping* periodical community, the women readers are not limited to silent absorption of writers' words. Especially in

[12] Beetham finds that even before the twentieth century, "practical advice on a career in journalism became a staple of girl's and women's magazines" ("Periodicals and the New Media" 236).

[13] In an interesting example of this trend, Roach documents the imaginative identification encouraged by interviews in periodicals.

articles about citizenship, the periodical writers call on readers to take action, to effect a transition from attentive reader to audible woman. As reading theorist Karin Littau puts it, "the politically engaged reader, spectator or critic must become an agent of change" (135). Helena Normanton's articles for *Good Housekeeping* in the 1920s call on readers to become such agents of change. Writing on the law as it affects women, Normanton draws on her extensive legal knowledge and deploys a flair for colorful historical anecdotes. In reminding readers of British women's activist history, she locates women's political engagement in noble traditions that need to be protected or revived by contemporary women.[14]

In "Breaking the Barriers: Some Great Women of the Past" (1922), appearing in the first volume of *Good Housekeeping*, Normanton explains the then-active petition of Viscountess Rhondda, who had inherited her late father's peerage, to sit and vote in the House of Lords. "Breaking the Barriers" provides a history of British women peeresses, situating Lady Rhondda at the end of a historical procession of women who have claimed the privileges legally available to them.[15] Normanton singles out for particular praise Alice Montacute, who in the fifteenth century successfully petitioned for her husband to take her name and sit for her in the House of Lords as well as in the Privy Council. Normanton judges that these are "the largest claims ever made by a woman in the history of England." She gently prods her readers to follow Lady Montacute's example of feminist activism: "It is mysterious why Englishwomen do not make more of the memory of so great and courageous a lady, a true protagonist of the rights of women" (11).

If Normanton typically identifies maternal forerunners as a source of women's obligation to pursue equity in the civic sphere, she also acknowledges contemporary male allies. In effect, she situates herself and her readers within a community that stretches beyond the

[14] Essays illustrating these hallmarks include: "Breaking the Barriers" (1922), "When a Woman's Married" (1922), "The Woman Juror" (1924), "Women Justices of the Peace" (1925), "Women and Diplomacy" (1925), "Women's Franchise Inequalities" (1926), "Representative Women of Great Britain" (1929), and "How Women Won the Vote" (1929).

[15] Margaret Haig Mackworth, 2nd Viscountess Rhondda (1883–1958), would have been familiar to many *Good Housekeeping* readers as the founder of the feminist weekly *Time and Tide*, in 1920. At the time of Normanton's writing, the House of Lords Committee for Privileges had ruled in favor of Lady Rhondda's petition to take her late father's seat in the House of Lords, but Normanton is aware that the Committee's ruling might be overturned. Her fear was borne out. Lord Birkenhead, the Lord Chancellor, who opposed the admission of women to the Lords, reconstituted the Committee, which then reversed the first Committee's decision.

Good Housekeeping periodical community, whose resources women would do well to use. In "The Woman Juror" (1924), Normanton explains the law governing women's jury service and demonstrates its civic and feminist value even where the law allows women to recuse themselves. "The Woman Juror" educates women about jury law, but its primary purpose is to convert more citizens to the view that women make good jurors. To do so, Normanton deploys her own confident, expertly prepared voice. She also draws on the opinions of well-respected professional men, who have presumably no personal interest in championing women jurors. Normanton's voice is strong enough to collaborate with other, male voices. Set alongside these, her own opinions are not stridently feminist, but reasonable, representative of the turning tide of public opinion.

Normanton educates her readers, supplying clear, precise information about jury service and taking special care to explain the rules under which juror candidates may be challenged by counsel or by a prisoner. In some cases, she explains, a challenge may be "peremptory," without need to show any reason for eliminating the juror. "It is here that the woman juror often fares badly, especially at the hands of such counsel as hold tenaciously certain preconceived views about women," she warns (173). Or a "judge sometimes *offers* [women] a special exemption" so that they may avoid hearing evidence of an offensive, unpleasant, or indecent character. Having explained the rules, Normanton turns to a recent legal case that set a valuable precedent for women jurors, which she subsequently formulates as a principle for her readers to follow: "the perpetual decency of duty, even when performed in the most repellent circumstances" (173). In the case, the plaintiff sued the defendant for slander. The jury found for the plaintiff and the defendant then appealed. At the appellate level, the defendant's counsel singled out two women jurors from the first trial who had been warned that the case was of "a very unpleasant character" and whom he had "called upon to retire," which they had declined to do. The objections of this counselor to the women jurors in turn prompted their praise by several justices, who pointed to the "honourable motive" of the women jurors who refused to be excused from serving. Like a colleague collaborating with the justices whose wisdom is on display, Normanton then chimes in: "Women at large ought to feel very grateful to those two unknown jurywomen, for if they did nothing else by remaining at their duty without flinching but elicit this important pronouncement upon the true function of the woman juror, they would have performed a remarkable public service" (174).

The judge's pronouncement allows the public to hear the opinion of a distinguished public servant who does not share the counselor's bias against women. But what is impressive about Normanton's modulation of various voices—the defendant's counsel, the jurors, the judge—is that it replicates the democratic process. Moreover, she patently wants to foster good citizenship rather than promote women at all costs. Indeed, the essay begins with a trusted male voice, writer and philosopher G.K. Chesterton, who speaks only to the democratic function of juries, not about the value of woman jurors. In his view, the jury is essential to counterbalance the judgments of police, lawyers, and judges, whose years on the job ultimately rob them of their sensitive perception of individuals. Normanton ends the essay with a second respected male voice, this time a judge who has been "converted" to the principle of women serving on juries. Sir E. Wild, K.C., is the Recorder of London. Normanton quotes his view that "women were in judicial matters less emotional, less sentimental than men." As a result, he continues, justice is more often the outcome: "Women convicted very much more readily than men if it were right to do so. Nowadays men get justice" (175).

The strength of "The Woman Juror" and a hallmark of Normanton's journalism for *Good Housekeeping* is her savvy negotiation of the contemporary political sphere, supported by her knowledge of the law and history. Normanton's essays are pragmatic as well as eye-opening: she persistently draws on history to demonstrate that women's inequalities with respect to men are relatively modern. There is nothing natural or inevitable about the inequalities, she shows. Indeed, in some instances, all that is needed is for women to assert a standing right.[16]

Normanton's recourse to British women's history kindles women's pride in their matrilineal legacy and reminds them that they collectively hold the power to drive change, as the history of the battle for women's suffrage illustrates. Even in an essay like "Women's Franchise Inequalities" (1926), in which Normanton calls out the cynicism of politicians who are thwarting the expansion of women's rights, she concludes by prodding women into action: "What do British women propose to do about [the franchise inequalities]? Why do they tolerate it? When will they end it? *As soon as they choose to do so*" (115).

[16] See, for example, "When a Woman's Married," *Good Housekeeping* vol. 2, no. 10 (December 1922), in which Normanton indicates that no law requires a woman to take her husband's name upon marriage. Normanton herself exercised this right.

The Woman Citizen's Difference

Normanton's and Dane's views of modernity are fundamentally shaped by their historical sense. But while Normanton often presents the vulnerability of British women's proud legacy of civic engagement, Dane more often affirms its fundamental strength. In "Sex and the Business Woman" (1926), for example, Dane argues that the full engagement of women in civic and cultural life occurs in the natural course of healthy civilizations. Women's recent emancipation from domesticity marks a landmark in the development of human civilization, she claims, calling it "the most remarkable development of the Human intelligence since the birth of the Christian conception of right living and wise thinking in the commandment—'Thou shalt love the Lord thy God, and thy neighbor *as thyself*!'" (36). She attributes this emancipation neither to feminist activism nor to women's war service; and she characterizes it not as a gain for women but a matter of national interest. In that light, women's ambition to work outside the home is a recognition of their civic roles and a sign of their national pride. Dane believes that "even the most prejudiced of the die-hards" now admit that it is economically and morally better for woman "to keep herself than be kept" (37). "They are even beginning to consider it not unthinkable that she should take her share, adjusted to her capacity, in supporting the country she was born in and the children she bears" (37). Dane exaggerates the supposed consensus about women's work outside the home; historical evidence points to a range of attitudes. Nor does Dane acknowledge the marriage bar that prevented women from working as teachers and civil servants. The rhetorical effect of her statement, then, is to insinuate that those who are opposed to women's "emancipation" are futilely resisting an advance in civilization much larger than they are. Here and in "The Mother Night," discussed in Chapter 4, Dane identifies women's foundational, and impliedly safeguarded, strength.

For Helena Normanton, women's full potential in the public sphere would be realized only when they had access to the same rights and privileges as men. Violet Bonham Carter and Clemence Dane, in contrast, often stress the value of women's *difference* from men. Bonham Carter, as we have seen, seeks to protect domestic women's privilege to be broadly educated in a society that demands increasing professional specialization. We should "treat our intellectual differences from men, not as an infirmity, but as an asset," she advises ("The Dilemma" 12). Dane maintains that women have long understood their difference as an asset. In "Sex and the Business Woman" this asset is characterized as a spiritual superiority that gives rise to women's serenity:

> [Woman] has chafed against the restrictions imposed upon her by her fellow-man, or she has submitted, smiling, to them, in each case for the same reason—because she knew her strength, because she understood her equality, because she even suspected herself of a certain superiority of spiritual development which she quite fairly reckoned against the physical superiority of man. (36)

Like Sophocles's Antigone who justifies her defiance of Creon by citing divine law, and like Mary Wollstonecraft, who recognizes and vows obedience only to God, Dane appeals above patriarchy to a higher authority.[17]

Dane's confidence in women's underlying strength paves the way for the risks she takes by defending female citizens' distinctive differences from male citizens. By valorizing woman's spiritual nature, imagination, and compassion, rather than her knowledge of history and politics, Dane might appear to invoke the age-old dichotomy between rational man and emotional woman. Yet she skirts that risk through her emphasis on the societal applications of woman's imagination. She makes clear that the cultivation of women's difference does not merely benefit or protect individual women within industrial society. Women may also use their difference to make ethical judgments that will *alter* society. In "Should the Girl of Twenty-One Have a Vote?" and "Women Voters and the Death Penalty," discussed below, Dane speaks to the role of woman's compassionate imagination in voting. Additionally, "The Educational Value of Acting in Schools" and "A Game of Speculation" (1924) identify imagination as a life skill for which women are particularly suited. The latter essay argues that women can use their independent thinking to reject the civilization of the city. Both essays describe how the faculty of imagination can remediate an ailing civilization.

Dane's "speculations" in "A Game of Speculation" obliquely exhort woman to act on her convictions and insist on living in the country so as to "impose upon the other half a civilisation of her own—a civilisation of the country, not of the towns!" (27).[18]

[17] Sophocles, *Antigone* (circa 441 BC); Mary Wollstonecraft, *A Vindication of the Rights of Woman* (1792).

[18] This essay first appeared in *The World's Work: A History of Our Time*, vol. 47 (April 1924), pp. 626–30.

"I cannot help believing," Dane continues, "that woman might do much more with her freedom than use it merely to help in elaborating a civilization which falls foul of her profoundest instincts" (28). In "Should the Girl of Twenty-One Have a Vote?" (1924), Dane counts both creative activity and civic action as the legitimate products of imagination. She briefly addresses the charge that women's creative output has been smaller than men's. Virginia Woolf was to address this historical problem extensively in *A Room of One's Own.* But in this essay, Dane locates imagination within a trio of faculties, claiming that brains and hearts together give birth to imagination; and woman's imagination in turn is a spur to action. Knowing that woman's brains and her imagination are hot buttons, Dane begins the essay by addressing these "troublesome" topics head-on: "The trouble about having a vote and being on juries and all the rest of it—the trouble that is to say of being a citizen instead of a cipher, is that a woman has always to be using her brains nowadays as well as her heart" (13).[19] Even more "troublesome," together women's brains and heart give birth to imagination. In mock dismay, Dane concedes that woman's imagination spells trouble: "once give a woman imagination to play with, and you know what happens!" (13). She quotes Master Ford in *The Merry Wives of Windsor* to document the long-held wisdom that if a woman's imagination is not curbed, "then she plots, then she ruminates, then she devises; and what [women] think in their hearts they may effect, they will break their hearts but they will effect" (2.2). Dane does not disagree, but she values this quality differently than Master Ford. In fact, she characterizes woman's imagination as "this terrific ardour and vigour and enterprise." Moreover, she argues, "this imagination is at its quickest, its fullest, its wildest vigour, round about twenty-one" (13).

"Should the Girl of Twenty-One Have a Vote?" thus links young women's imagination to civic energy. This energy and earnestness will make them work for reform rather than, like older citizens, "shrug our shoulders over the problem as beyond our strength to handle in 'the present state of civilisation'" (88). Young women voters in the mass will decrease the quotient of cynicism and resignation in the electorate as a whole, Dane adds. She predicts that women

[19] Dane refers mockingly to public debate about women's capacity for rational thinking, which was brought (back) into question during the interwar period as newspapers sought to reach readers in nondiscursive ways. Catherine Clay demonstrates that *Time and Tide* pushed back on this pejorative characterization of women readers in its use of the "thinking woman" as a catch phrase (*Time and Tide* 117–18).

voters' empathetic imaginations will likely mean changes to the laws concerning lunacy, prostitution, and divorce.

Through her emphasis on women's well-balanced faculties—imagination, empathy, energy, brains, and a proven record of serving their nation at war—Dane builds the case that the woman of twenty-one should have the vote. Women's minds, while not the focus of the essay, enter into the discussion in a crucial way, and link Dane's vision of women's citizenship to most of the *Good Housekeeping* essays about women's expanded public roles in modernity. Dane observes that as a new citizen, woman "has had to learn to think for herself" (13). She might have said, "She now has the freedom to think for herself."

Active Citizenship and Reading: Rebecca West and Clemence Dane

Earlier in this chapter, I argued that Violet Bonham Carter and Clemence Dane fostered political engagement through mirroring techniques in which *Good Housekeeping* readers were invited to see themselves in public roles analogous to that of the woman journalist. "Active Citizenship and Reading" builds on this argument in an analysis of Rebecca West's journalism. West embeds in her articles journalistic and literary forms such as symposia, drama, and satire, forms that model and prepare her audience for political engagement. Although West's articles for *Good Housekeeping* were not numerous, I argue that her gravitas and rhetorical versatility added to the collective strength of the feminist voices in the magazine. In one example of this amassed power, I demonstrate the alignment of West and Dane, based on their shared concern about citizens' reading practices. Both Dane and West establish a clear correlation between women's education, reading, and engaged citizenship.

West's essays for *Good Housekeeping* enriched its coverage of feminist concerns, which she treated with linguistic sophistication and sharpened with satire and wit. Moreover, West's stature was unmatched within the *Good Housekeeping* corps of journalists. By the time the first issue was launched in 1922, she was already a prolific and well-respected journalist. In articles and reviews written for, among other publications, *The Freewoman*, *The Clarion*, *The New Statesman*, and *Time and Tide*, West debated with and satirized opponents, often singling them out by name. The consistency of her voice across numerous publications, as well as the range of her satirical targets—the upper classes, MPs, newspaper editors, men, and "parasite women"[20]—indicate that her intended audience reaches beyond and is more heterogeneous than the middle-class women readers of *Good Housekeeping*, and this reach arguably increased her gravitas in the magazine. Through the continuity of her concerns and the resonance of her voice within a wide periodical network, when West spoke to *Good Housekeeping* readers she simultaneously spoke to her audiences in other periodicals.

A distinguished voice already established in socialist, feminist, and modernist periodicals, West brought those perspectives and sensibilities to *Good Housekeeping*.[21] Her book reviews and contributions to symposia like "The Function of the Weekly Review" appeared in *Time and Tide*, not in *Good Housekeeping*. But the principles and rhetorical tactics that animate those essays likewise inform her pieces for *Good Housekeeping*. West's handful of articles for *Good Housekeeping* in the early 1920s were on the sexual and societal differences between men and women, who are never reduced to their gender roles. This means, for example, that in an article like "In the Absence of a Possible Husband, What is a Girl to Do?" (1923), women's ability to marry is continuous with their tendency to think, with their function as wives and mothers, and with their ambition to secure employment so as to "lay hold on life and do something with it" (57). West's holistic treatment of women and men arises from her understanding of their situation within interwoven political, economic, and ideological mechanisms that can be resisted.[22]

West's incisive mind and rhetorical versatility were integral to the range of feminist voices that spoke to *Good Housekeeping*'s readers in the 1920s. She consistently looks beyond individuals to the systems in which they act. In "The White Slave Traffic Bill" (*The Clarion* 1912), for example, she implies that laws framed to arrest the

[20] Lyn Pykett finds that West most frequently applied this epithet to women in the upper and middle classes "who lived in prosperous or luxurious idleness" (178–9). In "The Dilemma of Woman's Education," Violet Bonham Carter also expresses concern about the vulnerability of educated "parasites" who have chosen love over a profession: "A carefully trained 'parasite' may be cast adrift on stormy seas without economic anchorage of any kind by the shipwreck of a romance which would also have meant a livelihood" (12).

[21] Margaret Stetz argues that *Time and Tide* capitalized on West's cross-publication to reach a larger and more hybrid audience: "in branding itself through the prominent and frequent display of West's 'subversive' forms, *Time and Tide* could feel assured simultaneously of being positioned at the cutting edge of literary taste while still appealing to a large readership" (192).

[22] Lyn Pykett rightly underscores West's consistent attention to material and economic factors.

procurers of prostitutes would not be necessary if the upper classes would give their women an education. Overturning any number of assumptions, West sarcastically observes that "the trouble, as usual, begins at the top," where "all the resources of civilisation are commandeered" to make the upper-class woman a "vivid human being with keen sensations and strong faculties" (119). This same civilization then demands that she remain idle. Society could do away with the necessity to penalize procurers "by giving every girl a full measure of knowledge and economic freedom" (121). West effectively argues that a society that withholds education from its women brings its problems upon itself.

West values the journalistic and literary forms that foster political education and debate, including symposia, drama, and satire. In "The Gospel According to Granville-Barker" (*The Freewoman* 1912), she singles out Harley Granville-Barker for his unabashed "joy of thinking" and applauds the dramatic debate that characterizes his plays, each of which is "an eager and happily passionate discussion ... of some important problem in life" (20). "Passionate discussion" of important problems is a mainstay of West's journalism, including those written for *Good Housekeeping*. West spars directly with opponents, as well as indirectly, through satire. Indeed, as a tool within West's critiques, satire often takes the form of dramatic argument, with West hauling to the debate floor the patriarchs who have left women in the lurch, even after they have slunk away. West's *Good Housekeeping* articles frequently challenge a previous speaker on a topic related to modern woman. "In the Absence of a Possible Husband, What is a Girl to Do?" signals such debate first through its title, the same used by Margery Swett, writing for an American magazine. Next West refutes the exaggerated feminist claim that, far from pitiable, the unmarried woman is enviable. But most emphatically, West calls men to account for their wrong-headed advice to woman, quoting their side of the dialogue so that she can contest what they have repeatedly "said to her" (57).

West uses satire to attack, but also to supply humorous relief within analyses of women's oppression in patriarchal civilization. This limited use of satire, deployed alongside more direct societal criticism, is exemplified by "In the Absence of a Possible Husband." West singles out women in two roles, the dancing instructress and the Belgian mother, who have been betrayed by men's guidance. The Belgian mother has accepted men's bargain that she leave politics to them, be a good wife and mother, and "we'll see to it that all's well with you" (57). But it was clear that all was not well when she appeared "at Charing Cross Station in the early days of the war ... homeless, seared by the unholy sights of war, deprived of her man, searching for her scattered children" (57). Like the Belgian mother, the dancing instructress has been selected for men's prescriptions—that she "be beautiful and graceful"—and she, too, has taken men at their word that they will "see to it that all's well with you." But she too has been betrayed. West uses refrains for satirical effect—"men have said to her"; "we'll see to it that all's well with you"—that in themselves signify the worn-out nature of men's "wisdom." These refrains moreover suggest the wearisome timelessness of women's listening to men. These ironic vignettes illustrating men's destructive promises might well justify anger and cynicism.

But although men's repetitive advice has stranded, baffled, and disempowered women, West supplements these bleak vignettes with a satirically gleeful passage that enacts something like a feminist revenge on men. Her non-ironic thesis is that "If a woman is to have her full ration of life she ought to have a husband and children. A husband as good as herself, that is" (56). West then devotes a full paragraph to a parody of men's typical criteria for a wife, replacing men with women as the mate seekers. The desirable husband should be good-looking, but not too intellectual. "Decidedly, his home must come before anything else for him," she continues. "And—yes, he must be religious. It doesn't matter so much for a woman, but it's nice for a man to go to church" (56). By positing women as the agents who will set the criteria for a mate and men as the objects sought, West inverts the usual male-female hierarchy, invites her readers' laughter, and rhetorically provides them with an imaginative and compensatory power.

What is the impulse that leads West to affirm women's intellectual power in nearly the same breath that she indicates their betrayal under patriarchy? If we imagine not just the cross-pollination of a single journalist's literary and political journalism, but the serendipity through which individual journalists enrich one another's voices in the periodical community, we can turn to Clemence Dane for another take on women's power. Reflecting on women's enfranchisement in 1918, Dane argues that woman takes the change quietly because she has always had a "curious inner knowledge of her real liberty, her unassailable position in the structure of society" ("Sex and the Business Woman" 36). West is confident that she can invite readers' laughter without undercutting their anger. She is sure of her own and her readers' "inner knowledge" of their fundamental strength. "In the Absence of a Possible Husband" and West's other articles for

Good Housekeeping exemplify these trademarks of her journalism: her critique of power structures that perpetuate economic and social inequalities, and her rhetorical empowerment of her readers. This simultaneous critique of power and its redistribution are essential to the intellectual energy of her journalism.

Both West and Dane offer a pragmatic solution to women's political weakness: reading. Both argue that informed citizenship depends on a culture of reading, with West making the strongest link of the journalists between reading news and opinion and citizens' confident agency within the political system. West makes her most direct case in articles written for *Time and Tide* in the 1920s, where she theorizes the centrality of news and opinion to shaping informed citizens, and where she finds such content in jeopardy. She holds editors to their responsibility to call out evasive or wrong-headed writers and politicians, and she champions the role of newspapers to provide citizens a "means of political expression" ("The Function of The Weekly Review" 1114), particularly at a time when "the modern newspaper persistently underrates the public's appetite for solid matter of serious interest" ("The Future of the Press IV" 196).[23]

Like West, Dane draws a connection between the "habit of learning," reading matter, and engaged citizenship ("Sex and the Business Woman" 37). Indeed, Dane is the only one of the *Good Housekeeping* journalists under discussion here to make these connections systematically. In contrast to West's call for journals to resume their political education of the public, however, Dane calls on readers to read better books. In two essays Dane explicitly steers women toward books that will profit the emancipated woman and cosmopolitan citizen. "The Sea and the Sex" (1924) and "Spring Fashions" (1929) both point to women's responsibility to read beyond what concerns them personally. "Spring Fashions" praises a recent trend in longer published books and a new fictional method of "group character drawing," both of which Dane connects to the reader-citizen's desire to be informed about national and international affairs (104). The portrayal of the mass at the expense of the individual is fitting, Dane says, because "when nations collapse like ninepins we have not time for individual tragedies" (104). The suggestion to her readers is to think globally, or at least, communally. Individuals still matter in these novels, but they are depicted as parts of a community: "we are given pictures of human beings and their

[23] For valuable discussions of both articles, see Clay, and Collier, "Journalism Meets Modernism."

passions used as bricks in a building, as parts of a machine—the machine of a community, a nation or a civilization" (104).

As we have seen, in this period longer blocks of newspaper text targeted male readers and posited rational thinking; graphic and shorter verbal texts were associated with entertainment and with female readers. Dane, however, challenges this dichotomy when she draws an analogy between longer texts and current fashions in women's clothing, thus feminizing long books. In the postwar era, she tells readers, "skirts are lengthening and growing fuller: and books are lengthening and growing fuller too" (35). The return of longer literary forms—Dane sees it in fiction, poetry, biography, and history—reflects the reader's "desire to know more about the subjects which cannot be dealt with in snippets" (35). (*Good Housekeeping* readers would have registered "snippets" as a pejorative term associated with curtailed delivery of information in the mass daily.[24]) In "Spring Fashions," Dane figures her readers as compassionate, intellectually curious, and cosmopolitan citizens.

In "The Sea and the Sex" (1924), Dane urges women readers to stop demanding books with a love interest, telling them point blank that such self-indulgent reading will jeopardize "our long-desired physical and legal freedom, our intellectual independence, this deep-rooted belief of ours that we are intended to move level with our menfolk in a shared existence" (173). No one will take women seriously, Dane continues, if for generation after generation, novelists must satisfy women's insatiable appetite for "the Art of Love and the Art of Getting Married" (48). Nor will this reading matter prepare them to stride alongside men as their intellectual equals. In "The Political Future of Women," Bonham Carter cautions that popular opinion about women's role in the public sphere lags behind her legal rights. Dane is likewise concerned about the public's perception of women, but she suggests that women hold the power to reshape public opinion. She turns the spotlight on their taste in books. Her assessment is in some ways discouraging: women are "the chief part of the reading public"; their "demand creates the supply" (173). And their exclusive interest in love stories is fast creating a national

[24] In one example, the snippet journalist was likened to a merchant who writes "to the yard measure" and to a "human machine[ ]." The *Saturday Evening* journalist concludes that "If all day long you do nothing but copy figures, or tot them up, or take down letters in shorthand, you can hardly be intellectually alive" ("The Literary Aspirant" 543).

Figure 5.2 Illustration for "The Sea and the Sex": an eighteenth-century engraving of female pirates Ann Bonny and Mary Read.

literary culture in which only stories of the sea can compete.[25] In some of the sternest language she was to use, Dane warned women readers that

> We should beware of our bookshelves, for our choice of books is bound to betray us. If we read principally sentimentalities and sex-novels, we show pretty plainly where our interest in life begins and ends, and I believe that the world cannot much longer afford to tolerate any human being whose interests are purely personal. (173)

In addition to their interference with what might otherwise be an organic and diverse literary production, women readers are stunting writers' creativity, "making it difficult for any but the rich and famous author to produce the stuff that is in him" (173). Yet precisely because they represent a powerful reading constituency, Dane knows women can reshape the course of literary production, and at the same time, alter the public's judgment that women's interests are "purely personal" (173). As Virginia Woolf was to do in *A Room of One's Own*, Dane calls for "stories of the arts, the sciences, the professions,

[25] Dane eliminates the detective story from the competition, since "it seldom is literature" (174).

and the trades." Why should these "be left to the technical experts? There is a human side to these things," she observes (48).

If West and Normanton spur women to demand change by arousing their anger, Dane inspires them. Consider how her poetic paean to Conrad entices them to embark on a new genre—tales of the sea—and to immerse themselves in a world-class author, outsider to England, but its "most honoured guest" (176). Conrad wrote of the sea "as most men write of the human universe, as if every wave had a distinct and conscious soul; and at the same time wrote of familiar humanity as of something unfamiliar, as if it were in turn a tossing ocean of identities so inextricably intermingled that to follow the fortunes of one wave meant a plumbing of the very mind of the universe" (178). Conrad made you wonder if the "human universe were indeed no more than a mirror of the sea, obeying no saner laws than the blind pull of the moon, and save for that one instinctive flow and ebb, utterly abandoned to its own currents and cross-currents, its winds and fogs and idle sunshines" (178). As Dane thought about how to cultivate less insular English readers, it was important that Conrad was not "one of us," that this "Pole who ... chose to write in English" (176) enlarged readers' provincial standards as he made strange things familiar.

Both Dane and West, albeit with different emphases, place reading at the center of women's preparation for democratic citizenship. But as we have seen, there is nothing passive about the reading they advocate. They call on women to apply the debate tactics of drama and political symposia to public life, and to read for understanding of the wider world, not for escape into romance. Rose Macaulay, as we will see, took quite a different rhetorical approach to the opportunities and "problems" of citizenship.

Rose Macaulay's Satire for the Citizen

In "Should the Girl of Twenty-One Have a Vote?" (1924), Clemence Dane argues that extending the franchise to women of twenty-one presents risks but is also cause for hope. She associates women's imagination with "terrific ardour and vigour and enterprise" (13). These qualities will spur young women to vote for reform rather than, like older citizens, "shrug our shoulders over the problem as beyond our strength to handle in 'the present state of civilization'" (88). Dane's earnest optimism is often shared, albeit more cautiously, by Violet Bonham Carter and Helena Normanton.

Figure 5.3 Illustration by Franklin Booth for "Women at the Ballot Box," by W.L. George. *Good Housekeeping*, June 1923. Courtesy of Hearst Magazines UK.

Rose Macaulay's "Problems for the Citizen" (1923) presents a satirical take on the topics covered seriously by Dane, Bonham Carter, and Normanton.[26] "Problems for the Citizen" seeks neither to inform nor advocate for the new woman voter, who was the source of much worry in the press.[27] Macaulay instead provided both a dose of realism and comic relief. Macaulay's satire also differed from West's in pieces like "In the Absence of a Possible Husband." As we have seen, West acknowledged oppressive political, economic, and ideological systems, but simultaneously insisted on individual agency. Macaulay instead turns readers' gaze on the factors that weaken individual voices in British democracy, including human bias and bureaucratic indifference.

Macaulay shifts among satirical targets while speaking through a single persona who adopts their points of view. Her first target is a curmudgeon who resents every civic responsibility as an infringement of his own liberty:

> The chief problem in the life of the citizen is, of course, how to exist with reasonable comfort while yet obeying just so many of

[26] Good recent scholarship on Macaulay's satire includes Collier, *Modernism on Fleet Street* and Wood, *Modernism and Modernity*.

[27] According to Sarah Lonsdale, nor did Macaulay go out of her way to defend the oft-denigrated woman reader, asking for "a more critical approach from the middlebrow reading public, especially women" ("Imprisoned in a Cage of Print" 71).

> the regulations of the Government under which we have the misfortune to live as to escape molestation by the minions of the law. This is not easy; perhaps it is impossible, while we have laws about paying away our hard-won earnings in taxes, not travelling in trains without buying a ticket, not obstructing the traffic, occasionally even muzzling our dogs, having to obtain a troublesome and ridiculous signed paper permit whenever we leave our native lands, and so on and so forth. (17)

Other targets include government bureaucracy, electoral culture, and public opinion about female political candidates. To stabilize multiple satiric targets, the conclusion of "Problems for the Citizen" supplies the overarching irony of the discrepancy between burdensome citizen responsibilities and the paucity of citizen privileges: "the rights of a citizen are few; but his (or her) duties are very numerous and onerous" (94). In counterpoint to the leavening effect of its comedy, then, "Problems for the Citizen" weighed down the group of *Good Housekeeping* citizenship articles with a dose of realism, and even of cynicism. Inverting Dane's, Normanton's, and Bonham Carter's emphasis on the advantages and privileges of civic engagement, Macaulay turns readers' attention to its less attractive duties. Satirizing the citizen who feels that her duties *are* onerous, Macaulay also holds the mirror up to her readers, each of whom has at some time felt as the curmudgeon citizen does.

Macaulay's satirical targets slide from the myopic and grudging citizen to the predictable, crude conventions of political campaigns, then to the citizen's tendency, amidst the abstraction of the political system, to fall back on the stereotypes and clichés absorbed from the daily press or from one's neighbor. The persona jettisons ethical principles as she blandly doles out advice about how to vote "if you wish to accept a bribe (such as a ride in a motor-car to the polls or a present in money or kind)"; and passes on popular prejudice against female candidates: "It is not thought good form to vote for a female candidate, unless she is the wife of your former member, who has disqualified himself from standing by means of death"; and "It is not thought very nice for a woman to get into Parliament merely on her own account; there is something a little unwomanly about it" (93).

Even as her targets shift, Macaulay's satire coalesces into a picture of faceless transactions in modern society. The citizen who learns how to avoid paying his income tax illustrates this point. The persona advises that he can ignore multiple notices delivered by mail, until he "reads" the seriousness of a final notice by decoding its color. Again the persona passes on received wisdom: "I am told that it is safe to ignore [all the notices] until they turn slate blue" (17). Macaulay suggests that the average person cannot feel his civic responsibilities urgently because he is far removed from the time and place of their impact. And if citizens opt out of their duties, nothing happens, at least initially. The tacit message to the citizen is *do nothing, resign yourself to things as they are.*

A similar experience awaits the voter. Macaulay briskly acknowledges that the citizen is "a political being, a creature with a right to a say in his country's government. Even women, above thirty years of age, have this right now" (17). But when it is time to vote in a Parliamentary election, the citizen will find that the candidates "will all be quite foolish, quite useless, and quite unable to show any reason why they should represent you" (17, 93). But "This cannot be helped. Members of Parliament are like that" (93). Initiation into the political system will bring women no sense of agency, only recognition that, as they enter the political system, candidates will inevitably conform to the politician "type" so as to join the ranks of those who have been molded by the machinery of politics.

The experiences of citizenship described in "Problems for the Citizen" share the feature of withdrawn or emptied agency. The real problem for the citizen is how to act so as to make an impact. Macaulay does not resolve this question, so humor offers a collateral or substitute satisfaction and enjoyment. In one sense, then, Macaulay is aligned with Dane, Normanton, Bonham Carter, and West; all five believe that individual citizens' contributions should make a meaningful difference in society. Macaulay is simply the pessimist seated at the table with her colleagues.

Citizenship and Literary Culture in *Good Housekeeping*

From its first issues, *Good Housekeeping* created a robust literary culture, offering readers serialized novels by distinguished female and male writers, poetry, regular columns on theater by St John Ervine, and regular literary criticism by Clemence Dane.[28] Dane took the lead in linking women's citizenship to what and how they read. Questions of citizenship figure in her book essays, and books permeate her feminist essays concerning women's citizenship. The fluid,

[28] For a broader consideration of literary culture in domestic and fashion magazines, see Wood, *Modernism and Modernity* chapter 3.

cross-referential dialogue between these two essay genres characterizes Dane's journalism in *Good Housekeeping*. Her critical contributions in multiple genres—social problem essays and literary-critical essays—themselves contributed to the periodical's "radical heterogeneity," the "fluid and heterogenous form" that empowered readers to "construct their own text from the printed version" by picking and choosing among the features and by reading them nonsequentially (Green, "The Feminist Periodical Press" 200; Beetham, *A Magazine* 12). The heterogeneity of magazines has also been linked to their function as public forums that "highlight the engagement of literary production with nonliterary discourse" (Morrisson 11).[29]

Recent scholarship has highlighted this agility, endemic to the periodical, to attend to the frequency and ease with which periodicals recirculate and repurpose discourse and cross-reference media.[30] In Dane's essays, we frequently find a cross-referential dialogue between her literary-critical and her feminist political essays, each discourse endorsing the other. Through this dialogue, each essay genre is enriched by the other and is freed from its primary purpose in order to realize multiple rhetorical effects. Dane's simultaneous engagement of women as readers of literature and women as citizens, of women's literary sensibility and their political consciousness, signals her holistic approach to the education of the modern woman and her confidence in the common reader's intellectual agility.

In the remainder of this chapter, I will show the variety of strategies Dane uses to enable literary discourse to inform political and civic questions. Dane routinely draws on imaginative literature to supply historical evidence, corroborate common human attitudes, and backdate modern conflicts. The chapter concludes with a discussion of "Women Voters and the Death Penalty," in which Dane features two well-known writers publishing in both political and imaginative genres, each genre enriched by the other. Such continuity

[29] Morrisson particularly has in mind periodical features such as correspondence sections and the *New Freewoman*'s Discussion Circles. In the latter, the feature itself grew out of Marsden's commitment to creating a public forum. Morrisson's close study of several modernist magazines also shows the limits of this strategy.

[30] In two pertinent examples, Fiona Hackney observes the "progressive cross-pollination" in Leonara Eyles's journalism for *Modern Woman* and for *Lansbury's Labour Weekly* in the late 1920s: "Eyles adapted strategies from the socialist press to give agency to *Modern Woman* readers, while shaping a feminist sensibility for the *Labour Weekly*'s readership" ("Getting a Living" 108). And Barbara Green demonstrates how the Edwardian *Votes for Women* "mixed traditional and advanced positions and rhetorics, presenting readers with both popular literary forms and decidedly avant-garde positions" ("Suffragette Celebrity" 235–6).

between an author's literary and political voices suggests that writers are not confined to the arts but also carry authority as humanist thinkers and concerned citizens.

In "Golden Opinions" (1928), Dane takes advantage of the characteristic cross-pollination of periodical materials by foregrounding the familiar literary essay's capacity to inform women's citizenship. Replicating the periodical's function as a forum, she sets quotations from the featured essayists in dialogue with one another. The selected essay collections, both new and classic, offer insight and opinion about how woman may face the demands of modern civilization. Dane quotes, endorses, and dissents from the theories of citizenship voiced in the essay collections under review. In so doing, she signals the extent to which the collections of literary essays under review inform modern political theories of citizenship. And in two ways, "Golden Opinions" illustrates the cross-referencing characteristic of Dane's literary and political essays. First, Dane's discussion of authors and of literary genre reinforces and extends the *Good Housekeeping* journalists' shared interest in citizenship.[31] Both within Dane's essay and within the magazine, a number of feminist authors share their expertise and opinions about modern women's roles beyond the home. Second, Dane's citation of individual women journalists allowed readers to link Dane's discussion of, say, Rebecca West's *Strange Necessity* with West's essays in *Good Housekeeping*, *Time and Tide*, and other progressive publications. Some of the essayists whose books Dane reviews—Vera Brittain, Dame Ethel Smyth, and Rebecca West—were also established journalists; West had in fact been a writer for *Good Housekeeping*, beginning with Volume 1 in 1922. (And she would be featured in a 1933 *Ladies of Literature* profile by Mary Craik.) Both Brittain and Smyth would later write for *Good Housekeeping*, Brittain beginning in 1929 and Smyth in 1932. Dane would thus have previewed these writers who would later appear as *Good Housekeeping* authors. In "Golden Opinions," Dane reviews *Women's Work in Modern England*, a volume of essays that Brittain developed from articles she had published in *The Outlook*. Reviewing the work of these women writers gave Dane an opportunity to promote individual journalists while recirculating their ideas within the periodical

[31] In additional attention to *Good Housekeeping*'s multi-vocality, Alice Wood analyzes feminist writing within the context of the "dominant domestic narrative of the magazine's service features" (*Modernism and Modernity* 110). Singling out Rose Macaulay and Storm Jameson, she argues that they present "feminist resistance to some of the magazine's core values" (115).

community, lending cohesion to the topic of citizenship treated in *Good Housekeeping*.[32]

But although she reinforced the status of these "famous feminists," her criticism of their essay collections was not necessarily an endorsement of their views.[33] Dane admires Rebecca West's *The Strange Necessity*, as a "remarkable confession of faith," but refers to Ethel Smyth, author of *A Final Burning of Boats*, as "a giantess in a temper," who evinces a "desire for domination in every word she writes" reminiscent of the Wife of Bath. The comparison of Smyth and George Bernard Shaw, two "vigorous ... fighter[s,]" helps Dane steer clear of mere cattiness, however (52, 122). Rather than promote sister journalists, "Golden Opinions" makes a contribution to a debate in a public forum.

The generic features of the essay likewise lend themselves to the quality of a forum or a community. Dane establishes the essay's "neighbor-to-neighbor" value, its direct address to the reader, with no veil of fiction or fantasy intervening between writer and reader (52). She implies that individuals' personal growth and the formation of values formerly occurred organically in the neighborly interactions of communities, but in "the appalling turmoil of modern city life," they must be acquired through reading, which can be a surrogate for those neighborly exchanges. Nor is the reader a mere listener, for the essayist often characterizes his thoughts as provisional, requiring the reader's intelligence and opinions to be complete. Dane quotes Langdon-Davies on this point, who says that the chapters in *A Short History of Women* "are intended rather to stimulate thought than to satisfy a quest for complete information" (qtd. in "Golden Opinions" 53). The essayist's provisional thoughts are linked to his desirable impersonality, a quality for which Dane praises both Gertrude Bell and Langdon-Davies. The latter has "no desire to prove a theory, to rid himself of an obsession or to indulge a spleen," and therefore welcomes the reader's contributions to the debate (53).

Dane's identification of the provisional character of the essayist's thought and her praise of two essayists' impersonality align with

[32] With the exception of Rebecca West, Dane's "Golden Opinions" precedes the featured essayists' authorship for *Good Housekeeping*. Smyth published at least four articles for *Good Housekeeping*, two in 1932 and two in 1934 (February and October). Brittain wrote numerous articles for *Good Housekeeping*, beginning in 1929 with "The Somerville School of Novelists." "Golden Opinions" also discusses essay collections by male authors such as George Bernard Shaw, J.B. Priestley, and John Langdon-Davies.

[33] "Famous Feminist on Sex-Antagonism" was the title of West's first article for *Good Housekeeping* in June 1922.

her belief that women's independent thought is essential to their effective citizenship. Both traits foster the reader's engagement with the author's ideas and allow room for her disagreement with them. Indeed, Langdon-Davies explains that the subjects treated in his book about women are controversial, and "the reader will therefore not expect to find more than a point of view" (qtd. in "Golden Opinions" 53). And Dane's own literary-critical approach likewise fosters readers' engagement with a range of voices in a single essay. Quotation allows her own voice to recede while she amplifies the voices of her primary sources. Dane's generous excerpt of Priestley's *Apes and Angels* in "Golden Opinions" is a good example. Priestley describes an encounter with a watercolor artist whom he wistfully upholds as an anachronism within industrial society. He opines that working in watercolor "demands a simple, unsophisticated soul ... content to mellow the beauty of the world without asking questions and tormenting itself." "In the rapid progress of thought and art and life," Priestley continues, the watercolor artist "has been left far behind ... in a place where it is possible to be innocent and industrious and happy" (qtd. in "Golden Opinions" 52).

But in contrast to the light essayist whose thoughts may be provisional, the literary critic develops a thesis, and Dane's quotation of Priestley is followed by her application of his insights to her project to help women navigate modern civilization. Priestley's opinion is "especially worth considering by women: and this is a woman's magazine," she begins. For "citizenship is no joke," and mental peace, Dane continues, is "of all the graces, virtues, knowledges, and equipment which modern woman is forced to acquire, the only one which is indispensable, and the only one which cannot be taught in the schools" (52). Not formal education, Dane finds, but self-directed reading, especially reading that fosters debate, best prepares women for "the daily growing bundles of responsibilities which are thrust upon [women's] shoulders, or which they themselves assume" (52).

Thus despite Dane's endorsement of essayists' impersonality, she aligns each featured essayist in "Golden Opinions" with her own concerns about industrial society, and indeed offers advice to her readers on this basis. Priestley may intend the vignette of the painter in *Apes and Angels* as a beautiful, anachronistic fragment, but Dane uses it to build her argument about women and modernity. In advising her readers on how to cope with the "turmoil of modern city life," she illustrates the definition of the essay that she offered readers at the outset of "Golden Opinions": "the considered opinions on life addressed directly to the reader without the veil or the framework of fantasy" (52). She also reinforces the spirit of the Shakespearean poetry that is the source of her essay title:

> He hath honored me of late, and I have bought
> Golden opinions from all sorts of people,
> Which would be worn now in their newest gloss,
> Not cast aside so soon. (*Macbeth* 1.7)

In quoting extensively, analyzing, and repurposing a range of literary voices then, Dane illustrates how literary criticism within *Good Housekeeping* provided the vehicle to deepen what Bonham Carter called women's "political conscience" ("Public Speaking: Part I" 12).

While Dane's literary criticism, as illustrated in "Golden Opinions," replicates the dynamics of a civic forum, her feminist essays about citizenship draw on the wisdom of imaginative literature. Dane routinely mines literature for insights that can be directly applied to societal problems. To provide illustration and evidence on any topic in human affairs, Dane refers to and quotes from beloved authors: Jane Austen, Bunyan, Shakespeare, and many other British, American, and European writers. In these sections of her essays, literary references serve to locate her audience in a familiar conversation among common readers. Dane's status as an expert who advises novices is suspended; she and her readers are on equal footing, as if meeting for a conversation in a sitting room. What could be more natural than for Dane to turn to any of these familiar books for "evidence" of almost any human phenomenon? Recall, for example, that in "The Educational Value of Acting in Schools," when Dane needs "proof" that the imagination is a valuable asset in civic life, she cites a Kipling novel.

Characteristically in Dane's social problem essays, literary authors past and present supply the expertise on human affairs. In "Sex and the Business Woman," Dane argues that women's desire to work outside the home is not merely ambition but arises from her "capacity for earning money for her children and for benefiting the community by the work of her brain or hand" (99). It is in fact a means of "supporting the country she was born in" (37). Women's emancipation, and with it her readiness for civic duty, arrive in the natural course of healthy civilizations, says Dane. Despite women's natural abilities, however, some civilizations have erected barriers to women's education. Dane reminds readers of the long-standing prejudice against educated women, and literature proves the best source of evidence for it. To understand the historical attitudes of men to women, she turns to Fanny Burney and to Jane Austen, the former for her faithful observation of men and women, and the latter for her deep knowledge of them. The topic is men's opinions of "sense" in women. Lengthy quotations from the novels, characteristic of Dane, reflect the primary authority of these texts, which for Dane provide truth refracted through the mind and heart of the novelist. Dane's critical corroboration of this authority was probably unnecessary for her readers. Nonetheless, she provides it: "Jane Austen, who knew more about men and women than any woman then or since, comments as follows ..." (36). Similarly, Dane follows a quotation from Charlotte Brontë with the reflection that her words "make it possible to understand the minds that thought it out of the question for a woman to give evidence in person at an enquiry, much less sit on a Board, even though that woman were Florence Nightingale, newly returned from the Crimea" (37).

"Women Voters and the Death Penalty"

The sustained, in-depth attention to women's literary culture in *Good Housekeeping* meant that its readers developed their political conscience not only by absorbing political news and opinion, but through *Good Housekeeping*'s diverse literary material. Moreover, for Dane, women's political conscience is inextricable from their ethical judgments. In "Women Voters and the Death Penalty" (1924), Dane validates the use of emotion, instinct, and reason to respond to ethical problems, and she calls on esteemed writers for support. First, however, she models ethical thinking about liberty, justice, and mercy.

All of Dane's essays about citizenship emphasize liberty. "News from the Country of Hardwork" and other essays advocate the evasion of educational authority in favor of self-regulation and of first-hand experience of the world, while essays like "Petty Tyrannies" (1925) remind women of the British legacy of individual liberty and call on them to protest recent infringements of it. Finally, in essays inviting the female citizen to intervene in public debate, including "Women Voters and the Death Penalty," Dane engages readers in heated discussions of prisoners' rights. In "Women Voters and the Death Penalty," Dane asks her audience to consider whether "because a man commits a crime, has he forfeited all his human rights?" (93). She raises the question in the context of activism to abolish the death penalty and contemporary debate about whether life sentences deprived the convict of basic human rights. The death penalty was not abolished in Britain until 1965, but the 1920s have been identified as the "firm beginnings" of the abolition movement (Knowles 29). Dane anticipates that opportunity to abolish it will come in the next few years, although in fact the first full parliamentary debate of the twentieth century on capital punishment took place in 1929. Dane's article reflects the tenor of 1920s' campaigns against capital punishment, based on its demonstrated failure to deter crime, its questionable legitimacy in a "civilized" society, and its shaky humanitarian grounds.

"Women Voters and the Death Penalty" raises additional ethical questions—vital, difficult questions that will soon come before the British voter: "Are we to be executioners or healers? We have a perfect right to choose which we will be. Custom and religion justify either attitude. The criminal is a diseased member of the social body. Shall we amputate, or shall we endeavour to heal?" (93). Choosing these stark terms, Dane demonstrates her own incisive mind. Yet she begins with, and never abandons, the claims of emotion. She refers to a recent and rare execution in England of a woman convicted of murder, and acknowledges that the public "wave of excitement" about the case pointed to the "instinctive" (18) feeling that to hang a woman was "indecent" (19). Women voters, she advises, will need to untangle in their own minds their "instinctive," "sentimental," and "reasonable" reactions. But so will male voters. Dane moves quickly from questions about the sex of the murderer and of the voter to questions about how to apply, and how to balance, justice and mercy.

Dane particularly wants to make room for experts on mercy and on compassion, because in the public debate about capital punishment, emotional responses are labeled sentimental or even morbid. Dane contests such a dismissal of emotion, finding that "whether the emotions roused when the life or death of a fellow-creature hangs in the balance" should be categorized as "morbid" "is an arguable matter" (18). Here, and throughout the essay, Dane identifies and valorizes emotional and instinctual reactions even while she treats them as matters for rational debate. Using this tactic throughout the essay, Dane models an ethical practice of public debate. For example, someone can admit the abstract justice of "kill and be killed" and yet feel "an instinctive repulsion from the idea of stringing up a woman. Such people will themselves admit that their instinct is unreasonable. Exactly! That is the trouble! It just exists, and you can't reason it away" (18).

In "Women Voters and the Death Penalty," Dane begins with irrational, instinctual responses to the death penalty but then plunges her audience of new women voters in ethical reasoning that draws on or builds on great books. Ethical thinking has its basis both in instinct and reason. Dane sets the opposing claims of justice and mercy against one another. Justice is represented by the Old Testament's "eye for eye, tooth for tooth" (94). To envision the quality of mercy and the forms it might take in modern civilization, Dane draws on classic and modern literature. Nearly all of the quoted voices of highly esteemed writers are on the side of mercy: Christ, Shakespeare, Anatole France, John Galsworthy, and William Morris. Toward the end of the essay, she asks her readers whether they remember *News from Nowhere* and the "intense compassion felt in that Utopia, not only for the murdered boy, but for the murderer" (94). Perhaps more than in any other of her essays on social and feminist questions, Dane relies on the wisdom of published literature.

In "Golden Opinions," as we have seen, Dane cites others, including *Good Housekeeping* authors, both to reinforce their status as important voices and to engage readers in debate of controversial ideas. In "Women Voters and the Death Penalty," Dane quotes literary authors to endorse their views on the political and ethical questions she raises. Imaginative writing provides authoritative *evidence* about human beings—their nature, their rights, their dilemmas—the very subject matters on which Dane and her readers must draw for support as they evaluate the death penalty in Britain.

Dane first calls on literary voices that are, in the eyes of most of her readers, indisputable and long-standing experts on the human condition, Shakespeare and Christ. Dane begins, "'The quality of mercy is not strained—' Is that sentimental? It is the sentimentality of Shakespeare then" (19). Dane quotes only the first of the nineteen lines on the topic of mercy in *The Merchant of Venice*, which conclude that mercy "is an attribute to God himself; / And earthly power doth then show likest God's / When mercy seasons justice" (4.1). And behind Shakespeare stands Christ, a point that Dane makes through the use of a refrain, "Is that sentimental?": "'Condemn not, and ye shall not be condemned.' Is that sentimental? Christ said it" (qtd. in "Women Voters and the Death Penalty" 19). Dane makes concise use of these foundational and highly respected authors.

Dane then turns to modern writers who have written on penal reform, authors who are not only authoritative and respected but whose voices have saturated the public consciousness. Both Anatole France (1844–1924) and John Galsworthy (1906–1930) support Dane's concerns about the justice of the death penalty. Both published imaginative writing, essays, and journalism, illustrating the double writerly roles Dane favors, the fluid passage of ideas across political journalism, fiction, and drama. Both authors won the Nobel Prize for Literature—France in 1921 and Galsworthy in 1932. They were among the most authoritative voices on prison reform Dane could have chosen. This was especially the case for Galsworthy. The well-known novelist and playwright, author of *The Forsyte Saga* novels, had visited prisons in London and Berlin in 1909, and persistently advocated for penal reform in open letters to government officials, in fiction and drama, and in numerous newspaper and journal articles. His play *Justice* (1910) is widely considered to have made an impact on such reform in Britain (Nellis 61).

Although each writer stands at the pinnacle of his profession, Dane reinforces their relevance by adopting a version of the continuity of authorial roles that characterizes her body of essays in *Good Housekeeping*. Just as Dane's voice as literary critic is continuous with her voice as a feminist journalist, each role stitched to and referring to the other, and just as her citation of books by Rebecca West and Vera Brittain in "Golden Opinions" both capitalizes on and reinforces their status as journalists, so do the modern writers quoted in "Women Voters and the Death Penalty" enjoy mutually endorsing literary and political voices. Galsworthy's and France's status as fiction writers is continuous with their gravitas in the realm of politics.

In "Women Voters and the Death Penalty," women's literary culture—the habit of reading and the choice of reading matter—is fundamental to their ethical citizenship. Yet trusted literary voices do not absolve women of their responsibility to think carefully, reason ethically, and inform themselves. To make a decision on the question of whether the death penalty should be abolished "is a responsibility that we cannot shift to other shoulders," and citizens must acquaint themselves "with the details of the problem" (94). But they should do so by drawing on all their human faculties: instinct, heart, and mind.

This chapter has surveyed the individual and collective work of Clemence Dane, Violet Bonham Carter, Helena Normanton, Rebecca West, and Rose Macaulay to conceptualize and foster women's active citizenship. *Good Housekeeping* characterized these writers as "women in the public eye, known for their sound grasp of their subject" who were "fearless, frank, and outspoken." At least initially, however, its editorial team believed that "women's interest" encompassed no more than "art, music, and the drama, and the social side of life" ("The Reason for *Good Housekeeping*").

The women journalists delivered much more. To be sure, art, music, and drama remained central to their vision of women's modernity, especially in the cases of Dane, Bonham Carter, and West. But they also understood and expected that women would use their aesthetic sensibilities, ethical powers, and expanded knowledge of the world, both past and present, to profoundly influence the direction of modern British society.

Works Cited

Altick, Richard. *The English Common Reader: A Social History of the Mass Reading Public, 1800–1900*. University of Chicago Press, 1957.

——. *Victorian People and Ideas*. Norton, 1973.

Anderson, Benedict. *Imagined Communities: Reflections on the Origins and Spread of Nationalism*. Verso, 1983.

Ardis, Ann. "Making Middlebrow Culture, Making Middlebrow Literary Texts Matter: The Crisis, Easter 1912." *Modernist Cultures*, vol. 6, no. 1 (2011), pp. 18–40.

Arlen, Shelley. "'For love of an idea': Jane Ellen Harrison, Heretic and Humanist." *Women's History Review* vol. 5, no. 2 (1996), pp. 165–90.

Assmann, Jan. *Religion and Cultural Memory*. Translated by Rodney Livingstone, Stanford University Press, 2006.

Atherton, Carol. *Defining Literary Criticism: Scholarship, Authority, and the Possession of Literary Knowledge, 1880–2002*. Palgrave Macmillan, 2005.

Bagehot, Walter. "The Trash of the Day." *Spectator*, 7 September 1861, pp. 976–7.

Baldick, Chris. *Criticism and Literary Theory 1890 to the Present*. Longman, 1996.

——. *The Oxford English Literary History. Volume 10: 1910–1940: The Modern Movement*. Oxford University Press, 2004.

——. *The Social Mission of English Criticism, 1848–1932*. Clarendon, 1983.

Barrow, Kenneth. *Winifred: The Life of Clemence Dane*. Unpublished manuscript. Undated. Box 4, Folder 70. THM 120 Theatre and Performance Archives, Victoria and Albert Museum, South Kensington, London, 27 September 2018.

Beaumont, Caitríona. *Housewives and Citizens: Domesticity and the Women's Movement in England, 1928–64*. Manchester University Press, 2013.

Beer, Gillian. *Virginia Woolf: The Common Ground.* University of Michigan Press, 1996.

Beerbohm, Max. "Something Defeasible." 1919. Republished in *And Even Now*, 1922. Project Gutenberg, www.gutenberg.org/files/1956/1956-h/1956-h.htm#link2H_4_0015.

Beetham, Margaret. *A Magazine of Her Own? Domesticity and Desire in the Woman's Magazine 1800–1914*. Manchester University Press, 1996.

——. "Periodicals and the New Media: Women and Imagined Communities." *Women's Studies International Forum* vol. 29, no. 3 (2006), pp. 231–40.

Bell, Michael. *Literature, Modernism and Myth: Belief and Responsibility*. Cambridge University Press, 2009.

Benjamin, Walter. *The Origin of German Tragic Drama*. Translated by John Osborne, Verso, 1998.

Bennett, Arnold. *Literary Taste: How to Form It*. 1909. Project Gutenberg, 25 October 2004, www.gutenberg.org/files/13852/13852-h/13852-h.htm#page76.

Bingham, Adrian. *Gender, Modernity, and the Popular Press in Interwar Britain*. Clarendon, 2004.

Bone, Gertrude. "Preface and Apology." *Provincial Tales*. Duckworth, 1904, pp. v–vii.

Bonham Carter, Violet. "Public Speaking: Part I." *Good Housekeeping* vol. 2, no. 11 (January 1923), pp. 11–12.

——. "The Dilemma of Woman's Education." *Good Housekeeping* vol.1, no. 5 (July 1922), pp. 11–12.

——. "The Last Battle." *Good Housekeeping* vol. 2, no.10 (December 1922), pp. 13–14, 136.

——. "The Political Future of Women." *Good Housekeeping* vol. 2, no. 2 (October 1922), pp. 11–12, 110.

Bourdieu, Pierre. *Distinction*. 1979. Routledge, 1986.

Braithwaite, Brian, and Joan Barrell. *The Business of Women's Magazines*. Kogan Page, 1988.

Brake, Laurel. "'The Profession of Letters': Walter Pater and Greek Studies." *Journalism, Literature, and Modernity: From Hazlitt to Modernism*, edited by Kate Campbell, Edinburgh University Press, 2000, pp. 121–40.

Britannica, The Editors of Encyclopaedia. "John Gerard." *Encyclopedia Britannica*, 28 January 2023, www.britannica.com/biography/John-Gerard.

——. "Octavia Hill." *Encyclopedia Britannica*, 9 August 2023, https://www.britannica.com/biography/Octavia-Hill.

——. "Revelation to John." *Encyclopedia Britannica*, 7 November 2023, www.britannica.com/topic/Revelation-to-John. ——. "Richard Jefferies." *Encyclopedia Britannica*, 2 November 2023, www.britannica.com/biography/Richard-Jefferies.

Brontë, Charlotte. "Which the Genteel Reader is Recommended to Skip, Low Persons Being Here Introduced." *Shirley*. 1849. Project Gutenberg, 16 November 2009, www.gutenberg.org/cache/epub/30486/pg30486-images.html#XVIII.

Brooker, Peter, and Andrew Thacker. "General Introduction." *The Oxford Critical and Cultural History of Modernist Magazines, Volume 1: Britain and Ireland*, edited by Brooker and Thacker, Oxford University Press, 2009, pp. 1–26.

Bunyan, John. *The Pilgrim's Progress*. 1678. Internet Sacred Text Archive, https://sacred-texts.com/chr/bunyan/pp08.htm.

Bush, Ronald. "Modernist Poetry and Poetics." *The Cambridge History of Twentieth-Century English Literature*, edited by Laura Marcus and Peter Nicholls. Cambridge University Press, 2004, pp. 232–50.

Campbell, Kate. "Introduction: On Perceptions of Journalism." *Journalism, Literature, and Modernity: From Hazlitt to Modernism*, edited by Kate Campbell, Edinburgh University Press, 2000, pp. 1–14.

——. "Journalistic Discourses and Constructions of Modern Knowledge." *Nineteenth Century Media and the Construction of Identity*, edited by Laurel Brake, Bill Bell, and David Finkelstein. Palgrave, 2000, pp. 40–53.

Campbell, R.J. "Why Don't You Go to Church?" *Good Housekeeping* vol. 6, no. 2 (October 1924), pp. 14–15, 88, 90.

Child, Francis James, editor. *The English and Scottish Popular Ballads*. Houghton Mifflin, 1882–98.

Clay, Catherine. *Time and Tide: The Feminist and Cultural Politics of a Modern Magazine*. Edinburgh University Press, 2018.

Clay, Catherine, Maria DiCenzo, Barbara Green, and Fiona Hackney, editors. *Women's Periodicals and Print Culture in Britain, 1918–1939*. The Edinburgh History of Women's Periodical Culture in Britain. Edinburgh University Press, 2018.

Colley, Linda. *Britons: Forging the Nation 1707–1837*. Yale University Press, 1992.

Collier, Patrick. "Journalism Meets Modernism." *Gender in Modernism: New Geographies, Complex Intersections*, edited by Bonnie Kime Scott, University of Illinois Press, 2007, pp. 186–96.

——. *Modernism on Fleet Street*. Ashgate, 2006.

Collis, Rose. "Ghost Writer: The Biography of Clemence Dane." *Rose Collis*, 2024, www.rosecollis.com/ghost-writer-the-biography-of-clemence-dane-by-rose-collis/.

Craik, Mary. "Rebecca West." *Good Housekeeping* vol. 22, no. 6 (February 1933), pp. 22–3, 99–100.

Cuddy-Keane, Melba. *Virginia Woolf, the Intellectual, and the Public Sphere*. Cambridge University Press, 2003.

Dane, Clemence. "A Bunch of Daisies." *Good Housekeeping* vol. 4, no. 6 (February 1924), pp. 29, 90, 92. Reprinted in *North American Review*, vol. 219, no. 819 (February 1924).

——. "A Game of Speculation." *The World's Work: A History of Our Time*, vol. 47 (April 1924), pp. 626–30. Reprinted in *The Women's Side*, George H. Doran, 1927, pp. 11–28.
——. "A Hidden Orchis." *Good Housekeeping* vol. 16, no. 1 (September 1929), pp. 39, 116–18, 120.
——. "A National Mirror." *Good Housekeeping* vol. 14, no. 5 (January 1929), pp. 71, 162–4.
——. "A Problem in Education." *The English Review* June 1918, pp. 531–9 (Part i); July 1918, pp. 39–48 (Part ii).
——. "American Primitives." *Good Housekeeping* vol. 5, no. 5 (July 1924), pp. 70, 184–6.
——. "As You Like It." *Good Housekeeping* vol. 9, no. 3 (May 1926), pp. 47, 190–2, 194–6.
——. "Autumn Lists." *Good Housekeeping* vol.16, no. 2 (October 1929), pp. 35, 143–7.
——. "Bibles." *Good Housekeeping* vol. 6, no. 1 (September 1924), pp. 16, 144, 146.
——. "Biographical." *Good Housekeeping* vol. 12, no. 3 (November 1927), pp. 51, 179–80, 182, 184.
——. "Bridges." *Good Housekeeping* vol. 13, no. 3 (May 1928), pp. 51, 154, 156–7.
——. "Britain's Heritage." Lay sermon delivered at St. Jude's, 2nd May 1942. Box 4, Folder 62. THM 120 Theatre and Performance Archives, Victoria and Albert Museum, South Kensington, London. 27 September 2018.
——. "Capes of Good Hope." *Good Housekeeping* vol. 8, no. 1 (September 1925), pp. 49, 110–12, 114.
——. "Children of Light." *Good Housekeeping* vol. 10, no. 5 (January 1927), pp. 41, 164–6, 168–70.
——. "Cities of God." *Good Housekeeping* vol. 9, no. 4 (April 1926), pp. 45, 132, 134, 136, 138, 140.
——. "Dream Holes." *Good Housekeeping* vol. 13, no. 2 (April 1928), pp. 33, 131–2, 134.
——. "Eighteenth-Century Amazons." *Good Housekeeping* vol. 13, no. 1 (March 1928), pp. 34–5, 139–42.
——. "Faerylands Forlorn." *Good Housekeeping* vol. 7, no.2 (April 1925), pp. 64, 150, 152–6.
——. "First Flights." *Good Housekeeping* vol. 10, no. 2 (October 1926), pp. 45, 175–6, 178, 180.
——. "Flapdragon." *Good Housekeeping* vol. 6, no. 4 (December 1924), pp. 49, 149, 194–5.
——. "Fools in the Forest." *Good Housekeeping* vol. 8, no. 3 (November 1925), pp. 71, 148, 150, 152, 154, 156, 158.
——. "Foreword." *The Women's Side*. George H. Doran, 1927, pp. v–vi.

——. "Fragments that Remain." *Good Housekeeping* vol. 9, no. 5 (July–August 1926), pp. 47, 162–4, 166.
——. "Golden Opinions." *Good Housekeeping* vol. 14, no. 2 (October 1928), pp. 52–3, 122, 124, 126.
——. "Goliath Slings the Pebble Back." *The Bookman* (December 1925), pp. 407–9.
——. "Interesting People." *Good Housekeeping* vol. 7, no. 2 (April 1925), pp. 16–17, 88, 90, 92.
——. "Jefferies of the Fields." *Good Housekeeping* vol. 11, no. 6 (August 1927), pp. 73, 188, 190–2, 194.
——. "Keys of Heaven." *Good Housekeeping* vol. 5, no. 4 (June 1924), pp. 53, 134–6.
——. "Melpomene and the Fat Boy." *Good Housekeeping* vol. 7, no. 1 (March 1925), pp. 22, 131–2, 134.
——. "Monuments." *Good Housekeeping* vol. 7, no. 6 (August 1925), pp. 59, 131–5.
——. "Mrs. Robinson's Bag." *Good Housekeeping* vol. 11, no. 5 (July 1927), pp. 49, 130–3.
——. "Near Home and Far Off." *Good Housekeeping* vol. 6, no. 2 (February 1925), pp. 50, 172, 174–8.
——. "News from the Country of Hardwork." *Good Housekeeping* vol. 5, no. 6 (August 1924), pp. 47, 136, 138–40.
——. "Petty Tyrannies." *Good Housekeeping* vol. 8, no. 1 (September 1925), pp. 12–13, 100. Reprinted in *The Women's Side*, pp. 39–50.
——. "Quality and Quantity." *Good Housekeeping* vol. 8, no. 4 (December 1925), pp. 61, 152, 154, 156, 158–9.
——. "Remarks About the Universe." *Good Housekeeping* vol. 15, no. 3 (May 1929), pp. 42–3, 158, 160, 162.
——. "Rolling Stones." *Good Housekeeping* vol. 12. no. 4 (December 1927), pp. 57, 146–8, 150.
——. "Sex and the Business Woman." *Good Housekeeping* vol. 8, no. 6 (February 1926), pp. 36–7, 98, 99.
——. "Short Stories." *Good Housekeeping* vol. 5, no. 1 (March 1924), pp. 20, 102, 104.
——. "Should the Girl of Twenty-One Have a Vote?" *Good Housekeeping* vol. 5, no. 3 (May 1924), pp. 13, 88.
——. "Some Questions on Divorce." *Good Housekeeping* vol. 1, no.1 (March 1922), pp. 23, 89–91, 93.
——. "Some Ramblers." *Good Housekeeping* vol. 4, no. 3 (November 1923), pp. 29, 95–6.
——. "Spring Fashions: Reflections on the New Trend of Literature as Revealed in the Newest Books." *Good Housekeeping* vol. 14, no. 6 (February 1929), pp. 35, 104–6, 108.
——. "The Consort Crown." *Good Housekeeping* vol. 11, no. 4 (June 1927), pp. 35, 132–4, 136–8.

——. "The Educational Value of Acting in Schools." *Good Housekeeping* vol. 2, no. 3 (November 1922), pp. 13, 79–82. Reprinted in *The Women's Side*, pp. 93–105.

——. "The English Eden." *Good Housekeeping* vol. 12, no. 6 (February 1928), pp. 48–9, 124–8.

——. "The Kingdom of Me." *Good Housekeeping* vol. 10, no. 6 (February 1927), pp. 61, 170, 172–6.

——. "The Looking Glass of Laughter." *Good Housekeeping* vol. 5. no. 2 (April 1924), pp. 45, 98–9.

——. "The Mother Night." *Good Housekeeping* vol. 8, no. 4 (December 1925), pp. 14–15, 114–15.

——. "The Painted Past." *Good Housekeeping* vol. 11, no. 2 (April 1927), pp. 25, 115–20.

——. "The Poet v. the Talkies." *Good Housekeeping* vol. 15, no. 5 (July 1929), pp. 57, 147–8, 150, 152.

——. "The Poet's Pen." *Saturday Review of Literature*, 27 June 1925. *Good Housekeeping* vol. 7, no. 5 (July 1925), pp. 39, 140, 142, 144–6.

——. "The Sea and the Sex." *Good Housekeeping* vol. 6, no. 3 (November 1924), pp. 48, 173, 174, 176, 178.

——. "The Sixth Commandment." *Good Housekeeping* vol. 9, no. 1 (March 1926), pp. 74, 201–4, 206.

——. "The Twelve Best Books for Women." *Good Housekeeping* vol. 4, no. 2 (October 1923), pp. 19, 104, 106.

——. *The Women's Side*. 1926. George H. Doran, 1927.

——. "The Writer's Partner." Paper read to The Royal Society of Literature, 15 May 1929. Reprinted in *Recapture, A Clemence Dane Omnibus*. Heinemann, 1932, pp. 3–26.

——. "Things That Go Bump in the Night." *Good Housekeeping* vol. 4, no. 5 (January 1924), pp. 32, 134, 136, 138–9.

——. "This Century's Religion." *Good Housekeeping* vol. 2, no. 12 (February 1923), pp. 10–11, 74, 76.

——. *Tradition and Hugh Walpole*. 1929. Heinemann, 1930.

——. "Two Eyes." *Time and Tide*, 21 May 1920, pp. 32–4.

——. "Women Voters and the Death Penalty." *Good Housekeeping* vol. 6, no. 3 (November 1924), pp. 18–19, 93–4. Reprinted in *The Women's Side*, pp. 51–60.

Deen, Stella. "Cultivating Citizen Readers: Clemence Dane's Historical Essays in *Good Housekeeping*." *Journal of Modern Periodical Studies* vol. 10, nos. 1–2 (2019), pp. 98–128.

——. "Remarkable Obscurity: Portraits of Professional Women." *Profession and Performance*, edited by Ben Hagen and Taya Jean Sazama. Forthcoming with Clemson University Press.

Delap, Lucy. *The Feminist Avant-Garde: Transatlantic Encounters of the Twentieth Century*. Cambridge University Press, 2007.

Demoor, Marysa. "Andrew Lang's Letters to Edmund Gosse: The Record of a Fruitful Collaboration as Poets, Critics, and Biographers." *The Review of English Studies* (new series) vol. 38, no. 152 (November 1987), pp. 492–509.

Dowson, Jane. "Interventions in the Public Sphere: *Time and Tide* (1920–1930) and *The Bermondsey Book* (1923–1930)." *The Oxford Critical and Cultural History of Modernist Magazines, Volume 1: Britain and Ireland*, edited by Peter Brooker and Andrew Thacker, Oxford University Press, 2009, pp. 530–51.

"Edith Sitwell." *The Poetry Foundation*, www.poetryfoundation.org/poets/edith-sitwell.

Elbert, N.S. Thompson. *The Seventeenth-Century English Essay*. 1926. Haskell, 1967.

Eliot, T.S. "Reflections on *Vers Libre*." *New Statesman*, 3 March 1917, pp. 518–19. Reprinted in *To Criticize the Critic*. Faber & Faber, 1978, p. 186.

——. "Ulysses, Order, and Myth." *The Dial* (November 1923), pp. 480–3.

"Epitomize." *Oxford English Dictionary*, https://www.oed.com/?tl=true.

Essayes or Moral Discourses on Several Subjects. Written by a Person of Honour. London, 1671. Reprinted in *Of Essays and Reading in Early Modern Britain*, Appendix D, by Scott Black. Palgrave Macmillan, 2006.

Esty, Jed. *A Shrinking Island: Modernism and National Culture in England*. Princeton University Press, 2004.

Flint, Kate. *The Woman Reader 1837–1914*. Clarendon, 1993.

Frost, Laura. *The Problem with Pleasure: Modernism and its Discontents*. Columbia University Press, 2013.

Gale, Maggie. "From Fame to Obscurity: In Search of Clemence Dane." *Women, Theatre and Performance: New Histories, New Historiographies*, edited by Maggie B. Gale and Viv Gardner, Manchester University Press, 2000, pp. 121–41.

Gerard, John. *The Herball or Generall Historie of Plantes*. 1597. *Early English Books Online Text Creation Partnership*, 2011, http://name.umdl.umich.edu/A01622.0001.001.

Gibbons, Phyllis. "How the Women's Institutes Came into Being." *Good Housekeeping* vol. 7, no. 4 (June 1925), pp. 14–15, 117–18.

Gikandi, Simon. *Maps of Englishness: Writing Identity in the Culture of Colonialism*. Columbia University Press, 1997.

Giles Judy. *The Parlour and the Suburb: Domestic Identities, Class, Femininity and Modernity*. Berg, 2004.

Giles, Judy, and Tim Middleton, editors. *Writing Englishness, 1900–1950*. Routledge, 1995.

Goethe, Johann. *Faust*. Translated by George Madison Priest, *The Alchemy Website*, http://www.levity.com/alchemy/faust25.html.

Goldschmidt, Nora. Abstract for *Fragmentary Modernisms: The Classical Fragment in Literary and Visual Cultures, 1896–1950*. Durham University, gtr.ukri.org/projects?ref=AH%2FS01201X%2F1.

Good, Graham. *The Observing Self: Rediscovering the Essay*. Routledge, 1988.

Green, Barbara. "Around 1910: Periodical Culture, Women's Writing and Modernity." *Tulsa Studies in Women's Literature*, vol. 30, no. 2 (2011), pp. 429–39.

——. *Feminist Periodicals and Daily Life: Women and Modernity in British Culture*. Palgrave Macmillan, 2017.

——. "Suffragette Celebrity at Home from Abroad: Feminist Periodicals and Transatlantic Circulation." *Edinburgh Companion to Atlantic Literary Studies*, edited by Leslie Elizabeth Eckel and Clare Frances Elliott, Edinburgh University Press, 2016, pp. 235–51.

——. "The Feminist Periodical Press: Women, Periodical Studies and Modernity." *Literature Compass*, vol. 6, no.1 (January 2009), pp. 191–205.

Grose, Francis. *A Glossary of Provincial and Local Words Used in England by Francis Grose, Esq., F. R. & A.S.S. To which is now first incorporated the Supplement by Samuel Pegge, Esq. F.S.A.* John Russell Smith, 1839. The Salamanca Corpus, Universidad de Salamanca, 2014.

Gualtieri, Elena. *Virginia Woolf's Essays: Sketching the Past*. St. Martin's Press, 2000.

Guedalla, Philip. "Emily Tennyson." *Good Housekeeping* vol. 13, no. 5 (July 1928), pp. 36–7.

——. "Mary Anne Disraeli." *Good Housekeeping* vol. 14, no. 2 (April 1928), pp. 14–15, 150, 152–3.

Guy, Josephine M., and Ian Small. "The British 'Man of Letters' and the Rise of the Professional." *The Cambridge History of Literary Criticism, Volume VII: Modernism and the New Criticism*, edited by A. Walton Litz, Louis Menand, and Lawrence Rainey, Cambridge University Press, 2000, pp. 377–88.

Habermann, Ina. *Myth, Memory and the Middlebrow: Priestley, du Maurier and the Symbolic Form of Englishness*. Palgrave Macmillan, 2010.

Hackney, Fiona. "Getting a Living, Getting a Life: Leonora Eyles, Employment and Agony, 1925–1930." *Women in Magazines: Research, Representation, Production and* Consumption, edited by Rachel Ritchie et al., Routledge, 2016, pp. 107–24.

——. *"They Opened Up a Whole New World": Feminine Modernity and the Feminine Imagination in Women's Magazines, 1919–1939*. 2010. Falmouth University, PhD dissertation.

——. "'Women are News': British Women's Magazines 1919–39." *Transatlantic Print Culture, 1880–1940: Emerging Media, Emerging Modernisms*, edited by Ann Ardis and Patrick Collier, Palgrave, 2008, pp. 114–33.

Hammill, Faye. *Women, Celebrity, and Literary Culture Between the Wars*. University of Texas Press, 2007.

Head, Alice M. *It Could Never Have Happened*. Windmill, 1939.
"Henry Thrale, MP: owner 1758–1781." Thrale.com, 2023, www.thrale.com/henry_thrale_mp_owner_1758_1781.
Hobson, J.A. *Imperialism*. James Pott, 1902.
Howkins, Alun. *The Death of Rural England: A Social History of the Countryside since 1900*. Routledge, 2003.
Humble, Nicola. *The Feminine Middlebrow Novel: 1920s to 1950s: Class, Domesticity, and Bohemianism*. Oxford University Press, 2001.
Hutchinson, Pamela. "C'mon feel the noise: what happened when the talkies came to Britain?" *The Guardian*, 21 September 2015, www.theguardian.com/film/filmblog/2015/sep/21/the-talkies-silent-film-british-cinema-alfred-hitchcock.
Hutton, Ronald. "The Neolithic Great Goddess: A Study in Modern Tradition." *Antiquity*, 71 (1997), pp. 91–9.
Jameson, Storm. "What Has Become of Victorian Vitality?" *Good Housekeeping* vol. 13, no. 1 (March 1928), pp. 49, 116–17.
Johnson, Samuel. *The Lives of the English Poets*. 1779–81. Jones, 1825, openlibrary.org/books/OL6623355M/The_lives_of_the_English_poets.
Julien, Heather. "School Novels, Women's Work, and Maternal Vocationalism." *NWSA Journal* vol. 19, no. 2 (2007), pp. 118–37.
Kaplan, Laurie. "Jane Austen and the Uncommon Reader." *Persuasions* 9 (1987), pp. 71–5, jasna.org/persuasions/printed/number9/kaplan.htm.
Kenner, Hugh. "The Muse in Tatters." *Arion: A Journal of the Humanities and the Classics* vol. 7, no. 2 (Summer 1968), pp. 212–33.
Kern, Stephen. *The Culture of Time and Space, 1880–1918*. Harvard University Press, 1983.
Kipling, Rudyard. "A School Song." *Stalky & Co.* Octavo, 1899.
——. "The Palace." 1903. The Kipling Society, 2023, www.kiplingsociety.co.uk/poem/poems_palace.htm.
Klikauer, T. *Hegel's Moral Corporation*. Palgrave Macmillan, 2016.
Knowles, Julian B. *The Abolition of the Death Penalty in the United Kingdom: How it Happened and Why it Still Matters*. The Death Penalty Project, 2015.
Lang, Andrew. "Introduction." *The Secret Commonwealth of Elves, Fauns, and Fairies: A Study of Folk-lore & Psychical Research*. David Nutt, 1893, pp. ix–lxv.
——. "L'Envoi to E.W.G." *Rhymes a la Mode*. Kegan Paul, 1885, p. 12.
Leavis, Q.D. *Fiction and the Reading Public*. 1932. Pimlico, 2000.
LeMahieu, D.L. *A Culture for Democracy: Mass Communication and the Cultivated Mind in Britain Between the Wars*. Clarendon, 1988.
Levine, Carol. "Public Art, Public Outcry: The Scandalous Sculptures of Jacob Epstein and Richard Serra." Paper delivered at Rutgers University, Camden, N.J., 23 April 2001, www.peterlevine.ws/epstein.pdf.
Lewis, Pericles. *Religious Experience in the Modernist Novel*. Cambridge University Press, 2010.

Light, Alison. *Forever England: Femininity, Literature and Conservatism Between the Wars*. Routledge, 1991.

Littau, Karin. *Theories of Reading: Books, Bodies and Bibliomania*. Polity, 2006.

Lonsdale, Sarah. "Imprisoned in a Cage of Print: Rose Macaulay, Journalism and Gender." *Rose Macaulay, Gender, and Modernity*, edited by Kate Macdonald, Routledge, 2018, pp. 57–74.

——. *Rebel Women Between the Wars*. Manchester University Press, 2020.

Lowe, Peter. *English Journeys: National and Cultural Identity in 1930s and 1940s England*. Cambria, 2012.

Lowndes, [Mrs.] Belloc. "The Effects of Easy Divorce." *Good Housekeeping* vol. 1, no. 2 (April 1922), pp. 27, 94.

Lucas, John. *The Radical Twenties: Writing, Politics, and Culture*. Rutgers University Press, 1999.

McAleer, Joseph. *Popular Reading and Publishing in Britain 1914–1950*. Oxford University Press, 1992.

Macaulay, Rose. "Problems for the Citizen." *Good Housekeeping* vol. 4, no. 3 (November 1923), pp. 17, 93–4.

McDonald, Louise. *Clemence Dane: Forgotten Feminist of the Inter-War Years*. Routledge, 2021.

McKibben, Ross. *Classes and Cultures: England 1918–1951*. Oxford University Press, 1998.

Marks, Peter. "Making the New: Literary Periodicals and the Construction of Modernism." *Precursors and Aftermaths: Literature in English 1914–45*, vol. 2, no. 1 (2004), pp. 24–39.

Masterman, C.F.G. [Lucy]. "Those Horrid Tourists!" *Good Housekeeping* vol. 1, no. 7 (September 1922), pp. 64–6.

Matless, David. *Landscape and Englishness*. Reaktion, 2005.

Miller, N. "Cicero's Cosmos: Somnium Scipionis ('The Dream of Scipio')." *The Inspiration of Astronomical Phenomena VI, Proceedings of a conference held 18–23 October 2009 in Venezia, Italy*, edited by Enrico Maria Corsini. Astronomical Society of the Pacific, 2011, p. 375, ui.adsabs.harvard.edu/abs/2011ASPC..441..375M/abstract.

Morrisson, Mark. *The Public Face of Modernism: Little Magazines, Audiences, and Reception 1905–20*. University of Wisconsin Press, 2001.

Nash, Christopher. "Myth and Modern Literature." *The Context of English Literature 1900–1930*, edited by Michael Bell, Holmes and Meier, 1980, pp. 160–85.

Nead, Linda. *Victorian Babylon: People, Streets and Images in Nineteenth-Century London*. Yale University Press, 2000.

Nellis, Mike. "John Galsworthy's Justice." *The British Journal of Criminology*, vol. 36, no. 1 (1996), pp. 61–84.

Normanton, Helena. "Breaking the Barriers: Some Great Women of the Past." *Good Housekeeping* vol. 1, no. 3 (May 1922), pp. 10–11, 68.

——. "How Women Won the Vote." *Good Housekeeping* vol. 14, no. 5 (January 1929), pp. 35, 96, 98–9.

——. "The Woman Juror." *Good Housekeeping* vol. 5, no. 1 (March 1924), pp. 64, 172–5.

——. "Waters of Babylon." *Good Housekeeping* vol. 16, no. 6 (February 1930), pp. 58, 147–8.

——. "Women Justices of the Peace." *Good Housekeeping* vol. 7, no. 1 (March 1925), pp. 64, 154, 156, 158.

North, Michael. *Reading 1922: A Return to the Scene of the Modern.* Oxford University Press, 1999.

Norwood, Gilbert. "Too Many Books." *The Wooden Man.* Macmillan, 1926, pp. 53–71.

Outka, Elizabeth. *Consuming Traditions: Modernity, Modernism, and the Commodified Authentic.* Oxford University Press, 2009.

Owen, Alex. *The Place of Enchantment: British Occultism and the Culture of the Modern.* University of Chicago Press, 2004.

"Paradox." *Catholic Dictionary.* Catholic Culture, www.catholicculture.org/culture/library/dictionary/index.cfm?id=35394.

Parsons, Jacynth, illustrator. *Songs of Innocence*, by William Blake, with a Prefatory Letter by W.B. Yeats. Hale, Cushman and Flint/Medici Society, 1928.

Philpotts, Matthew. "Defining the Thick Journal: Periodical Codes and Common Habitus." Paper delivered at the Modern Language Association 2013 Special Session *Towards a Theory of Periodical Studies*, seeeps.princeton.edu/wp-content/uploads/sites/243/2015/03/mla2013_philpotts.pdf

"Phrynichus." *Encyclopedia Britannica*, 14 May 2008, www.britannica.com/biography/Phrynichus-Greek-tragic-poet.

Plock, Vike Martina. "'A Journal of the Period': Modernism and Conservative Modernity in *Eve: The Lady's Pictorial* (1919–29)." Clay et al. pp. 28–41.

Proudfoot, Richard, Ann Thompson, and David Scott Kastan, editors. *The Arden Shakespeare Complete Works*, revised edition. Thomson, 2001.

"Psychical." *Cambridge Dictionary.* Cambridge University Press, dictionary.cambridge.org/us/dictionary/english/psychical.

Pulbrook, E.C. "Preface." *The English Countryside.* Batsford, 1915, pp. v–vii.

Pykett, Lyn. "The Making of a Modern Woman Writer: Rebecca West's Journalism, 1911–1930." *Journalism, Literature, and Modernity: From Hazlitt to Modernism*, edited by Kate Campbell, Edinburgh University Press, 2000, pp. 170–90.

Quiller-Couch, Arthur. *On the Art of Writing: Lectures Delivered in the University of Cambridge 1913–1914.* Cambridge University Press, 1917.

——., editor. *The Oxford Book of English Verse: 1250–1900*. Clarendon, 1919.

Review of *The Giant of Oldborne*, by John Owen. *The Spectator*, 13 November 1926, p. 30.

Richards, I.A. *Practical Criticism: A Study of Literary Judgment*. 1929. Kegan Paul, 1930.

——. *Principles of Literary Criticism*. 1924. Routledge, 2001.

Richardson, A.E., and H.D. Eberlein. *The English Inn, Past and Present*. Batsford, 1925.

Roach, Rebecca. "'The Lady Interviewer and Her Methods': Chatter, Celebrity, and Reading Communities." Clay et al., pp. 170–84.

Royden, A. Maude. "Religion in Modern Fiction and on the Stage." *Good Housekeeping* vol. 8, no. 4 (December 1925), pp. 20–1, 125–8.

Shakespeare, William. *Macbeth*. Proudfoot et al., pp. 774–99.

——. *The Merchant of Venice*. Proudfoot et al., pp. 831–57.

——. *The Merry Wives of Windsor*. Proudfoot et al., pp. 859–87.

Shattock, Joanne. *Politics and Reviewers: The "Edinburgh" and the "Quarterly" in the Early Victorian Age*. Leicester University Press, 1989.

Snyder, Carey. "Key Literary Figures: Introduction." *Women, Periodicals, and Print Culture in Britain, 1890s to 1920s: The Modernist Period*, edited by Faith Binkes and Carey Snyder, Edinburgh University Press, 2019, pp. 165–8.

Staveley-Wadman, Rose. "Understanding the 1920s Spiritualism Revival." Blog, The British Newspaper Archive, The British Library, https://blog.britishnewspaperarchive.co.uk/2021/10/14/understanding-the-1920s-spiritualism-revival/.

Steel, Ronald. *Walter Lippmann and the American Century*. Little, Brown, 1980.

Stetz, Margaret D. "Time and Tide Waited for Her: Rebecca West's Journalism in the 1920s." *Women, Periodicals, and Print Culture in Britain, 1890s–1920s: The Modernist Period*, edited by Faith Binckes and Carey Snyder, Edinburgh University Press, 2019, pp. 183–94.

Strachey, Lytton. "Preface." *Eminent Victorians*. Chatto and Windus, 1918, pp. vii–ix.

Sullivan, Melissa, and Sophie Blanch. "Introduction: The Middlebrow—Within or Without Modernism." *Modernist Cultures*, vol. 6, no. 1 (2011), pp. 1–17.

Taylor, John. *A Dream of England: Landscape, Photography and the Tourist's Imagination*. Manchester University Press, 1994.

Tennyson, Alfred. *The Princess: A Medley*. 1847. Project Gutenberg, 2 August 2008, https://www.gutenberg.org/files/791/791-h/791-h.htm.

The Bible. King James Version, Bible Gateway, www.biblegateway.com/versions/King-James-Version-KJV-Bible.

"The Literary Aspirant." *The Saturday Review*, 1 November 1902, p. 543.

"The Press: *John O'London's* Dies." *Time*, 20 September 1954, content.time.com/time/subscriber/article/0,33009,820250,00.html.

"The Reason for *Good Housekeeping*." *Good Housekeeping* vol. 1, no. 1 (March 1922), p. 11.

"The Results of Our Reading Questionnaire." *Good Housekeeping* vol. 15, no. 1 (March 1929), pp. 35, 141–2, 144.

"The Witch-Cult in Western Europe." *Wikipedia*, en.wikipedia.org/wiki/The_Witch-Cult_in_Western_Europe.

Thorndike, Sybil. "Clemence Dane." *Drama: The Quarterly Theatre Review*, new series, no. 78 (Autumn 1965), p. 42.

Thurston, Robert W. *Witch, Wicce, Mother Goose: The Rise and Fall of the Witch Hunts in Europe and North America*. Longman, 2001.

Tracy, Daniel. "From Vernacular Humor to Middlebrow Modernism: *Gentlemen Prefer Blondes* and the Creation of Literary Value." *Arizona Quarterly: A Journal of American Literature, Culture, and Theory*, vol. 66, no. 1 (2010), pp. 115–43.

Tusan, Michelle Elizabeth. *Women Making News: Gender and Journalism in Modern Britain*. University of Illinois Press, 2005.

Verdon, Nicola. "'The Modern Countrywoman': Farm Women, Domesticity and Social Change in Interwar Britain." *History Workshop Journal*, vol. 70, no. 1 (Autumn 2010), pp. 86–107.

Viswanathan, Gauri. "Secularism in the Framework of Heterodoxy." *PMLA*, vol. 123, no. 2 (2008), pp. 466–76.

Vogeler, Martha S. *Austin Harrison and the "English Review."* University of Missouri Press, 2008.

Waller, P.J. *Writers, Readers, Reputations: Literary Life in Britain, 1870–1918*. Oxford University Press, 2006.

Walpole, Hugh. *Reading*. Jarrolds, 1926.

Weiner, Martin J. "England is the Country: Modernization and the National Self-Image." *Albion, A Quarterly Journal Concerned with British Studies*, vol. 3, no. 4 (Winter 1971), pp. 198–221.

West, Rebecca. "In the Absence of a Possible Husband, What is a Girl to Do?" *Good Housekeeping* vol. 4, no. 4 (December 1923), pp. 56–7, 188–9.

——. "The Function of The Weekly Review." *Time and Tide*, 9 December 1927, p. 1114.

——. "The Future of the Press IV: The Journalist and the Public." *Time and Tide*, 2 March 1928. Reprinted in *Gender in Modernism* and introduced by Patrick Collier, *Gender in Modernism: New Geographies; Complex Intersections*, edited by Bonnie Kime Scott, University of Illinois Press, 2007, pp. 196–201.

——. "The Gospel According to Granville-Barker." *The Freewoman*, 7 March 1912. *The Young Rebecca: Writings of Rebecca West 1911–1917*, selected and introduced by Jane Marcus, Indiana University Press, 1982, pp. 19–23.

——. "The White Slave Traffic Bill." *The Clarion*, 22 November 1912. *The Young Rebecca: Writings of Rebecca West 1911–1917*, selected and introduced by Jane Marcus, Indiana University Press, 1982, pp. 119–23.
Williams, Constance. "Political Work as a Profession for Women." *Good Housekeeping* vol. 1, no. 6 (August 1922), pp. 35, 117.
Williams, Raymond. *Culture and Society: 1780–1950*. 1958. Columbia University Press, 1983.
Wintringham, Margaret. "What Makes a Home-Maker?" *Good Housekeeping* vol. 2, no. 1 (September 1922), pp. 15, 82–3.
Wood, Alice. "Housekeeping, Citizenship, and Nationhood in *Good Housekeeping* and *Modern Home*." Clay et al., pp. 210–24.
——. *Modernism and Modernity in British Women's Magazines: Ultra-Modern Eves*. Routledge, 2020.
Woolf, Virginia. *A Room of One's Own*. 1929. Harcourt, 1957.
——. *Mrs. Dalloway*. 1925. Harcourt, 2005.
——. "The Common Reader." *The Common Reader* (First Series). Harcourt, 1925, pp. 11–12.
——. "Why?" *The Death of the Moth and Other Essays*. Harcourt, 1942, pp. 227–34.
Wootton, Barbara. "Where Your Money Goes: What Every Woman Ought to Know." *Good Housekeeping* vol. 1, no. 2 (April 1922), pp. 49, 106.
Workman, Joanne. "Normanton, Helena Florence (1882–1957), barrister and feminist campaigner." *Oxford Dictionary of National Biography*. 2011. 20 April 2019, www.oxforddnb.com/view/10.1093/ref:odnb/9780198614128.001.0001/odnb-9780198614128-e-39091.
Yeats, W.B. "Adam's Curse." 1903. *The Collected Poems of W.B. Yeats*. Macmillan, 1956, pp. 78–9.

Index

Good Housekeeping articles by Dane are shown in bold. Page numbers for illustrations and excerpts from *Good Housekeeping* are shown in *italics*. Footnotes are identified by page number followed by the suffix 'n'.

EU Authorised Representative:
Easy Access System Europe Mustamäe tee 50, 10621 Tallinn, Estonia
gpsr.requests@easproject.com

Printed and bound by CPI Group (UK) Ltd, Croydon, CR0 4YY
29/09/2026
02224984-0001